First International Workshop on Construction Grammars and NLP (CxGsNLP 2023)

Washington, DC, USA
9-12 March 2023

ISBN: 978-1-7138-9049-2

Printed from e-media with permission by:

Curran Associates, Inc.
57 Morehouse Lane
Red Hook, NY 12571

Some format issues inherent in the e-media version may also appear in this print version.

Association for Computational Linguistics
209 N. Eighth Street
Stroudsburg, Pennsylvania 18360

Phone: 1-570-476-8006
Fax: 1-570-476-0860

acl@aclweb.org

Additional copies of this publication are available from:

Curran Associates, Inc.
57 Morehouse Lane
Red Hook, NY 12571 USA
Phone: 845-758-0400
Fax: 845-758-2633
Email: curran@proceedings.com
Web: www.proceedings.com

CxGsNLP 2023

The First International Workshop on Construction Grammars and NLP (CxGs+NLP, GURT/SyntaxFest 2023)

Proceedings of the Conference

March 9-12, 2023

The CxGsNLP organizers gratefully acknowledge the support from the following sponsors.

The Georgetown College of Arts & Sciences, the Georgetown Faculty of Languages and Linguistics, and the Georgetown Department of Linguistics

Introduction

Construction Grammar (CxG) approaches recognize all levels of linguistic structures as contributing meaning, which makes them a powerful tool for considering a wide variety of linguistic problems. Similarly, recent advances in NLP, driven in large part by the introduction of pre-trained language models, have led to the development of computational methods independent of a linguistic grounding. In an effort to close the gap between the recent direction of NLP research and the field of CxGs, The First International Workshop on Construction Grammars and NLP (CxGs+NLP 2023) will take take place at GURT2023, an annual linguistics conference held at Georgetown University, which this year co-locates four related but independent events:

- The Seventh International Conference on Dependency Linguistics (Depling 2023)
- The 21st International Workshop on Treebanks and Linguistic Theories (TLT 2023)
- The Sixth Workshop on Universal Dependencies (UDW 2023)
- The First International Workshop on Construction Grammars and NLP (CxGs+NLP 2023)

The Georgetown University Round Table on Linguistics (GURT) is a peer-reviewed annual linguistics conference held continuously since 1949 at Georgetown University in Washington DC, with topics and co-located events varying from year to year.

In 2023, under an overarching theme of 'Computational and Corpus Linguistics', GURT/SyntaxFest continues the tradition of SyntaxFest 2019 and SyntaxFest 2021/22 in bringing together multiple events that share a common interest in using corpora and treebanks for empirically validating syntactic theories, studying syntax from quantitative and theoretical points of view, and for training machine learning models for natural language processing. Much of this research is increasingly multilingual and cross-lingual and requires continued systematic analysis from various theoretical, applied, and practical perspectives. New this year, the CxGs+NLP workshop brings a usage-based perspective on how form and meaning interact in language.

For these reasons and encouraged by the success of the previous editions of SyntaxFest, we —the chairs of the four events— decided to facilitate another co-located event at GURT 2023 in Washington DC.

As in past co-located events involving several of the workshops, we organized a single reviewing process, with identical paper formats for all four events. Authors could indicate (multiple) venue preferences, but the ultimate assignment of papers to events for accepted papers was made by the program chairs.

33 long papers were submitted, 11 to Depling, 16 to TLT, 10 to UDW and 10 to CxGs+NLP. The program chairs accepted 27 (82%) and assigned 7 to Depling, 6 to TLT, 5 to UDW and 9 to CxGs+NLP.

16 short papers were submitted, 6 of which to Depling, 6 to TLT, 10 to UDW and 2 to CxGs+NLP. The program chairs accepted 9 (56%) and assigned 2 to Depling, 2 to TLT, 3 to UDW, and 2 to CxGs+NLP.

Our sincere thanks go to everyone who is making this event possible: everybody who submitted their papers; Georgetown University Linguistics Department students and staff—including Lauren Levine, Jessica Lin, Ke Lin, Mei-Ling Klein, and Conor Sinclair—for their organizational assistance; and of course, the reviewers for their time and their valuable comments and suggestions. Special thanks are due to Georgetown University, and specifically to the Georgetown College of Arts & Sciences and the Faculty of Languages and Linguistics for supporting the conference with generous funding. Finally, we would also like to thank ACL SIGPARSE for its endorsement and the ACL Anthology for publishing the proceedings.

Owen Rambow, François Lareau (Depling2023 Chairs)
Daniel Dakota, Kilian Evang, Sandra Kübler, Lori Levin (TLT2023 Chairs)
Loïc Grobol, Francis Tyers (UDW2023 chairs)
Claire Bonial Harish Tayyar Madabushi (CxG+NLP2023 Chairs)
Nathan Schneider, Amir Zeldes (GURT2023 Organizers)
March 2023

Organizing Committee

Depling2023 Chairs

Owen Rambow, Stony Brook University
François Lareau, Université de Montréal

TLT2023 Chairs

Daniel Dakota, Indiana University
Kilian Evang, Heinrich Heine University Düsseldorf
Sandra Kübler, Indiana University
Lori Levin, Carnegie Mellon University

UDW2023 Chairs

Loïc Grobol, Université Paris Nanterre
Francis Tyers, Indiana University

CxGs+NLP2023 Chairs

Claire Bonial, U.S. Army Research Lab
Harish Tayyar Madabushi, The University of Bath

GURT2023 Organizers

Amir Zeldes, Georgetown University
Nathan Schneider, Georgetown University

GURT2023 Student Assistants

Lauren Levine, Georgetown University
Ke Lin, Georgetown University
Jessica Lin, Georgetown University

Program Committee

Program Committee for the Whole of GURT2023

Lasha Abzianidze, Utrecht University
Patricia Amaral, Indiana University
Valerio Basile, University of Turin
Emily Bender, University of Washington
Bernd Bohnet, Google
Claire Bonial, Army Research Lab
Gosse Bouma, University of Groningen
Miriam Butt, Universität Konstanz
Marie Candito, Université de Paris
Giuseppe G. A. Celano, Universität Leipzig
Xinying Chen, Xi'an Jiaotong University
Silvie Cinkova, Charles University Prague
Cagri Coltekin, Universität Tübingen
Stefania Degaetano-Ortlieb, Universität des Saarlandes
Éric Villemonte de la Clergerie, INRIA
Miryam de Lhoneux, KU Leuven
Valeria de Paiva, Topos Institute
Lucia Donatelli, Saarland University
Timothy Dozat, Google
Kim Gerdes, Université Paris-Saclay
Koldo Gojenola, University of the Basque Country
Loïc Grobol, Université Paris Nanterre
Bruno Guillaume, INRIA
Dag Trygve Truslew Haug, University of Oslo
Jena Hwang, Allen Institute for Artificial Intelligence
András Imrényi, Eötvös Lorand University
Alessandro Lenci, University of Pisa
Lori Levin, Carnegie Mellon University
Markéta Lopatková, Charles University Prague
Sylvain Kahane, Université Paris Nanterre
Jordan Kodner, State University of New York, Stony Brook
Sandra Kübler, Indiana University
Jan Macutek, Mathematical Institute, Slovak Academy of Sciences
Harish Tayyar Madabushi, University of Sheffield
Nicolas Mazziotta, Université de Liège
Alexander Mehler, Johann Wolfgang Goethe Universität Frankfurt am Main
Simon Mille, Dublin City University
Pierre André Ménard, Computer research institute of Montréal
Yusuke Miyao, The University of Tokyo
Simonetta Montemagni, ILC-CNR
Alexis Nasr, Aix Marseille Univ
Joakim Nivre, Uppsala University
Pierre Nugues, Lund University
Timothy John Osborne, Zhejiang University
Petya Osenova, Bulgarian Academy of Sciences
Robert Östling, Stockholm University

Simon Petitjean, Heinrich-Heine Universität Düsseldorf
Dirk Pijpops, Université de Liège
Michael Regan, University of Colorado, Boulder
Mathilde Regnault, Universität Stuttgart
Laurence Romain, University of Birmingham
Rudolf Rosa, Charles University Prague
Haruko Sanada, Rissho University
Beatrice Santorini, University of Pennsylvania
Giorgio Satta, Università degli studi di Padova
Sebastian Schuster, Universität des Saarlandes
Olga Scrivner, Rose-Hulman Institute of Technology
Ashwini Vaidya, Indian Institute of Technology, Delhi
Remi van Trijp, Sony Computer Sciences Laboratories Paris
Giulia Venturi, Institute for Computational Linguistics "A. Zampolli" (ILC-CNR)
Nianwen Xue, Brandeis University
Eva Zehentner, University of Zurich
Amir Zeldes, Georgetown University
Daniel Zeman, Charles University Prague
Heike Zinsmeister, Universität Hamburg
Hongxin Zhang, Zhejiang University

Table of Contents

Exploring the Constructicon:
Linguistic Analysis of a Computational CxG

Jonathan Dunn
Department of Linguistics and
New Zealand Institute for Language, Brain and Behaviour
University of Canterbury
Christchurch, New Zealand
jonathan.dunn@canterbury.ac.nz

Abstract

Recent work has formulated the task for computational construction grammar as producing a constructicon given a corpus of usage. Previous work has evaluated these unsupervised grammars using both internal metrics (for example, Minimum Description Length) and external metrics (for example, performance on a dialectology task). This paper instead takes a linguistic approach to evaluation, first learning a constructicon and then analyzing its contents from a linguistic perspective. This analysis shows that a learned constructicon can be divided into nine major types of constructions, of which *Verbal* and *Nominal* are the most common. The paper also shows that both the token and type frequency of constructions can be used to model variation across registers and dialects.

1 Introduction

Construction Grammar (CxG) is a usage-based approach to language which views grammatical structure as a set of form-meaning mappings called a *constructicon* (Langacker, 2008). From this usage-based perspective, a *construction* could belong in the grammar either (i) because it is sufficiently entrenched (i.e., frequent) that it is stored and processed as a unique item or (ii) because it is sufficiently irregular (i.e., idiomatic) that it requires a unique grammatical description (Goldberg, 2006). The advantage of CxG from this perspective is that it focuses on explaining the creativity, the flexibility, and the idiosyncrasy of actual language use in real-world settings (Goldberg, 2019).

Given this focus of CxG as a linguistic theory, the ideal computational implementation must be data-driven and unsupervised. For example, approaches which rely on manual annotations derived from individual introspection (Steels, 2017) fail to capture the usage-based foundations of CxG, in addition to being unreproducible and difficult to scale. For this reason, most recent work on computational CxG has taken an unsupervised learning approach to forming constructicons (Dunn, 2017, 2022). Such an unsupervised approach has its own challenges, however, especially the challenge of evaluation. Grammars from other syntactic paradigms can be evaluated by annotating a gold-standard corpus and then measuring the ability of both supervised and unsupervised models to predict those same sets of annotations (cf., Zeman et al. 2017, 2018). Given its usage-based foundations, this approach to evaluation is simply not feasible for computational CxG because the standard for what counts as a construction depends to some degree on the corpus or the community of speaker-hearers that is being observed.

For this reason, recent work on computational CxG has undertaken both internal and external evaluations for determining which one of a set of posited constructicons is better. An internal metric measures the fit between a grammar and a given corpus to determine which alternative constructicon offers a better description (Dunn, 2018b, 2019a). This work has drawn on Minimum Description Length (Goldsmith, 2001, 2006) as an evaluation metric because it combines both descriptive adequacy (i.e., the fit between the grammar and the test set) and model complexity (i.e., the number and the type of constructions in the grammar).

An external metric evaluates and compares constructicons using their performance when applied to a specific prediction task. Recent work has focused on the use of computational CxG for modelling individual differences (Dunn and Nini, 2021), register variation (Dunn and Tayyar Madabushi, 2021), and population-based dialectal differences (Dunn, 2018a, 2019c,b; Dunn and Wong, 2022). Because CxG is a usage-based paradigm, the definition of a construction that is referenced above depends on both entrenchment and idiomaticity. Both of these are properties of a corpus of usage rather than properties of a language as a whole.

Proceedings of the First International Workshop on Construction Grammars and NLP (CxGs+NLP, GURT/SyntaxFest 2023), pages 1 - 11
March 9-12, 2023

In other words, it is only meaningful to describe *entrenchment* relative to a particular individual, dialectal community, or context of production. These external tasks have therefore focused on the degree to which computational CxG can in fact account for differences in usage across these dimensions.

The contribution of this paper is to undertake a detailed qualitative and quantitative evaluation of a learned grammar. While it is not possible to start with gold-standard linguistic annotations of constructions, it is possible to apply a linguistic analysis to the output of an unsupervised, usage-based framework. We start by describing the model and the data which are used to learn the constructicon (Section 2) before presenting examples of types of constructions that it contains (Section 3). We then proceed to a quantitative analysis of the grammar (Section 4). Finally, we end with a discussion of the challenge of parsing a nested and hierarchical grammar which contains representations at different levels of abstraction (Section 5).

2 Methods and Data

Computational CxG is a theory in the form of a grammar induction algorithm that provides a reproducible constructicon given a corpus of exposure (Dunn, 2017, 2022). The theory is divided into three components, each of which models a particular aspect of the emergence of constructicons given exposure to a corpus of usage.

First, a psychologically-plausible measure of association, the ΔP, is used to measure the entrenchment of potential constructions (Ellis, 2007; Dunn, 2018c). These potential constructions are sequences of lexical, syntactic, and semantic slot-constraints. The problem of *category formation* is to define the inventory of fillers that are used for slot-constraints. In this implementation, lexical constraints are based on word-forms, without lemmatization. Syntactic constraints are formulated using the universal part-of-speech tagset (Petrov et al., 2012) and implemented using the Ripple Down Rules algorithm (Nguyen et al., 2016). Semantic constraints are based on distributional semantics, with k-means clustering used to discretize fastText embeddings (Grave et al., 2018). The semantic constraints in the examples in this paper are formulated using the index of the corresponding clusters, a simple notational convention.

Second, an association-based beam search is used to identify constructions of arbitrary length by finding the most entrenched representations in reference to a matrix of ΔP values (Dunn, 2019a). The beam search parsing strategy allows the grammar to avoid relying on heuristic frames and templates for producing potential constructions.

Third, a measure of fit based on the Minimum Description Length paradigm is used to balance the increased storage of item-specific constructions against the increased computation of more generalized constructions (Dunn, 2018b). The point is that any construction could become entrenched but more idiomatic constructions come at a higher cost.

The contribution of this paper is to evaluate this existing model of CxG (Dunn, 2022) rather than to alter its overall method of learning a constructicon. We therefore apply the model without further discussion of its implementation and focus instead on a linguistic analysis of the resulting constructicon. The data used to learn grammars is collected from three sets of corpora: social media (Twitter), non-fiction articles (Wikipedia), and web pages (from the Common Crawl) drawn from the *Corpus of Global Language Use* (Dunn, 2020). This training corpus contains 2 million words per register for a total of 6 million words.

From a usage-based perspective, exposure to language continues after the grammar has been acquired and such exposure might change the entrenchment of particular constructions. The model thus undertakes a second pruning stage which updates the constructicon given an additional 2 million words of exposure (Dunn, 2022). The model observes sub-corpora from each of the three registers in increments of 100k words. Each construction in the grammar receives an activation weight with an initial value of 1. For each sub-corpus in which a construction is not observed, its weight decays by 0.25. For each sub-corpus in which a construction is observed, its weight is returned to 1. When a construction's weight falls below 0, it is forgotten and removed from the grammar.

This is a simple model of the way in which continued exposure leads to the forgetting of previously entrenched constructions. While somewhat arbitrary, the decay rate (0.25) is chosen to ensure that a construction is not forgotten simply because it occurs primarily in a specific register: this decay rate means that a construction must be absent from four successive sub-corpora, thus ensuring that each of the three registers has been observed. Thus, this pruning method removes unproductive constructions given additional exposure while ensuring that all three registers remain represented. A package for reproducing this grammar induction algorithm is available[1] as well as the specific grammars used in this study.[2]

This method produces a constructicon that contains 12,856 constructions. The analysis in this paper is based on using this constructicon to annotate samples of 1 million words from 12 independent corpora: Project Gutenberg (Rae et al., 2019), Wikipedia (Ortman, 2018), European Parliament proceedings (Tiedemann, 2012), news article comments (Kesarwani, 2018), product reviews (Zhang et al., 2015), blogs (Schler et al., 2006), and tweets from six countries (with 1 million words representing each country; Dunn 2020). This range of corpora allows us to consider both register (different contexts of production) and dialect (different populations using the same register) when measuring the frequency and the productivity of individual constructions in the grammar.

3 Categorizing Constructions

In this section we categorize the learned constructions to aid our quantitative analysis of the contents of the constructicon. We annotate a random sample of 20% of the constructions using the categorization described below, thus allowing an estimate of the overall composition of the grammar. The primary categories are *Verbal*, *Nominal*, *Adjectival*, *Adpositional*, *Transitional*, *Clausal*, *Adverbial*, *Sentential*, and *Fixed Idioms*. These categories are defined and exemplified in this section.

The first category consists of VERBAL constructions. As shown in (1), we notate the construction using its slot-constraints, with each slot separated by dashes. Lexical constraints are shown in italics; syntactic constraints are shown in small caps; and semantic constraints are shown using the index of their distributional cluster (e.g., <521>). Using this notation, the construction in (1) is a simple passive verb phrase in a continuous aspect, defined using primarily syntactic constraints.

(1) [AUX – *being* – VERB]
(1a) were being proposed
(1b) was being spread
(1c) is being invaded
(1d) am being kept

The verbal construction in (2) now contains a semantic constraint (<521>). This domain contains lexical items like *house* and *carriage*, all locations that can be moved into or out of. The construction thus captures a meaning-based pattern of movement in relation to some area.

(2) [VERB – ADP – DET – <521>]
(2a) come to this house
(2b) leaped into a carriage
(2c) seated at that window
(2d) hurried across the room
(2e) lying on the floor

A lexical constraint for the main verb is shown in the construction in (3). This leads to an idiomatic usage of *play*, a set of utterances whose behaviour differs from the basic transitive verb phrase. The construction in (4) shows the influence of a lexical constraint in a different position, here *time* as a noun introducing the verb phrase. This again results in idiomatic utterances with behaviour more specific than a construction with only syntactic constraints. Finally, the lexical constraint in (5) defines a particle verb, again with idiomatic semantics resulting for the utterances in (5a) through (5e). This series of examples shows how a lexical constraint in different locations within a verb phrase leads to different types of idiomatic verbal constructions.

(3) [*play* – DET – NOUN]
(3a) play the game
(3b) play the part
(3c) play the coquette
(3d) play the king

(4) [*time* – *to* – VERB]
(4a) time to plead
(4b) time to write
(4c) time to tell
(4d) time to consider
(4e) time to worry

(5) [*to* – VERB – *down*]
(5a) to sit down
(5b) to put down
(5c) to settle down
(5d) to bring down
(5e) to strike down

While these examples are relatively simple verbal constructions, a more complex example is shown in (6). This construction contains a main

[1] https://www.github.com/jonathandunn/c2xg
[2] https://doi.org/10.18710/CES0L8

verb with an infinitive complement followed by an argument that takes the form of a noun phrase. The entrenchment of these more complex constructions shows the flexibility of computational CxG as well as the infeasibility of relying on the introspection of individual linguists.

(6) [VERB – *to* – *be* – <830> – ADP – DET – NOUN]
  (6a) seem to be unaware of the fact
  (6b) came to be known as the *Newcastle*
  (6c) have to be supplied from that source
  (6d) is to be found in the world
  (6e) expect to be ushered into the temple

Moving to NOMINAL constructions, the first examples show the influence that a semantic constraint in one slot exerts across the entire construction. We focus here on complex nominal constructions, with both of these first examples containing a subordinate adpositional phrase within the noun phrase. In each case, the noun in the adpositional phrase is constrained to a specific semantic domain. In (7), this leads to lexical items like *empire* and *palace* and, in (8), like *ground* and *road.* Not all examples of a construction are perfect matches; an example of this is shown in (8e), marked with an asterisk, in which the first word is actually a mistagged verb rather than a noun.

(7) [NOUN – *of* – DET – <587>]
  (7a) part of the empire
  (7b) inmates of the palace
  (7c) guardianship of the wanderer
  (7d) pursuit of a chimera
  (7e) circuit of the citadel

(8) [NOUN – ADP – *the* – <484>]
  (8a) feet on the ground
  (8b) side of the road
  (8c) law of the land
  (8d) entrance of the path
  (8e) journey through the forest
  (8e) *wanders around the forest

(9) [*one* – ADP – *the* – *best* – NOUN]

  (9a) one of the best paintings
  (9b) one of the best apologies
  (9c) one of the best examples
  (9d) one of the best books

More idiomatic noun phrases, with lexical constraints, are shown in (9) and (10). In the first, an adpositional phrase *one of the best* functions as a single adjective. In the second, a superlative adjective frames the core noun phrase. In both cases, these constructions provide additional flexibility to describe unique nominal phrases, made into constructions by their entrenchment and their idiosyncrasy in this set of usage.

(10) [*the* – *most* – ADJ – NOUN]
  (10a) the most amusing instance
  (10b) the most violent writhings
  (10c) the most astounding instances
  (10d) the most important generalizations
  (10e) the most unfavourable circumstances

A single example of an ADJECTIVAL construction is shown in (11). While the previous nominal constructions included adjectival material within them, this construction as a whole provides a modifier for a noun phrase. For example, (11e) as an abstract adjective could be combined with a variety of nouns like *immigrants*, *the elderly*, or *house sparrows* to form a larger nominal construction.

(11) [*huge* – NOUN – *of*]
  (11a) huge pair of
  (11b) huge influx of
  (11c) huge clumps of
  (11d) huge piece of
  (11e) huge population of

The next category is ADPOSITIONAL constructions, as shown in (12) through (14). As before, a semantic constraint leads to a meaning-based group of utterances, as with the terms specific to legal language in (12). In other words, this adpositional construction is specific to the category of nouns contained within it. A potentially problematic case is shown in (12e), here with what is likely a fixed idiom, where *case* is not used in the legal sense. A lexical constraint for the head noun in (13) leads to idiosyncratic adpositional phrases with *beginning*. Other adpositional constructions are more syntactically complex. For example, the phrase in (14) transitions from a noun into a relative clause which describes that noun.

(12) [ADP – DET – <959>]
  (12a) in the case
  (12b) of the provisions
  (12c) as a rule
  (12d) from the petitioners
  (12e) ?in which case

(13) [ADP – *the* – *beginning*]
  (13a) towards the beginning
  (13b) at the beginning
  (13c) from the beginning
  (13d) in the beginning
  (13e) for the beginning

(14) [ADP – *the* – NOUN – *where*]
  (14a) in the world where
  (14b) at the spot where
  (14c) from the point where
  (14d) near the ceiling where

The example of an adpositional phrase that transitions into a relative clause in (14) introduces another category of constructions, those which capture TRANSITIONAL material connecting other types of constructions. In particular, the constructions in this category capture different types of transitions without containing the substance of the involved structures themselves. For example, in (15) there is the introduction of a new main clause with a first-person verb phrase. In (16) there is the introduction of a subordinate clause. In (17) there is a comparison between two nominal constructions. The final example in (17e) represents a problematic parse: the phrase is likely *at least* rather than *least* alone. These examples show how this category serves to link other constructions together.

(15) [*but* – *i* – VERB]
  (15a) but i think
  (15b) but i knew
  (15c) but i regret
  (15d) but i noticed

(16) [SCONJ – VERB – *to*]
  (16a) without seeming to
  (16b) because according to
  (16c) as opposed to
  (16d) while listening to
  (16e) in resorting to

(17) [ADV – <917> – *than*]
  (17a) far deeper than
  (17b) considerably better than
  (17c) now more than
  (17d) much smaller than
  (17e) *least better than

While transitional constructions focus mainly on the connecting element, CLAUSAL constructions are those which contain a significant portion of a subordinate clause. For instance, (18) is an example of a relative clause embedded within a larger noun phrase and (19) of a relative clause in which the subject is defined by the proceeding element. A problematic example is shown in (19e), where the phrase *a lot* is treated as two separate slots. The complex subordinate clause in (20) consists of a gerund within an adpositional phrase, where the verb is further defined by a semantic constraint. Finally, a reduced relative clause is captured by (21), again with a semantic constraint on the verb. This series of examples shows the way in which subordinate clauses are captured in the grammar.

(18) [NOUN – ADP – *those* – *who*]
  (18a) hearts of those who
  (18b) arguments of those who
  (18c) side of those who
  (18d) minds of those who
  (18e) tactics of those who

(19) [*which* – VERB – *a* – NOUN]
  (19a) which formed a snare
  (19b) which occasioned a detour
  (19c) which presented a problem
  (19d) which contained a letter
  (19e) ? which looked a lot

(20) [SCONJ – <113> – DET – NOUN – *of*]
  (20a) by taking the life of
  (20b) in sacrificing the rights of
  (20c) after collecting the remains of
  (20d) by applying a drop of
  (20e) in neglecting the cultivation of

(21) [DET – NOUN – *he* – <830>]
  (21a) the loan he solicited
  (21b) the temple he discovered
  (21c) the words he used
  (21d) the life he led
  (21e) the flask he carried

While these clausal constructions are connected into the main clause itself, the category of ADVERBIAL constructions contain clauses which are more independent of the structure of the main clause. For example, in (22) there is a gerund clause within an adpositional phrase, now with a semantic constraint. In (23) there is an adposition introducing a finite verb. And in (24), with a lexical constraint,

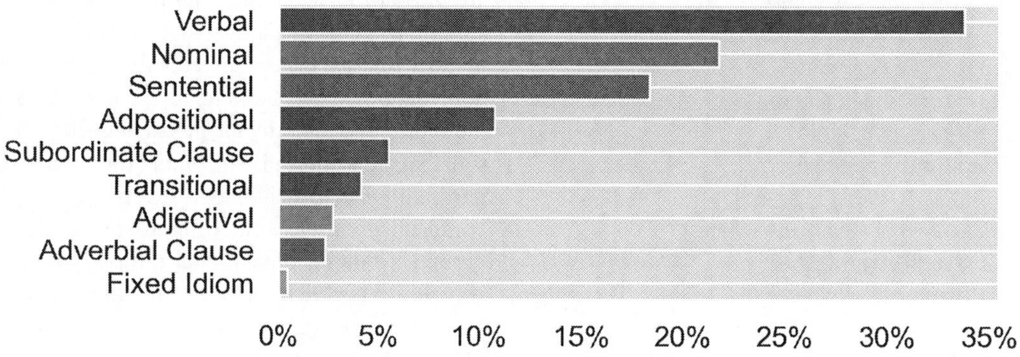

Figure 1: Distribution of Construction Types in the Grammar

there is a similar construction again with a finite verb. While similar to the clausal category, this class of constructions is less integrated with the main clause structure.

(22) [SCONJ – VERB – ADP – DET – <512>]
(22a) in dealing with that section
(22b) after referring to the matter
(22c) as bearing on the question
(22d) without glancing within the volume
(22e) by bringing up the subject

(23) [SCONJ – PRON – AUX – VERB – *to*]
(23a) that it would come to
(23b) if he had lived to
(23c) as they were trying to

(24) [*when* – DET – NOUN – *is*]
(24a) when the end is
(24b) when a man is
(24c) when the heart is
(24d) when the patient is
(24e) when the temperature is

(25) [PRON – *were* – VERB – ADP]
(25a) we were accosted by
(25b) they were employed by
(25c) these were succeeded by
(25d) they were drilled by
(25e) ? who were barred from

SENTENTIAL constructions contain the structure of the main clause. This category overlaps to some degree with verbal constructions; the key difference is that the sentential constructions contain the subject while verbal constructions do not. A simple passive clause is shown in (25), together with an adpositional argument. In many examples, this adpositional argument specifies the agent, but the example in (25e) differs in specifying a location. An active clause introducing an indirect speech clause is shown in (26), constrained to the subject *he*. Finally, a sequence of main verb and infinitive is shown in (27), with the final verb defined using a semantic constraint.

(26) [*he* – VERB – *that*]
(26a) he remembered that
(26b) he said that
(26c) he realised that
(26d) he discovered that
(26e) he promised that

(27) [*they* – VERB – PART – <583>]
(27a) they began to draw
(27b) they threatened to destroy
(27c) they chose to assert
(27d) they wanted to persuade
(27e) they began to look

A more complex passive construction is shown in (28), containing both a semantic constraint on the main verb as well as an adpositional argument. Finally, a main clause with an existential *there* as subject is shown in (29). As with the clausal constructions, these sentential constructions overlap with verbal constructions, thus illustrating the problem of parsing as clipping (c.f., Section 5).

(28) [NOUN – *are* – ADV – <830> – ADP]
(28a) villages are thickly scattered about
(28b) recruits are never measured for
(28c) substances are universally regarded as
(28d) lines are then drawn from

	Blogs		Comments		Parliament		Gutenberg		Reviews		Wikipedia	
	Freq	*Type*	*Freq*	*Type*	*Freq*	*Type*	*Freq*	*Type*	*Freq*	*Type*	*Freq*	*Type*
Adjectival	57	36	69	43	66	40	79	59	80	45	73	43
Adpositional	207	141	222	150	433	215	401	272	221	145	327	181
Adverbial	118	87	107	80	117	79	95	80	127	88	56	45
Idiom	32	3	33	2	54	13	12	4	27	3	13	2
Nominal	95	82	128	109	261	184	189	163	123	101	179	138
Sentential	199	115	144	103	176	107	144	110	195	111	109	77
Clausal	156	99	157	112	182	117	154	112	152	97	70	58
Transitional	102	75	96	77	103	72	107	89	108	82	49	43
Verbal	137	104	143	116	188	142	139	122	144	108	116	86

Table 1: Mean Frequency and Productivity of Constructions by Category and Register

(29) [*there* – VERB – *a* – NOUN – ADP]
(29a) there was a kind of
(29b) there is a habit of
(29c) there were a number of
(29d) there were a couple of
(29e) there came a sort of

The final category of constructions are FIXED IDIOMS, which here are mainly lexical constructions. These have a very limited number of types for each construction because the constraints are lexical: *in favor of*, *seems to be*, *all the best*, or *no matter* ADV. Taken together, the categories illustrated in this section describe the contents of the learned constructicon. A quantitative analysis of the distribution of construction types and their properties follows in the next section.

3.1 Marginal Examples of Categories

Not all constructions that are classified as belonging to a given category are equally good examples of that category. This section provides a few examples of such marginal tokens in order to provide a more transparent picture of the grammar as a whole. Starting with a construction categorized as adjectival in (30), we could also see this being categorized as a nominal construction. The reason behind this annotation decision is that the overall unit is used to describe a part of some piece of writing.

(30) [*beginning* – ADP – DET – NOUN]
(30a) beginning of this note
(30b) beginning of the article

A marginal example of a nominal construction is shown in (31). Here, this sequence of noun and adpositional phrase, when taken in context, is quite likely to be two separate arguments of a double object verb phrase: for example, "They [ran [this country] [with the help...]]. However, the construction itself only includes the two arguments on their own. At the same time, (31) would clip together nicely with a verbal construction (c.f., Section 5).

(31) [*this* – NOUN – ADP – *the* – NOUN]
(31a) this country with the help
(31b) this morning to the surprise

(32) [VERB – *by* – DET – <88>]
(32a) occcupied by a foreign
(32b) used by the american

A final marginal example is shown in (32), here within the verbal category. This example is a passive verb together with a prepositional phrase that expresses the agent. The issue here is that only part of the noun phrase specifying the agent is explicitly defined, and the slot constraint is semantic. From the perspective of clipping constructions, many noun phrases could be merged here but would not experience the same emergent relationships between slot-constraints. In other words, the impact of the semantic constraint would not transcend the construction boundary. These examples are meant to show some weaknesses of both the categorization scheme and the constructions themselves.

4 Distribution of Construction Types

The first step in quantifying the contents of the constructicon is to estimate the relative distribution across these nine categories. This is shown in Figure 1 using annotations of 20% of the grammar to estimate the overall distribution. The y-axis contains a bar chart for each category of construction

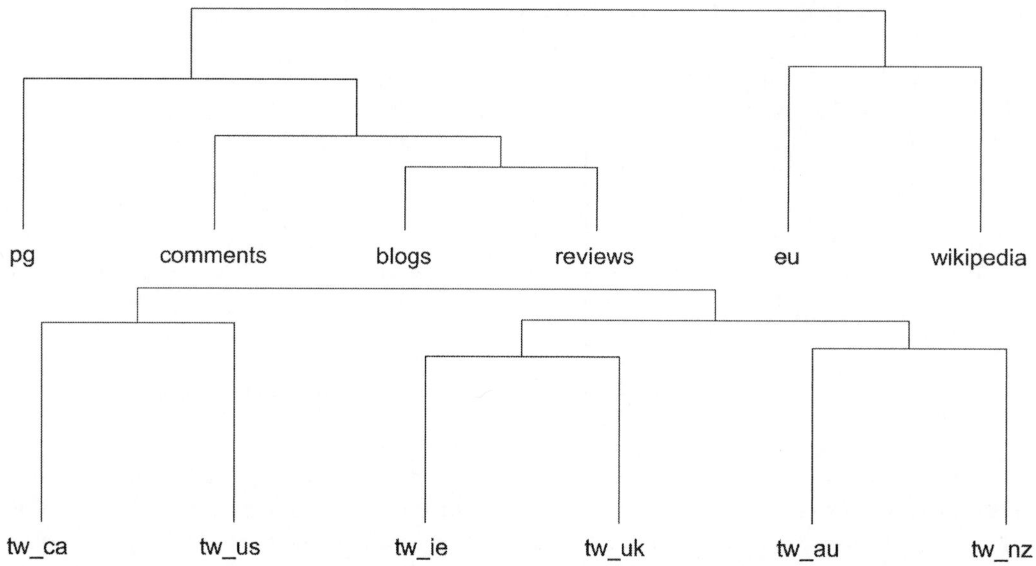

Figure 2: Clustering of Corpora Using Burrow's Delta, Register (Above) and Dialect (Below)

and the x-axis shows the percent of the constructicon which falls into that category.

Thus, for example, the most frequent type of construction is *verbal* at 33.7% of the grammar, followed by *nominal* at 21.7% and *sentential* at 18.3%. This distribution is not surprising given that verbs and nouns are the most common open-class lexical items and that sentential clauses form the basic structure of sentences.

The next step is to measure the frequency of each construction and the number of its unique types, thus capturing its productivity. These measures of frequency and productivity are corpus-specific in the sense that different constructions are more likely to be used in specific contexts or by specific populations. We thus consider 12 distinct corpora of 1 million words each, six representing distinct registers and six representing distinct populations within the same register.

Starting with a comparison across registers, Table 1 shows the mean frequency of tokens and the mean number of types for each class of constructions in each register-specific corpus. For example, the Project Gutenberg corpus has significantly more types per adpositional construction than the corpus of blogs. While some categories of construction are more common in the grammar, the measures in Table 1 take the average for each category. While there are more verbal constructions in the grammar, for example, adpositional and sentential constructions have more tokens per construction.

The frequency of each category of construction (i.e., the mean number of tokens) also provides a view of the grammatical differences between these six registers. For instance, blogs contain fewer adpositional constructions than other registers while published books and speeches in parliament contain approximately twice as many overall. Wikipedia articles contain many fewer cases of clasual and transitional constructions, indicating a register with fewer embedded clauses. Further, blogs have nearly twice as many sentential constructions (i.e., base main clauses) as Wikipedia, but many fewer adpositional phrases. This would indicate that information can be packaged in short sentences or in additional adpositional constructions, depending on the register. Note that another set of Wikipedia corpora was available during the grammar learning process, so that the reduced frequencies of these types are not simply a matter of under-fitting the register.

The next question is whether the differences in frequency of individual constructions across corpora are random or whether they reveal underlying relationships between the corpora themselves. In other words, given the frequencies of each construction in the grammar, we would expect a meaningful grammar to create meaningful relationships between conditions. A *condition* in this case refers to the register or the population represented by the corpus. This is shown in Figure 2 using Burrow's Delta to calculate the distances between corpora and then hierarchical clustering to visualize relationships based on these distances.

The figure shows relationships between registers on the top. The two core clusters are with modern formal documents (EU and WIKIPEDIA) and digital crowd-sourced documents (COMMENTS and BLOGS and REVIEWS). The books from Project Gutenberg, from a different historical period, are an outlier. On the bottom the figure shows relationships between different dialects within the same register (tweets). The core pairs are the countries which are closest in geographic terms: Ireland and the UK together with Australia and New Zealand, with Canada and the US as a distant pair. In both cases, we see that the frequencies of constructions in the grammar provide meaningful relationships between both registers and dialects. This is important because it shows that the differing frequencies of constructions are not simply arbitrary patterns from this particular model but also reproduce two sets of real-world relationships.

5 Clipping: The Problem of Parsing

The analysis in this paper has categorized and described the kinds of constructions that are contained in a learned constructicon, has quantified the frequency and productivity of each kind, and has shown that the usage of these constructions can reconstruct meaningful relationships between corpora. The analysis of construction types in Section 3, however, reveals a major challenge in this approach to computational CxG: the unification or *clipping together* of these constructions into complete utterances during parsing (Jackendoff, 2013).

The idea in CxG is that word-forms are not the basic building blocks of grammar. Rather, the types of constructions analyzed in this paper form the basic units, themselves built out of slot-constraints that depend on basic category formation processes. With the exception of short utterances, however, no single construction provides a complete description of a linguistic form. These constructions must be clipped together: a sentential construction, for example, joined with a verbal construction and then a nominal construction. CxG posits a continuum between the lexicon and the grammar, so that the constructicon contains basic units at different levels of abstraction. We must distinguish, however, between **first-order constructions** of the type discussed in this paper and **second-order constructions** which are formed by clipping together these lower constructions. A complete constructicon would thus also contain emergent structures formed from multiple first-order constructions.

As a desideratum for future developments, we can conceptualize two types of second-order constructions: First, SLOT-RECURSION would allow a higher-order construction to contain first-order constructions as slot-fillers. For example, the set of sentential constructions could be expanded by allowing verbal constructions to fill verbal slots. Second, SLOT-CLIPPING would allow two overlapping constructions to be merged, for instance connecting a transitional construction with a verbal construction. An overlapping shared slot-constraint would license such slot-clipping unifications.

6 Conclusions

The main contribution of this paper has been to provide a qualitative linguistic analysis of a learned construction grammar, providing a new perspective on grammars which have previously been evaluated from a quantitative perspective. We presented a division of construction types into nine categories such as *Verbal* and *Nominal*, with those two open-class categories the most common. The discussion of examples shows both the range and the robustness of computational construction grammar.

This linguistic analysis does point to two current weaknesses: First, not all constructions fit nicely into the categories used for annotation (c.f., Section 3.1). A truly usage-based grammar does not necessarily align with introspection-based analysis, especially in regards to boundaries between constructions. Introspection often focuses on constructions which are complete or self-contained units, while the computational constructions place common pivot points at boundaries. Second, these constructions do not generally describe entire utterances, so that we must consider a form of clipping to provide complete parses (c.f., Section 5).

From a quantitative perspective, the analysis of register and dialectal differences shows that the productivity of these constructions also reproduces expected relationships between corpora. This is important for providing an external evaluation of the grammar: the differences between registers, for example, show how functions which are salient in a given communicative situation ultimately drive constructional frequencies. In other words, the frequencies of different types of constructions reflect meaningful patterns in real-world usage.

References

J Dunn. 2017. Computational Learning of Construction Grammars. *Language & Cognition*, 9(2):254–292.

J. Dunn. 2018a. Finding Variants for Construction-Based Dialectometry: A Corpus-Based Approach to Regional CxGs. *Cognitive Linguistics*, 29(2):275–311.

J Dunn. 2018b. Modeling the Complexity and Descriptive Adequacy of Construction Grammars. *In Proceedings of the Society for Computation in Linguistics*, pages 81–90.

J Dunn. 2018c. Multi-Unit Association Measures: Moving beyond pairs of words. *International Journal of Corpus Linguistics*, 23(2):183–215.

J. Dunn. 2019a. Frequency vs. Association for Constraint Selection in Usage-Based Construction Grammar. In *Proceedings of the Workshop on Cognitive Modeling and Computational Linguistics*, page 117–128.

J. Dunn. 2019b. Global Syntactic Variation in Seven Languages: Toward a Computational Dialectology. *Frontiers in Artificial Intelligence*, 2:15.

J. Dunn. 2019c. Modeling Global Syntactic Variation in English Using Dialect Classification. In *Proceedings of the Sixth Workshop on NLP for Similar Languages, Varieties and Dialects*, pages 42–53.

J. Dunn. 2020. Mapping Languages: the Corpus of Global Language Use. *Language Resources and Evaluation*, 54:999–1018.

J. Dunn. 2022. Exposure and Emergence in Usage-Based Grammar: Computational Experiments in 35 Languages. *Cognitive Linguistics*, 33:659–699.

J Dunn and A Nini. 2021. Production vs Perception: The Role of Individuality in Usage-Based Grammar Induction. In *Proceedings of the Workshop on Cognitive Modeling and Computational Linguistics*, pages 149–159.

J. Dunn and H Tayyar Madabushi. 2021. Learned Construction Grammars Converge Across Registers Given Increased Exposure. In *Conference on Natural Language Learning*, pages 268–278.

J. Dunn and S. Wong. 2022. Stability of Syntactic Dialect Classification over Space and Time. In *Proceedings of the 29th International Conference on Computational Linguistics*, pages 26–36.

N. Ellis. 2007. Language Acquisition as Rational Contingency Learning. *Applied Linguistics*, 27(1):1–24.

A. Goldberg. 2006. *Constructions at Work: The Nature of Generalization in Language.* Oxford University Press, Oxford.

A. Goldberg. 2019. *Explain Me This.* Princeton University Press.

J. Goldsmith. 2001. Unsupervised Learning of the Morphology of a Natural Language. *Computational Linguistics*, 27(2):153–198.

J. Goldsmith. 2006. An Algorithm for the Unsupervised Learning of Morphology. *Natural Language Engineering*, 12(4):353–371.

E. Grave, P. Bojanowski, P. Gupta, A. Joulin, and T. Mikolov. 2018. Learning Word Vectors for 157 Languages. In *Proceedings of the International Conference on Language Resources and Evaluation*, pages 3483–3487.

R. Jackendoff. 2013. Constructions in the Parallel Architecture. In *The Oxford Handbook of Construction Grammar*, pages 70–92. Oxford University Press.

A. Kesarwani. 2018. New York Times Comments. Kaggle.

R. Langacker. 2008. *Cognitive Grammar: A Basic Introduction.* Oxford University Press, Oxford.

Dat Quoca Dai Quocb Dat Quoca Dai Quocb Nguyen, Dat Quoca Dai Quocb Dat Quoca Dai Quocb Nguyen, Dang Ducc Pham, and Son Baod Pham. 2016. A Robust Transformation-based Learning Approach Using Ripple Down Rules for Part-of-Speech Tagging. *AI Communications*, 29(3):409–422.

M. Ortman. 2018. Wikipedia Sentences. Kaggle.

S. Petrov, D. Das, and R. McDonald. 2012. A Universal Part-of-Speech Tagset. In *Proceedings of the Eighth Conference on Language Resources and Evaluation*, pages 2089–2096. European Language Resources Association.

J. Rae, A. Potapenko, S. Jayakumar, and T. Lillicrap. 2019. Compressive Transformers for Long-Range Sequence Modelling.

J. Schler, M. Koppel, S. Argamon, and J. Pennebaker. 2006. Effects of Age and Gender on Blogging. In *Proceedings of 2006 AAAI Spring Symposium on Computational Approaches for Analyzing Weblogs.*

L. Steels. 2017. Basics of Fluid Construction Grammar. *Constructions and Frames*, 9(2):178–255.

J. Tiedemann. 2012. Parallel Data, Tools and Interfaces in OPUS. In *Proceedings of the Eighth International Conference on Language Resources and Evaluation*, pages 2214–2218.

D. Zeman, J. Hajič, M. Popel, M. Potthast, M. Straka, F. Ginter, J. Nivre, and S. Petrov. 2018. CoNLL 2018 Shared Task: Multilingual Parsing from Raw Text to Universal Dependencies. In *Proceedings of the CoNLL 2018 Shared Task: Multilingual Parsing from Raw Text to Universal Dependencies*, pages 1–21.

D. Zeman, M. Popel, M. Straka, J. Hajič, and Others. 2017. CoNLL 2017 Shared Task: Multilingual parsing from raw text to Universal Dependencies. In

Proceedings of the CoNLL 2017 Shared Task: Multilingual Parsing from Raw Text to Universal Dependencies, pages 1–19.

Xiang Zhang, Junbo Zhao, and Yann LeCun. 2015. Character-level convolutional networks for text classification.

Constructions, Collocations, and Patterns: Alternative Ways of Construction Identification in a Usage-based, Corpus-driven Theoretical Framework

Gábor Simon
Eötvös Loránd University Budapest
simon.gabor@btk.elte.hu

Abstract

There is a serious theoretical and methodological dilemma in usage-based construction grammar: how to identify constructions based on corpus pattern analysis. The present paper provides an overview of this dilemma, focusing on argument structure constructions (ASCs) in general. It seeks to answer the question of how a data-driven construction grammatical description can be built on the collocation data extracted from corpora. The study is of meta-scientific interest: it compares theoretical proposals in construction grammar regarding how they handle co-occurrences emerging from a corpus. Discussing alternative bottom-up approaches to the notion of construction, the paper concludes that there is no one-to-one correspondence between corpus patterns and constructions. Therefore, a careful analysis of the former can empirically ground both the identification and the description of constructions.

1 Introduction

If there is a dichotomy between construction grammar and NLP technologies, it can be considered a multidirectional theoretical problem as well. On the one hand, NLP models and methods need constant theoretical support from CxG approaches to language. On the other hand, constructionist frameworks also need to devote more attention to data extraction techniques, because this may result in a more appropriate bottom-up modelling of the complex system of the constructicon. The present paper aims at bridging the gap between data-driven collocation analysis and the theoretical endeavor of construction grammar, focusing on argument structure constructions (ASCs). Thus, the following pages (merging the genres of a metatheoretical proposal and a critical review) provide the reader not with an empirical analysis of a specific issue, but with an overview of how we can refine our knowledge of constructions based on collocation patterns.

In the most general sense, grammatical constructions are form-meaning pairs that are at least partially arbitrary (Croft 2001: 18), i.e., some aspect of their form or function cannot be predicted from their components or from other existing constructions (Goldberg 2006: 5). Building on this definition, constructionist grammatical approaches model our knowledge of the language as a network of constructions of varying complexity: morphemes, word forms and syntactic structures (Goldberg 2019: 36; Croft 2001).

This kind of fluidity and flexibility certainly has a liberating effect on theorizing, since a single concept can explain an extremely wide range of phenomena previously isolated into rigid taxonomies. However, it may paralyse corpus-driven research based on data analysis, since it does not even provide the researcher with clear concepts for defining and/or identifying the central phenomenon. What should be the size (and complexity) of the structure whose occurrences are to be analyzed? How large a sample should we take? What quantifiable data will be relevant in mapping the diversity of the phenomenon?

Illustrating the emerging problems with a specific example, consider the following issues: is the noun of the expression *kick the bucket* a construction in its own right, or can it only be

Proceedings of the First International Workshop on Construction Grammars and NLP (CxGs+NLP, GURT/SyntaxFest 2023), pages 12 - 20

described as a component of the construction as a whole? If we accept the former, what is the relation between *bucket* and the nouns in the expressions *kick the ball* (in a soccer match) or *kick the habit*?

Moving a step further, is the structure *kicked the bucket* merely a realization of the initial example above, or is it an independent construction, given that in the COCA corpus the past tense verb form has almost the same frequency (55) as the infinitive (70), much more than the present tense singular third person form of the verb (19)?[1] And to what extent can a CxG analysis distinguish between the structure *kicking the bucket* and the structure *emptying the bucket*, if the collocation strength of the two verb forms does not differ significantly (7.85 and 8.83 in MI score)?

William Croft (2001: 17) summarizes this dilemma in an illuminating way: "[t]he constructional tail has come to wag the syntactic dog: everything from words to the most general syntactic and semantic rules can be represented as constructions." This leads us to the following questions: (i) How can the researcher delineate individual constructions as empirical facts in language use? (ii) How can data-driven analysis of corpus patterns support construction grammatical description?[2]

A possible solution to the problem of construction identification in a corpus may lie in the adaptation of the distributional approach to construction grammar (Goldberg 2019: 39): to decide what will be a construction in a language, we must first identify the units that express the same thing in a similar or identical way, then observe their distribution and what other constructions might belong to that category. However, the main assumption of a distributional analysis is that there is invariability either in meaning or in form. Since constructions are holistic representations, considerable formal differences (e.g., person or tense marking) may instantiate the same schematic construction, while relatively small modifications in the form (e.g., replacing a nominal argument with another) may lead to a new construction.

One problem obviously arises from the predetermination of either the form or the meaning without having observed the data themselves. Our decision can only be theoretical, which then either works on a wide range of data (with the risk of overgeneralization and the loss of explanatory power) or necessarily narrows the scope of the construction analysis. Another one comes from the analysis of overlapping distribution. Is it the morphological elaboration of verb forms? Does it extend to word order? Or to the presence or absence of additional (potential) arguments? In other words: how many details do we need to take into consideration when describing the variability of a hypothetical construction to draw conclusions from the data at a higher level of abstraction?

Again, these questions cannot be answered from the perspective of construction grammar, which presupposes a usage-based approach in which different levels of generalizations constitute our knowledge about language. Goldberg (2006: 64), for example, defines the essence of a usage-based approach as taking into account both the facts of the actual use of linguistic expressions (frequencies, specific patterns) and the cases of generalizations (schema-level knowledge). That is, in addition to instance-based representations, knowledge of more generic constructions is also assumed, and the network of the constructicon is therefore multilevel. (See also Croft 2001: 25 and Bybee 2013 on further claims of a usage-based construction grammatical approach.) Consequently, there is no distinguishing feature which, if observed, makes the distinction between constructions clear.

It is instructive how Croft (2001: 28) formulates this dilemma: "the degree of generality of construction schemas, and the location of grammatical information in the taxonomic network is an empirical question to be answered by empirical studies of frequency patterns and psycholinguistic research on entrenchment and productivity of schematic constructions". Nevertheless, to extract assumed constructions from a data set, we need to posit the construction beforehand.

The data type of collocations may seem a good candidate for a data-driven construction identification. However, we do not know to what extent collocations can be considered constructions in themselves, or to what extent they can be used as

[1] The data are from the COCA corpus (`https://www.english-corpora.org/coca/`), last access: 11/09/2022.

[2] For the sake of clarity, it is worth noting that the present study focuses only on corpus-driven methodological framework. Therefore, corpus-based and/or corpus-assisted investigations are not the target of the paper.

a parameter for describing a construction. Consequently, collocations cannot be considered a priori data for construction identification, therefore any corpus analysis needs to determine in advance what kind of construction it wants to explore. This in turn may make scientific reasoning more circular. The primary aim of the present paper is to provide the reader with alternative ways out of this circularity.

To summarize the theoretical and methodological dilemmas raised here, we can conclude that the conceptualization of the construction and the multi-level network model of construction grammars are not very conducive to systematic and data-driven corpus analyses. As Thomas Herbst and his colleagues note, "while many usage-based researchers in cognitive linguists have, of course, embraced the corpus method, it is still true to say that they have been more interested in arriving at generalizations than in reaching the level of descriptive granularity and specificity that is typical of more traditional corpus-based approaches" (Herbst et al. 2014: 4).

In the following, first I outline the possibilities and limitations of using data types of corpus linguistics in construction descriptions (2). Then those proposals building on collocation-like patterns for mapping constructions are discussed (3). The paper ends with concluding remarks (4).

2 How can corpus data help to identify constructions?

This section aims to provide a brief outline of those corpus linguistic data types that may ground the analysis of construction based only on observable facts of language use. As Stefan Gries (2013) points out, the inclusion of corpus linguistic tools in the description of constructions is a significant shift from the early introspective methods of construction linguistic analysis. The simplest data is if there is no data, i.e., the lack of any occurrence of a construction in the corpus. It serves as an argument against the hypothetical existence of the construction based on intuition. Starting from the absence of occurrence as an extreme case, the corpus provides two types of data for construction identification: frequency and co-occurrence. However, the question is not only how and by what means we measure and make these phenomena observable, but also how we interpret them.

Absolute frequency, the total number of occurrences of a unit in the corpus, proves to be informative when one wants to observe the central variants of a structure. For example, the most frequent verb + argument combinations for each verb, or the arguments most frequently realized with a verb. The methodological limitations of this data type stem from the fact that the calculation of the absolute frequency assumes a prior definition of the unit to be measured.

Compared to the number of occurrences, the co-occurrence rate, i.e., the degree to which two (or more) words are associated in the corpus seems to be more informative. The most familiar category of co-occurring words is the one of collocation. Two words are collocated if their association is statistically significant. Collocation extraction can be performed with two kinds of method (Seretan 2011: 3): according to the n-gram method, a sequence of consecutive words can be considered fixed units of collocability (therefore, n-grams shed light on fixed word-order patterns); whereas the window method takes the context in a broader sense and explores all potential collocates that typically occur in the corpus within a certain context of the node.

Beyond counting the number of co-occurrences of words in a corpus, the other aspect of collocability is the strength of co-occurrence patterns. It can be measured using different association scores (see Evert 2009; Levshina 2015: 234–235 for more details). Without going into details about the different methods of calculation, it is worth pointing out that each value highlights a different aspect of the observed patterns. For example, the Mutual Information (MI) score is sensitive to fixed lexical units (e.g., names, phraseological units, idioms) and favors infrequent terms, the so-called hapaxes. Therefore, MI measures are particularly useful for lexicography. Other values (e.g., log likelihood, $\chi 2$ score or t-score) tend to make frequent grammatical patterns observable (Evert 2009: 1230). Thus, both idiomatic and more schematic constructions might be identified with the help of collocation extraction.

The association scores can also be distinguished according to their directionality: for instance, the ΔP value is unidirectional (i.e., the node associates the collocate or the collocate associates the node), while most of the values are bidirectional (i.e., they demonstrate a mutual association between members of the collocation). Even though ΔP is unidirectional, it is suitable for constructional measures (see Gries 2013), because one version of it can be used to measure association from the verb (ΔP, verb as cue, construction as response), and another version of it can give us data about the attraction of verb lexemes from the perspective of the construction (ΔP, construction as a cue, collexeme as response, Levshina 2015: 234). Therefore, directionality plays an important role in distinguishing the specific and schematic parts of a co-occurring pattern.

From this overview, it is perhaps clear that the observation of collocability may lead to a rich variety of verb + argument associations. But the question of whether these are real constructions remains open, which is why a more detailed methodological grounding is needed for this type of analysis. Indeed, the fact of collocability tells us how typical the occurrence of other words is in the narrower or wider context of a verb, but the reason for the occurrence of such word combinations, i.e. whether there is indeed a constructional behavior in the background or not, cannot be explained from the collocation data themselves. Seretan (2011: 4) argues that even if a pair of words does indeed typically occur together within a particular window, it is not certain that they are truly syntactically related terms, rather than random juxtapositions or mere noise (e.g., occurrences separated by a clause boundary or additional terms). Barnbrook et al. (2013: 164) draw a similar conclusion: collocations, despite their apparent significance as data type, are not really integrated into linguistic modelling.

The main problem of collocation measurement for constructional grammar is, therefore, that collocations themselves are not transparent in terms of constructions. Thus, just as we do not arrive at the empirical identification of constructions from the theoretical definition of the concept, we do not arrive at the identification of constructions on the basis of data types provided by the corpus. By way of explanation, there is no one-to-one correspondence between a pattern in a corpus and the concept of construction. Corpus analysis can help us to describe verb constructions with a variety of data, explore the features of the verbal components in them (via frequency patterns), identify fixed or flexible word order patterns (n-grams), reduce our effort to measure the variability of the construction by statistical measurements, and increase the efficacy of observing the variability of a given construction (collocation analysis). But the question of what counts as a construction in the corpus data remains unanswered even in quantitative analysis. As a consequence, for a corpus-driven description of constructions, it is necessary to narrow the gap between CxGs and corpus linguistics. In the following section, I present alternative theoretical proposals for such an attempt at integration.

3 Collocation-based construction analysis: alternative proposals

Three alternative theories of construction grammar that attempt to link the notions of construction and collocation are discussed here: radical construction grammar, the valence-based construction approach, and pattern grammar. While these theories initiate collocation-based construction identification in different ways, a common point is that extracting collocation patterns serves as the initial step to exploring higher levels of argument structure constructions.

3.1 Collocational dependencies

Croft (2001: 176-185) presents an analysis in which he considers two types of dependencies: coded and collocational dependencies. As shown in examples (1a-b), these relations are essentially syntactic in nature.

(1a) I have folks like you to open my eyes to see that love is weird, love is strange, love is good
(1b) Every time I open my eyes she is looking down at me.[3]

In both cases, the verb *open* has a subject and an object argument. The reflexive usage of the verb in (1b) demonstrates, however, that the process of opening the eye instantiates differently. In the first case, the multi-word unit can be interpreted as 'to see the truth', but in the second case, the meaning of the structure is 'open the eyes/begin to see'. The examples thus show that the encoded and collocational dependencies do not coincide (despite all apparent similarities).

Similar observations led Croft to define collocational dependencies, which prescribe

[3] The data are from the COCA corpus (`https://www.english-corpora.org/coca/`), last access: 11/09/2022.

specific phrases besides the verb (e.g. the structure *into flower* in the context of the verb *burst*) or a group of phrases (e.g. the lemmata of *cherry tree/almond tree/fruit tree* etc. in the context of the phrase *burst into flower*), as symbolizing semantic rather than syntactic relations. The figure below summarizes this interpretation, using the English idiom *spill the beans* as an example.

The collocational relationship thus links two concepts at the semantic pole (e.g. *open* → MAKES TO SEE, *eyes* → TRUTH, cf. Figure 1), and the association observed in the corpus stabilizes these semantic correspondences in language use.

On this basis, collocational relations are inherently semantic in nature, which are then represented to varying degrees in a syntactically transparent way. Consequently, Croft postulates a continuum from purely semantic collocational relations through syntactically encoded collocations to those collocations that are not transparent in any way. For instance, the verb *blossom* has the following stable collocations in the COCA corpus: *flower* (6.43), *tree* (4.48), *rose* (5.50), and *garden* (3.52). [4] These collocations imply a selectional restriction, according to which the verb under consideration is combined with words referring to flowering plants (individually or in a group). In other words, the selectional restrictions that can be identified through collocations are purely semantic collocational dependencies that help to identify constructions. However, among the collocations, one can observe *romance* (7.09), *relationship* (3.54), *friendship* (6.47) or *career* (4.18). Since the latter violate the selectional restrictions emerging from the previously observed group of collocations, it follows that we are dealing here with another construction with a figurative meaning, in which the verb means 'increases in intensity, unfolds vigorously'. Selectional restrictions are therefore not directly encoded syntactically, but they do help to identify the constructions organized around the verbs, and as collocational dependencies, they allow analyses based on word combinations.

Compared to purely semantic collocational dependencies, collocations proper represent a shift towards syntactic transparency. In Croft's system (Croft 2001: 180) collocations proper listed above function as lower-level constructions and can be subordinated to more general constructions. The occurrences of *blossom* + *flower/tree/rose/garden* (etc.) are instances of the construction [*blossom* PLANTNOUN], while the data of *blossom* + *love/friendship/career/relationship* are instances of the construction [*blossom* PROCESSNOUN]. This is a productive approach because we can describe figurative constructions without attributing any specific linguistic marker (e.g., morpheme or syntactic feature) to the figurative meaning in the language system.

The extreme cases of collocational dependencies are the so-called idiomatically combining expressions (Croft 2001: 181): in this category, the syntactic and the semantic pattern correspond to each other, as we saw in the case of *open the eyes*. As another example, the following collocates are at the top of the list next to the verb *burst* (*into*): *flames* (11.33), *tears* (10.97), *flame* (10. 04), *giggles* (9.67). While the first and the third cases represent the primary meaning of the verb *burst*, since they refer to a sudden change of physical state, the second and the fourth collocates cannot be categorized as instances of the general construction [*burst* + CAUSED CHANGE OF STATE]. In the case of *tears* or *giggles*, the construction can be described with the correspondences *burst* → START (SUDDENLY), *tears/giggles* → EXPRESSION OF EMOTION. Finally, in the case of *bloom* (8.07) the correspondences are the following *burst* → START TO PRODUCE, *bloom* → BLOSSOMING /FLOWERING. The idiomatic combinations are thus not only independent constructions, but also cannot be assigned to a higher, more general constructional schema. Put it differently, they are

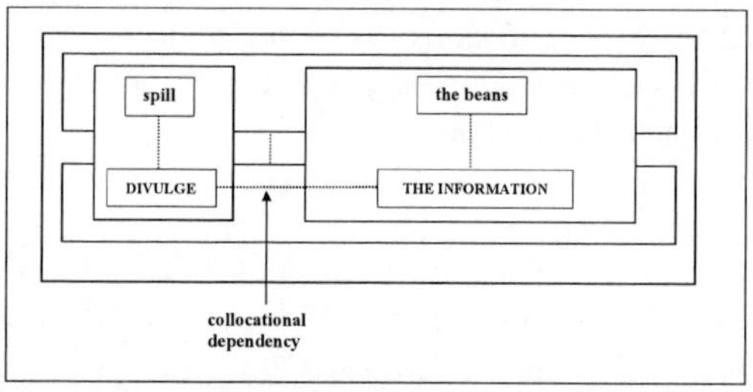

Figure 1: The schematic diagram of collocational dependencies in the idiom *spill the beans* (Croft 2001: 183)

[4]The data are from the COCA corpus (https://www.english-corpora.org/coca/), last access: 11/09/2022. The strength of collocations is measured with the MI score in the corpus.

not simply nodes on the lower level of the network of the constructicon but are nodes in themselves.

In Croft's proposal, the decisive criterion is not the presence or absence of compositionality, although it is true that – precisely because of the semantic relations symbolized by collocational dependencies – even idiomatic combinations are characterized by a degree of transparency. (Non-compositional idiomatic phrases, such as *kick the bucket*, are not transparent at all, and are therefore collocations, but not syntactically meaningful constructions – they are rather independent elements of the mental lexicon.) The crucial parameter is genericity, i.e., whether a structure can be subordinated to a higher-order construction. Collocations help to explore constructions of different degrees of abstraction along this aspect.

3.2 Valency constructions

In Herbst's constructional analysis proposal (Herbst 2014) based on valence theory, the term *collocation* does not occur, but he takes such formal patterns as a starting point for the constructional analysis that are element-specific (i.e., argument structure constructions (ASCs) are organized around specific verbs), may have a fixed word order pattern (which can be mapped with n-grams), and are based on the fact that verbs as valency carriers can open up argument positions (valency slots) in the course of construing a sentence. These initial patterns are called valency constructions in this approach which contain the potential valencies arising from the usage of a given verb and all its possible forms. As an example, two different valency constructions of the verb *give* are as follows:[5]

(2a) [SCU: NP "GIVER"]_give$_{act}$_[PCU1: NP "GIVEE"]_[PCU2: NP "ITEM GIVEN"] || Sem
(2b) And now you want to give them reputation bonus?

(2c) [SCU: NP "GIVER"]_give$_{act}$_[PCU1: NP "ITEM GIVEN"]_[PCU2: NP "GIVEE"] || Sem
(2d) they had to give it to a different teacher to be used for a different purpose

Herbst proposes not to synthesize the different valency patterns with optional constructions (e.g., implicit but expressible object arguments in the context of the verb *read*), but to treat the presence and absence of valency as different instances of valency constructions.

From valency constructions, we can generalize form, meaning, or form-meaning structures. In the first case, we obtain valence patterns that describe the context of the valency carrier with formal labels (e.g., NP, to INF in English). In the second case, we obtain participant patterns that characterize the participant roles of the event marked by the verb in a more general way (e.g., agent, patient, benrec, i.e. beneficient/recipient). At the same time, participant patterns are abstractions that can be realized by several different valency patterns. In other words, they do not prescribe the occurrence of arguments in the context of the verb. Finally, in the dimension of form-meaning pairs, the observation of concrete valency constructions arrives at general valency constructions, i.e., ASCs.

Herbst also maintains the two-step method, in which first the specific valency patterns are explored by observing the occurrences of word combinations in the corpus, and in a further step the more general ASCs can be identified, which are allostructions of the specific valency constructions at the same time. Although this approach does not give a general answer to the question of how valency constructions can be assigned to general ASCs, it takes the participant pattern (i.e., semantic motivation) as a guiding principle: all valency patterns that realize the same participant pattern can be considered allostructions of a construction. This brings us to the level of the constructeme, which is the set of a given participant pattern and all the valency constructions realizing this pattern.

The valency-based approach has not yet received a monographic explanation; thus, the applications of the analytical framework may lead to further questions. However, it seems to be a promising initiative for a data-driven description of constructions because it essentially gives priority to observable valency constructions in the description. This is also shown by the fact that Herbst while adopting the semantic coherence principle of Goldberg, complements it with the so-called valence realization principle: according to it, if the valency construction of a verb is fused with a general argument structure construction, and its

[5] The data are from the COCA corpus (https://www.english-corpora.org/coca/), last access: 01/25/2023.

participant roles are constructed as arguments, then the formal realization of the ASC must coincide with the pattern of the valency construction. This ensures that the language user's constructional knowledge does not only cover the higher-order, more general representations but element-specific constraints, i.e., lower-level patterns, are also reflected in it. Overall, Herbst considers the description of argument constructions and valency constructions as complementary steps: he calls his theory an empirical valency-based approach to argument constructions.

3.3 Patterns

Hunston's proposal (Hunston 2014) does not use the category of collocations again, but it is akin to previous approaches in that its central concept, the pattern, which is a re-occurring linguistic context around a core word, characterized by grammatical devices (e.g., dependency relations), must be identified in a rigorous corpus-driven way. No prior interpretation or grammatical theory can be assumed in the analysis until the pattern (and its semantic groups) has been identified. "Patterns, then, are a way of describing the common grammatical environment of different words and, building on these descriptions, identifying the co-occurrence of pattern and meaning. They are intentionally naïve in that they do not presuppose any particular way of interpreting word-pattern combinations" (Hunston 2014: 106).

Pattern grammar grew out of the annotation process of the Collins COUBILD English Dictionary and is thus based on the Bank of English corpus. The re-occurring grammatical context associated with each word was coded by the annotators along the lines of part of speech category, clause type and grammatical elements (e.g., prepositions) occurring in the structure. This endeavor produced a word-centered repository of patterns in English that includes also word combinations from a semantic point of view (see also Hunston and Francis 2000). Thus, the enterprise did not originally develop within the framework of collocation analysis, nor was it originally a branch of construction grammar.

Yet patterns integrate the notions of collocation (repeated co-occurrences) and colligation (grammatical choices specific to a phrase) since they contain both specific collocates and components characterized by a lexical category, the order of which is fixed. (It is no coincidence that Hunston (2014: 99) considers both Sinclairian notions as precursors to her proposal.) Thus, further analysis of the identified patterns is open to various semantic interpretations, among which Hunston highlights valency theory and frame semantics. Indeed, the patterns can be understood as element-specific valency constructions, although pattern grammar does not rely on valency theory as a theoretical background.

Hunston (2014: 112-115) emphasizes that pattern grammar is akin to construction grammar in many ways, and it can be harmonized with cognitive grammar as well. The similarities include (i) the rejection of the syntax/lexicon dichotomy, (ii) the acceptance of a tight relation of form and function, (iii) the construction-based/pattern-based conception of meaning (i.e., the rejection of word-centered meaning description), (iv) a preference for the word form over the lemma (favoring element-specific patterns over higher-level generalizations), and finally (v) a rejection of grammatical rules as abstract representations (instead, rules are redefined as generalizations of frequently reoccurring structures). Consequently, the analysis of patterns can be integrated into the cognitive constructionist approaches from a linguistic theoretical point of view.

However, patterns themselves are not constructions. While there is a large overlap between the two categories, not all constructions are patterns. For example, inversion, which is not related to specific words but rather to a group of words, such as auxiliaries, is not a specific pattern, but a general construction. Moreover, patterns are not mental representations but rather observable and identifiable usage tendencies in the corpus. By way of explanation, Hunston explicitly rejects any mentalization in modelling, although she leaves open the possibility of further interpretation of patterns. It is no coincidence that she does not regard pattern grammar as a theory of grammar, but rather as a way of describing language: "[p]ut another way, pattern grammar is not an incomplete constructional grammar, but a part of a description built on units of meaning. Pattern identification establishes order in the mass of data, but does not propose a set of mental constructs" (Hunston 2014: 115). Patterns, like collocations or valency constructions, seem to be thus the "lobby" of construction description: pattern extraction constitutes the first step of construction identification, minimizing the role of introspection on the construction grammatical approaches and maximizing the involvement of corpus data in linguistic research.

3.4 Discussion

As a modest summary, three lessons can be drawn from the overview. First, all of them instantiate methodological unidirectionality: in a bottom-up approach, these proposals start with raw data and observation, and the generalization from them towards higher-level constructions is tightly controlled. Due to this methodological commitment, a corpus-driven construction analysis can find a way out of theoretical circularity and results in not a heuristic but rather an empirically grounded interpretation of the notion of construction. The weakness of this approach is, however, that a large-scale description of the constructional network of a language is really time-consuming and needs a vast amount of effort since it begins with the exploration of corpus patterns (collocations, valency constructions or simply patterns).

Second, the presented frameworks make it possible to decrease the fluidity of the notion of construction while maintaining its flexibility. Based on corpus pattern analysis we can arrive at pure semantic generalizations (e.g., selectional restrictions), more or less schematic grammatical structures (e.g., valency carriers and their syntactic context), figurative expressions (e.g., idiomatically combining expressions) or the family of higher-level constructions (i.e., the constructeme). Put differently, the analyst can map a larger section of the constructicon without relying on their own intuition. However, the process of analyzing corpus patterns as more abstract grammatical and/or semantic configurations remains theory-driven, which means that the researcher has to make a decision what kind of theoretical perspective they will adopt, what grammatical theories (e.g., dependencies, valencies or the cognitive grammatical modelling of construal) are preferred by them. Thus, a pure empirical investigation of constructions does not seem to be achievable; nevertheless, a solid methodological foundation may serve as a vantage point for further theoretical decisions and considerations.

Third, and maybe the most important for the NLP community from the whole issue: pattern extraction is the point where NLP tools provide invaluable support to CxGs. Data are messy and do not match necessary with our expectations; but if we turn first to patterns and then form theoretical proposals about potential constructions, it may increase the reliability of our research without closing the door to discover new phenomena of language use. Moreover, it can speed up the process of analysis since the sooner we face raw data the better the precision and the recall of our analysis will be. An automatized pattern extraction process designed and tested in accordance with the demands of CxG research may also provide a remedy to the problem of a large-scale but bottom-up exploration of constructions.

4 Conclusion

This meta-theoretical and methodological study attempted to reflect on the interpretation of the concept of construction from a corpus-driven perspective. The main question of the study was how verb argument constructions can be identified in corpus analysis, and which expressions can be said to be (potential) constructions. Closely related to this is the question of whether there is a data type in corpus linguistics that can be equated with the broad notion of construction.

If the reader considers my attempt successful, they will probably agree with the following two more general conclusions. First, the notion of construction can be used in empirical research neither without reflection nor on the basis of some theoretical consensus. In a corpus-driven approach, the researcher does not rely on a pre-given model of the phenomenon under investigation but arrives at a definition and description of the phenomenon after observing and processing the data. This does not mean, of course, that we should not be aware of the diversity of linguistic constructions. It is, however, suggested that for any given construction under investigation, attributing the label of construction to a set of linguistic phenomena should not be the starting point but the end point (or at least the intermediate result) of an analysis.

Secondly, the corpus does not provide the constructions directly, therefore, a procedure needs to be developed to move from the raw data of the corpus to the constructions. Collocations can be interpreted as dependency relations with varying degrees of symbolization, valency patterns, or recurrent and grammatically more or less transparent patterns. Their precise analysis can lead us to the identification of more generic form-meaning pairings. Whichever proposal is adopted (or even if we develop our own analytical approach), the corpus contains only patterned verb–word combinations, so we should think in two steps: first, by exploring these combinations to identify constructions, and then, by further methods (e.g., by collostructional analysis), to perform a comprehensive description of the identified constructions. These two steps need not necessarily follow each other, but it is still important not to assume a priori constructions in a corpus-driven analysis.

Construction grammar and corpus linguistics can therefore be integrated in a number of ways, and we need large-scale investigation to decide which way of them will be the most appropriate. The integration is by no means pre-given, however, by achieving it we will have a better understanding of the organization of the construction.

Acknowledgments

The research was supported by the NKFI project K 129040, "Verbal Constructions of Hungarian".

References

Adele E. Goldberg. 2006. Constructions at Work: The Nature of Generalization in Language. Oxford University Press. Oxford.

Adele E. Goldberg. 2019. Explain Me This: Creativity, Competition, and the Partial Productivity of Construction. Princeton University Press, Princeton, Oxford.

Geoff Barnbrook, Oliver Mason and Ramesh Krishnamurthy. 2013. Collocation: Applications and Implications. Palgrave Macmillan, Houndmills, New York.

Joan L. Bybee. 2013. Usage-based Theory and Exemplra Representations of Constructions. In The Oxford Handbook of Construction Grammar. Eds. Thomas Hoffmann and Graeme Trousdale. Oxford University Press, New York. 49–69.

Natalia Levshina. 2015. How to do Linguistics with R. Data exploration and statistical analysis. John Benjamins, Amsterdam, Philadelphia.

Stefan Evert. 2009. Corpora and collocations. In Corpus Linguistics. An International Handbook. HSK. 29.2. Eds. Anke Lüdeling and Merja Kytö. Walter de Gruyter, Berlin, New York. 1212–1248.

Stefan H. Gries. 2013. Data in Construction Grammar. In The Oxford Handbook of Construction Grammar. Eds. Thomas Hoffmann and Graeme Trousdale. Oxford University Press, New York. 93–109.

Susan Hunston. 2014. Pattern grammar in context. In Constructions Collocations Patterns. Eds. Thomas Herbst, Hans-Jörg Schmid and Susen Faulhaber. De Gruyter Mouton, Berlin, Boston. 99–120.

Susan Hunston and Gill Francis. 2000. Pattern Grammar: A corpus-driven approach to the lexical grammar of English. John Benjamins, Amsterdam, Philadelphia.

Thomas Herbst. 2014. The valency approach to argument structure constructions. In Constructions Collocations Patterns. Eds. Thomas Herbst, Hans-Jörg Schmid and Susen Faulhaber. De Gruyter Mouton, Berlin, Boston. 167–216.

Thomas Herbst, Hans-Jörg Schmid and Susen Faulhaber. 2014. From collocations and patterns to constructions – an introduction. In Constructions Collocations Patterns. Eds. Thomas Herbst, Hans-Jörg Schmid and Susen Faulhaber. De Gruyter Mouton, Berlin, Boston. 1–8.

Violeta Seretan. 2011. Syntax-Based Collocation Extraction. Springer, Dordrecht.

William Croft. 2001. Radical Construction Grammar: Syntactic Theory in Typological Perspective. Oxford University Press, Oxford.

CALaMo: a Constructionist Assessment of Language Models

Ludovica Pannitto
CIMeC
University of Trento
ludovica.pannitto@unitn.it

Aurélie Herbelot
CIMeC/DISI
University of Trento
aurelie.herbelot@unitn.it

Abstract

This paper presents a novel framework for evaluating Neural Language Models' linguistic abilities using a constructionist approach. Not only is the usage-based model in line with the underlying stochastic philosophy of neural architectures, but it also allows the linguist to keep meaning as a determinant factor in the analysis. We outline the framework and present two possible scenarios for its application.

1 Introduction

Over the years, linguists have given a lot of thought to what language *is*, and how it can be best formally described. Different approaches with sometimes contradictory aims have produced an extremely rich array of conceptual tools to describe linguistic phenomena. Such tools play diverse roles in explaining the phylogenetic, ontogenetic or historical-cultural facets of language and are often heavily interlaced with one another. In this research landscape, computational modelling has largely been used to simulate and investigate speaker behaviour at various levels of granularity. A specific area within the computational community is known as *(Neural) Language Modelling*, which aims at reproducing linguistic surface structure by means of (pseudo)-probabilistic models. Neural architectures have played a special role in this subfield of research, due to their flexibility.

The extreme complexity of theoretical tools found in linguistics gets cut down by order of magnitudes when it comes to the analysis of language processing using computational modelling. For instance, when the term *language* is mentioned in relation to Artificial Neural Networks, it seems that the word is often used as a mere synonym of *grammar*: while it is clear from a broader theoretical perspective that the two objects do not overlap, the distinction gets blurred in many computational studies. That is, assumptions which would be clearly stated in theoretical linguistics (e.g. how grammatical abstraction fits into the concept of *language*), are not explicitly discussed by computational studies: it is often the case that a specific set of choices concerning the description of language are taken as default. Most current work also seems to implicitly make a number of assumptions about what kind of grammar is supposed to emerge from neural language models (henceforth, NLMs), and this underlying choice is often echoed in the most common evaluation settings and in the conclusions that are being drawn from such experiments. Most of these default assumptions are inherited from the nativist Chomskian tradition and the Universal Grammar (UG) framework (Chomsky, 1986; Smith and Allott, 2016), which has pervaded a lot of the computational work on grammar, and continues to do so in the recent literature on neural models.

Ironically, the nativist assumptions that permeate the mainstream computational methodology are at odds with the very nature of the models created by the field. Neural models are essentially based on pattern learning and are completely agnostic about the nature of the data they are made to process. The idea that language can be abstracted from a general purpose statistical mechanism is more akin to usage-based (henceforth, UB) approaches (Barlow and Kemmer, 2000; Goldberg, 2003; Tomasello, 2003), and NLMs would provide a much more natural testbed for that theoretical strand. In the cognitive and UB accounts, the exploitation of predictability during language development (and again we refer to development at all the three tiers of philogeny, ontogeny and cultural evolution) is the root of a number of fundamental mechanisms such as schematization, entrenchment and distributional analysis (Lewkowicz et al., 2018). In the light of these processes, language, seen as a structured inventory of constructions, gets build through generations (Cornish et al., 2017) and throughout a speaker's lifetime: shared linguistic

Proceedings of the First International Workshop on Construction Grammars and NLP (CxGs+NLP, GURT/SyntaxFest 2023), pages 21 - 30
March 9-12, 2023 ©2023 Association for Computational Linguistics

material among utterances, such as morphological markers for instance, enable the identification of particular patterns or constructions as units bearing meaning (Croft, 2001).

The perceived gap between the nativist and non-nativist traditions with respect to computational modelling probably stems from historical factors. The Chomskian school and its formal approach offered a definition of language that, in the past, could easily be interpreted and implemented by emergent computational approaches. But there is no reason for this bias to perdure. In this paper, we argue in favour of a usage-based framework to analyse language acquisition in ANNs. We first point out the aspects of nativist theories that have so far influenced the evaluation of NLMs (§2). We then introduce a framework for a quantitative and qualitative analysis of NLMs linguistic abilities within the constructionist perspective (§3). We finally show some preliminary analyses performed with the proposed formalization (§4).

2 Nativist vs. non-nativist approaches to language acquisition

All theories of language use and development recognize that at the root of human linguistic ability is the capacity to handle symbolic structures. But they disagree on the specific content of speakers' linguistic knowledge, the mode of acquisition of such content, and the extent to which linguistic productivity is affected by this stored knowledge (Bannard et al., 2009a). Theories diverge with respect to three aspects: input, stability and systematicity. The perspective taken on each of these aspects has consequences for the conclusions drawn from NLMs' responses to the evaluation setting. In the following, we consider each aspect in turn and specifically highlight how the evaluation of computational models becomes biased due to a lack of explicitness in relating experimental and theoretical aspects of the research question.

Input. One of the main arguments introduced by nativist frameworks is the *poverty of the stimulus*: the input children are exposed to is underdetermined and does not explain acquisitional generalizations observed in learners (Crain and Pietroski, 2001). Such theories assume that children navigate a hypotheses space defined by innate constraints (Eisenbeiß, 2009). Constructionist approaches, instead, posit that language emerges from the input through domain-general mechanisms: this implies that the input is shaped and skewed in a specific way in order to enhance learnability (Boyd and Goldberg, 2009). A well established line of research has shown how children are proficient statistical learners (Gómez and Gerken, 2000; Romberg and Saffran, 2010; Christiansen, 2019). The emergence of language-like structure from purely linear signal has also been shown in recent experiments such as (Cornish et al., 2017), which demonstrated how important aspects of the sequential structure of language may derive from adaptations to the cognitive limitations of human learners and users (Christiansen and Chater, 2016b). The crucial difference between the nativist and the non-nativist approach here is how strict the relation between the received input and the acquired linguistic structure is: if we commit to a view in which the input only serves as a trigger of an almost pre-determined cognitive structure, we are naturally driving our attention far from the features of the input and primarily to the features of the structure. On the other hand, deriving the linguistic structure from the input structure itself requires investigating the two aspects together. So far, most studies on NLMs have disregarded the effect of the input on experimental results (Pannitto and Herbelot, 2022).

Stability. The *continuity assumption* was first introduced by Pinker (1984) in order to reconcile aspects of developmental language with the generative framework. It posits that the differences between adult and children linguistic structures is negligible and merely due to performance factors. In contrast, what we can refer to as the *developmental hypothesis* claims that the mechanisms underlying acquisition remain the same throughout a life-long acquisition process, but the structures and abstractions they generate evolve over time. UB models also put emphasis on the linear and time-dependent nature of the linguistic signal (Christiansen and Chater, 2016b; Cornish et al., 2017). According to the UB account, generalizations appear gradually, as productivity emerges from item-specific knowledge (Bannard et al., 2009b).

Another aspect of stability is inter-speaker differences. UG posits that all speakers eventually converge to the same grammar (Lidz and Williams, 2009; Crain et al., 2009). Individual differences have however been found in almost every area of grammar, depending on a variety of factors including environmental ones (Street and Dąbrowska, 2010). The 'sameness' assumption pervades the computational linguistics literature, where evaluation is performed according to a single 'gold standard' per task. For traditional tasks such as sentiment analysis or word similarity ratings, the annotations of human subjects are averaged, and the system is evaluated against the average. For language modeling, model perplexity is computed with respect to the statistical features of a large corpus, which aggregates the writing styles and linguistic habits of thousands of speakers. While this state of affairs has started to be criticised by various researchers, it remains for now the status quo. When considering language development as a speaker-dependent process, strongly affected by the nature of the input, an evaluation based on an 'average speaker' becomes truly unsatisfactory. We cannot assume the existence of a ground truth, and must rely on softer evaluation measures: it is clear that the linguistic behaviours of different speakers must overlap sufficiently to allow for communication, but that we also want to observe in the output of the network the kind of variability that is seen in humans.

Systematicity. The ability to understand and generate an unbounded number of novel sentences, using finite means, is considered one of the hallmarks of our language faculty. The boundaries of this systematicity remain however largely unclear: provided that we agree on what the finite means at our disposal are, not all the possibilities are actually realised by speakers and not all realised possibilities share the same cognitive or linguistic status.

One way to look at systematicity is that of compositionality, for which the most widely known version is probably due to Katz and Fodor (1963), that port Chomsky's innateness theory to semantics: a set of rules or constraints is needed in order to systematically build the meaning of sentences by integrating meaning of words. Even the Montagovian formal approach to compositionality (Montague, 1970) relies on Chomskian-derived ideas of a stable lexicon that stores meanings, and the existence of a set of precise interpretation rules that allow for those meanings to be mixed and modulated *through* the filter of syntax. The core of both visions is still very much syntax-centered (to which semantics has to be isomorphic) and very little space is left for indeterminacy, negotiation between speakers and other aspects related to the interactive and communicative nature of language (different individuals can retain in fact quite different concepts associated to the same lexical label for instance, Labov, 1973). In a nutshell, if we see systematicity from the standpoint of compositionality, the quasi-regularities of linguistic structure represents a major hurdle to surpass.

Quasi-regularity is instead the engine of productivity, as in the ability of speakers to use all the available linguistic means to cue the intended meaning. Just like compositionality, productivity deals with the domain in which a grammatical pattern can be employed in a linguistic context without losing interpretability, and it deals with what is actually possible in the language and where to draw the boundaries of acceptability. The shift has not just been syntactic: in the formal representation of these two aspects of systematicity in semantics, for instance, composition-oriented (Katz and Fodor, 1963) or productivity-oriented (Fillmore, 1976) theories have conceptualized the idea of selectional constraints differently.

Knowledge on systematicity is in both cases considered as implicit knowledge that the speaker has about their language. Nativist approaches have however primarily dealt with compositionality, and so are NLMs often evaluated: given grammar rules and lexicon, what are the computational mechanisms that allow them to combine? UB theories, on the other hand, have primarily been dealing with productivity: how far can meaning boundaries be forced? What are the mechanisms that allow for linguistic creativity? This of course entails, in the UB community, a relation to surface properties of the input as well: Croft and Alan Cruse (2004), for instance, note how the maximally schematic constructions, such as `sbj verb obj`, are also the most productive ones, and that this has a relation to their frequency too, both as a type and for each of their instantiations.

3 CALaMo

In our proposed methodology, CALaMo (Constructionist Assessment of Language Models), we incorporate the UB perspective across all three aspects: input, stability and systematicity.

As far as *input* is concerned, CALaMo differs from standard approaches by considering input data an important factor in determining the shape of the learner's grammatical knowledge. In traditional scenarios, the input only serves as a triggering factor and its features play little to no role in the analysis. From a UB perspective, instead, the relation between the abstract grammatical structure of the input and the acquired grammar, which then constrains the production of the learner, is strict.

Regarding *stability*, depending on the view that is taken on the continuity hypothesis, we can see NLM's grammatical competence either as a binary or as a gradient property. In the first case, we test whether the network is able or not to handle some linguistic phenomenon, while in the second case, as advocated by CALaMo, we are interested in seeing how and why some linguistic aspect becomes more and more salient to the network during training.

The *compositionality vs. productivity* perspectives, finally, entail a different organization of linguistic knowledge: the mainstream compositionality perspective tends to set meaning aside, and treat the lexicon as an organized repository of meanings (it makes sense therefore to test NLM's capabilities on semantically nonsensical sentences or to extend the known rules to completely unknown lexical items). In the productivity perspective, instead, meaning is intrinsically part of the process and is treated as a systematic aspect of grammar, too.

3.1 Acquiring language

When talking about NLMs and their linguistic capabilities, the issue of language acquisition (A) is often formalized as how much language Λ can be learned by the (artificial) speaker, given a certain level of computational complexity C by being exposed to a certain type of data I:

$$A : C \times I \mapsto \Lambda \qquad (1)$$

All the components of the equation have been central to the linguistic debate. However, starting from this basic formalization, we identify two major focus points that we specifically address in our framework. Firstly, the above formula describes acquisition as instantaneous, but it is actually better described as a process $A = (a_0, a_1, \cdots a_N)$ (§3.2). From a cognitive perspective the process is fully continuous, while in the artificial scenario, input data is often fed in 'batches'. We can however imagine that, if we had the ability to increase the number of steps at will (i.e., make N larger while keeping constant the amount of data), we could formalize steps small enough to make the two processes comparable.

Secondly, language is often seen as something that the learner has acquired and gained knowledge of. We want to bring back in the framework the role of the linguist-observer, that builds an abstraction over the linguistic behavior of the speaker (§3.3). As the actual knowledge acquired by the speaker is undetectable and only explainable metalinguistically, in a way that is not viable with neural networks (i.e., we cannot ask NLMs what they know about linguistic regularities), we must take into account the fact that we are always analyzing both the linguistic input received by the speaker and the output produced as an effect of the acquisition process through analytical categories that are created and used by the linguist-observer. In other words, Λ is not a property of the speaker, but rather a function operated by the linguist-observer. It does not evolve per se during the acquisition process, but rather it helps us detect and characterize the evolution of the speaker's abilities.

3.2 The process of acquisition

All the elements of Equation 1 ideally change throughout time as the acquisition process unfolds.

The input I to which the learner is exposed, in a real-life scenario, changes continuously. We can therefore define $I = (\iota_0, \iota_1, \cdots, \iota_N)$, where ι_i is the collection of input data to which the learner has been exposed to in-between a_i and a_{i+1}. Again ideally, with N large enough, each ι_i could even correspond to a single sentence. The computational complexity also co-evolves with the acquisition function, as linguistic knowledge gets incorporated into it. In the human case, the initial state is unobservable and in the artificial scenario it is often not interesting as initialization of neural models is random. At step i, instead, the computational mechanism that has incorporated knowledge up to step $i-1$ is exposed to ι_i. For these reasons, we define $C = (c_\emptyset, c_0, \cdots, c_{N-1})$. As an effect, Λ identifies different subsets $\lambda_0, \lambda_1, \cdots, \lambda_N$ throughout the acquisition process, namely $\Lambda = \bigcup_{i=0}^{N} \lambda_i$

Each step of the broader process A can be therefore defined as:

$$\begin{cases} a_0 : \iota_0 \times c_\emptyset \mapsto \lambda_0 \\ a_i : \iota_i \times c_{i-1} \mapsto \lambda_i \end{cases} \qquad (2)$$

3.3 How do we observe *learned* language?

The notion of language that we introduced incorporates that of grammar, namely the analytical categories that we superimpose on the linguistic stream in order to analyze it and its unfolding over time. We do not test language as a cognitive state of the speaker: we intend it instead a set of categories that the observer (i.e., the linguist) considers relevant to the description of the linguistic stream produced by the (artificial) speaker. There exists, therefore, a striking difference between the linguistic stream (either the input perceived or the output produced by the speaker) and its representation through the lens provided by *language*.

If we wanted to be more precise with the notation, we should acknowledge the fact that language, i.e. Λ, as we mean it is actually a function by itself, that takes as input some linguistic stream (some observable data) and returns a representation of it. We could therefore rewrite the definition of a_i as $a_i : \iota_i \times c_{i-1} \mapsto \Lambda(o_i)$ where o_i is the linguistic stream produced by the speaker as a result of acquisition step a_i.

As we are interested in the categories that are acquired by the speaker and deployed during language comprehension and production, defining $\lambda_{o_i} = \Lambda(o_i)$ allows us to apply the same transformation on the input ι_i to which the speaker is exposed, thus obtaining λ_{ι_i} that is comparable to λ_{o_i} in terms of linguistic categories.

Sticking to the constructionist perspective while trying to make the fewest possible assumptions on the actual content of linguistic knowledge, we hypothesize language as made up of a network of structures that are supposed to approximate constructions. As constructions are form-meaning pairs, the notion of grammar incorporates that of a meaning space spanning beyond the lexical level. This can be easily implemented by extending the notion of vector space models that has been extensively explored and used in distributional semantics (Lenci, 2008; Erk, 2012; Lenci, 2018). This represents a major difference with nativist approaches and the standard evaluation framework: meaning cannot be factored out of grammar effects and the acquisitional framework must account for its role in the process. If we had to formalize the content of any λ_i, therefore, we could expand it as $\lambda_i = \{(\kappa, \vec{\kappa}) \mid \kappa \text{ is a construction wrt. some linguistic stream}\}$

Unpacking this, we are saying that each obtained constructicon λ_i is a network of structures. These can be more or less lexicalized, with their abstractness being a proxy for linking the structures in the network as we will explain in the next paragraph. Each construction is associated with a distributional vector (Figure 1), which represent its meaning.

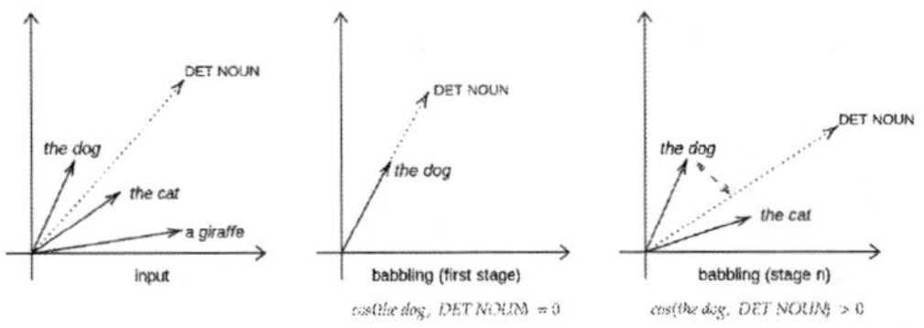

Figure 1: Let's assume that Λ contains both contructions *DET NOUN* and *the dog*, with the latter being a lexicalized instance of the former. At different steps during acquisition, the two constructions can assume different meanings and be therefore associated with different distributional vectors. A distributional vector condenses in fact information about co-occurrences between linguistic items in a given piece of text. In the figure, we see that a cluster of vectors gather around *DET NOUN* in the constructicon built from the input data (leftmost panel). This means that a variety of lexicalized instances exist for the construction *DET NOUN*. During learning, the constructicons built from generated output show different distributions for the construction *DET NOUN*. In the central panel, the cosine distance between *DET NOUN* and *the dog* is 0, meaning that their distributional contexts (i.e., their co-occurrences) perfectly overlap. In the rightmost panel instead, the distance between the two vectors has increased as another lexicalized instance (i.e., *the cat*) is being produced. In this scenario, the contexts where *DET NOUN* appears do not perfectly overlap with those where *the dog* appears.

3.4 Desiderata: the structure induced by Λ

We defined Λ as a function that takes as input a linguistic stream τ and returns a *constructicon* λ_τ: a structured repository of form-meaning pairs. In order to define and explore the internal structure of the constructicon, we introduce a few auxiliary functions and definitions:

(i): having meaning defined as a distributional space allows for distance computation $d(\kappa_i, \kappa_j)$ with $d : \Lambda \times \Lambda \mapsto [0, 1]$. $d(\cdot, \cdot)$ is a metric function that computes the distance between two meaning vectors. Usually, $d(\kappa_i, \kappa_j) = 1 - cos(\vec{\kappa_i}, \vec{\kappa_j})$, where $cos(\vec{\kappa_i}, \vec{\kappa_j})$ is the cosine similarity between the two vectors associated to κ_i and κ_j;

(ii): constructions bearing different abstraction levels are linked in the network. In order to navigate the network we introduce the function $c(\kappa_i, \kappa_j)$ with $c : \Lambda \times \Lambda \mapsto \{0, 1\}$ being a boolean function that computes whether two constructions constitute an *abstraction chain*. For instance, κ_i = nsubj, GIVE, iobj, dobj and κ_j = nsubj, root, iobj, dobj form a chain with κ_i being a partially lexicalized (hence, less abstract) instance of κ_j.

3.5 Use scenarios

3.5.1 Individual acquisition over time

The framework can be used to observe how the acquisition process unfolds over time. We can in fact set a number of steps n and observe: (i) how the shape of grammar changes over the course of learning, comparing the various steps, as in: $\Lambda(o_1) \sim \Lambda_(o_2) \sim \cdots \sim \Lambda_(o_n)$, (ii) how the grammar of the input can be compared to that acquired by the speaker, as in: $\Lambda(I) \sim \Lambda(o_n)$. Given a subset $K \subseteq \Lambda(I)$[1] of interesting constructions, we can observe their behaviour over the learning process.

A popular constructionist hypothesis (Goldberg, 2006), for example, states that the meaning of a construction (e.g., the ditransitive pattern *Subj V Obj Obj2*), and therefore its productivity, emerges from the association with specific lexical items in the input received by the learner (e.g., *give* in the case of the ditransitive): part of the lexical meaning remains attached to the meaning of the syntactic pattern, and therefore its distributional properties with it. Let's assume that the speaker has acquired some construction κ (e.g., the ditransitive construction). Once they're able to use it in a productive and creative way (i.e., in a more varied contexts than the *give* contexts the construction is strongly associated with in the input), we can use the proposed framework to check whether the distributional meaning of two constructions $\kappa_i, \kappa_j \in \Lambda(I)$ with $c(\kappa_i, \kappa_j) = 1$ (i.e., with κ_i being a less abstract instance of κ_j) influences the learnability of κ_j as an independent construction.

The notion of *abstraction chain* introduced before helps us testing this hypothesis as we can check the behaviour of the chain (κ_i, κ_j) at each timestep. We can denote $\kappa_i^{\lambda_k}$ the construction $\kappa_i \in \lambda_k$ and similarly $\kappa_j^{\lambda_k}$ the construction $\kappa_j \in \lambda_k$, through distributional analysis we can capture how the contexts in which κ_i and κ_j vary, and whether this variation is associated with grammatical generalization. We expect, in fact, $d(\kappa_i, \kappa_j)$ to increase during acquisition:

$$d(\kappa_i^{\lambda_a}, \kappa_j^{\lambda_a}) \leq d(\kappa_i^{\lambda_b}, \kappa_j^{\lambda_b}) \ \forall\, a, b \mid a \leq b \quad (3)$$

If κ_j is produced in contexts that do not perfectly overlap with those where κ_i is produced, this indicates that the speaker has gained a productive use of construction κ_j, which is recognized as an independent construction from κ_i. If conversely their distance decreases during acquisition, we might deduce that the speaker has recognized κ_j as unnecessary by restricting its application cases to those of κ_i.

3.5.2 Language as the expression of a population of speakers

We are often interested in defining grammar in terms of what can be considered shared linguistic knowledge among the speakers. A core aspect of construction grammar is in fact conceiving language primarily as a social and external phenomenon, as opposed to nativist theories that focus on its inner nature. By means of the framework, we can analyze grammar as an abstraction over the linguistic productions of a population of P speakers $\Pi = (\sigma_1, \sigma_2, \cdots, \sigma_P)$. We can define the grammatical conventions deployed by the community Π as $\Lambda_\Pi = (\lambda_{\sigma_1}, \lambda_{\sigma_2}, \cdots, \lambda_{\sigma_P})$. This allows for modelling variation between the acquisition process of the different speakers. Speaker σ_i might be exposed to a unique series of input material $\iota_0^{\sigma_i}, \cdots, \iota_N^{\sigma_i}$ that does not necessarily coincide with that of speaker σ_j.

In this setting, we can for instance investigate what is learned *no-matter-the-input*, and what is instead specific or idiosyncratic for each speaker. We can define:

$$G_{\geq p} = \left\{ \kappa \mid \sum_{i=0}^{P} X(\kappa, \sigma_i) \geq p \right\} \quad (4)$$

as the set of constructions that we can observe in the linguistic productions of p or more speakers. With:

$$X(\kappa_i, \sigma_j) = \begin{cases} 1 & \text{if } \kappa \in \Lambda^{\sigma_j} \\ 0 & \text{otherwise} \end{cases} \quad (5)$$

being an auxiliary function that evaluates to 1 if the construction κ appears in the production of speaker σ_j and 0 otherwise (this just helps us count how many speakers use construction κ productively). G_P would for instance be the set of constructions shared by all speakers in a population, and could be therefore identified as the set of *core* constructions in Λ^Π. When, instead, $p \ll P$, we are observing constructions that are not shared by a significant amount of speakers in the population, and their use can therefore depend on specific input

[1]Actually, we have to make sure that $K \subseteq \Lambda(I) \cap \lambda_0 \cap \lambda_1 \cap \cdots \cap \lambda_n$

instances or tendencies in subgroups of speakers. Following the same logic we can of course also just define $G_{(\sigma_i,\sigma_j)}$ as the constructions that are common to the two speakers σ_i and σ_j. By means of G, we can define $\widetilde{\Lambda_G}$ as an approximation of the function Λ, which only uses the categories that are retained in G. $\widetilde{\Lambda_{G_{\geq P}}}$ would for instance be a function that considers only linguistic knowledge shared by the entire population Π, while $\widetilde{\Lambda_{\sigma_i}}$ would be restricted to the constructicon λ_{σ_i}. Considering speakers σ_i and σ_j, with their respective produced linguistic outputs O_{σ_i} and O_{σ_j}, we can produce and compare $\widetilde{\Lambda_{G_{\sigma_i}}}(O_{\sigma_j})$ and $\widetilde{\Lambda_{G_{\sigma_j}}}(O_{\sigma_i})$: respectively, what speaker σ_i is able to retrieve from O_{σ_j} and what speaker σ_j is able to retrieve from O_{σ_i}.

The fact that speakers use the same constructions κ to build their linguistic productions does not of course ensure that the corresponding meanings $\vec{\kappa}$ coincide.[2] Different speakers, depending on the input they have been exposed to, and to the partial randomness attributed to computational mechanisms, could associate different meaning spaces to the same construction. Given two speakers σ_i and σ_j, and a sentence s, we could therefore compare the portions of λ_{σ_i} and λ_{σ_j} meaning spaces that are activated to linguistically (de)compose the sentence s.

4 Exploratory experiments

In order to explore the potential applications of the framework described in §3, we built a simple instance using the CHILDES corpus (MacWhinney, 2000) as input data I and a vanilla character-based LSTM (Hochreiter and Schmidhuber, 1997) as computational mechanisms C. With this simple setting, we explored two aspects: (i) we tested whether distributional similarities in λ_I would influence the acquisition of constructicons $\lambda_1, \cdots, \lambda_n$, and (ii) we tried to describe grammar as it emerges from a population of speakers. Constructions were approximated through *catenae* (Osborne et al., 2012): subtrees extracted from a dependency parsing syntactic representation (see Figure 2).

4.1 Abstracting grammar over training

We first replicate an analysis presented in Pannitto and Herbelot (2020), where a character-based LSTM was trained on CHILDES corpus. The authors fixed 7 steps during the LSTM's acquisition process, each after 5 epochs of training. In our formalization, this equates to 7 constructicons λ_1 to λ_7. The distributional space for each λ_i is obtained by counting co-occurrences between constructions within the same sentence. We can then consider abstraction chains (κ_i, κ_j) in I (i.e., in Λ(CHILDES) and computed $d(\kappa_i^{\lambda_7}, \kappa_j^{\lambda_7}) - d(\kappa_i^{\lambda_1}, \kappa_j^{\lambda_1})$ for each abstraction chain, namely the difference in cosine similarity between step 7 and step 1. Grouping all chains by κ_i and κ_j, it is possible to compute the average distributional shift as shown in Table 1 (i.e., for each κ_i to its more abstract instances and for each κ_j to its more concrete instances).

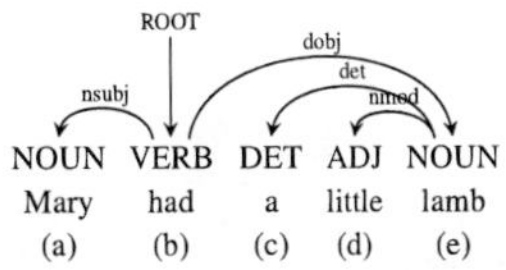

Figure 2: The dependency representation of the sentence *Mary had a little lamb*, annotated with morpho-syntactic and syntactic information. In this structure, we can identify the following *catenae*: a, b, c, d, e, ab, abce, abde, abcde, abe, bce, bde, be, ce, de, cde. Other possibilities would have been *strings* (e.g., a, ab, abc, ... b, bc, ...e) or *constituents* (i.e., a, abcde, c, d, cde).

κ_i	shift	cosine	κ_j	shift	cosine
@nsubj @root so	0.18	0.43	more @root	0.2	0.21
@nsubj only @root	0.18	0.41	_AUX know @obj	0.19	0.66
what @root @obj	0.18	0.39	@advmod tell	0.17	0.64
what @advmod _VERB	0.16	0.19	@aux know @obj	0.16	0.71
only @root	0.16	0.38	@advmod can _VERB	0.15	0.76
more @root	0.16	0.23	know @obj	0.15	0.62
@root it @xcomp	0.15	0.61	a _NOUN	0.13	0.52
@det minute	0.15	0.25	might @root	0.13	0.70
_PRON only @root	0.15	0.53	_PRON @root n't	0.12	0.53
_VERB _DET minute	0.15	0.33	@root that _VERB	0.12	0.65
_PRON @root so	0.14	0.54	_VERB 'll @ccomp	0.12	0.71
_DET minute	0.134	0.33	_VERB me @obl	0.12	0.76

Table 1: Constructions with highest average shifts.

Three bins are considered, based on average distributional shift: the hypothesis is that constructions that underwent the highest shifts during training are those showing intermediate levels of similarities in the input distributional space. Indeed, chains with very high input similarities are unlikely to exhibit abstraction: according to constructionist intuition, their distributional similarity means that the construction that is part of the *Constructicon* is the least schematic one, and there is no need for the more schematic (and therefore, *abstract*) category to be created. Low similarity pairs, on the other hand, may simply contain unrelated constructions.

[2] This makes sure that G_{σ_i} does not coincide with λ_{σ_i}

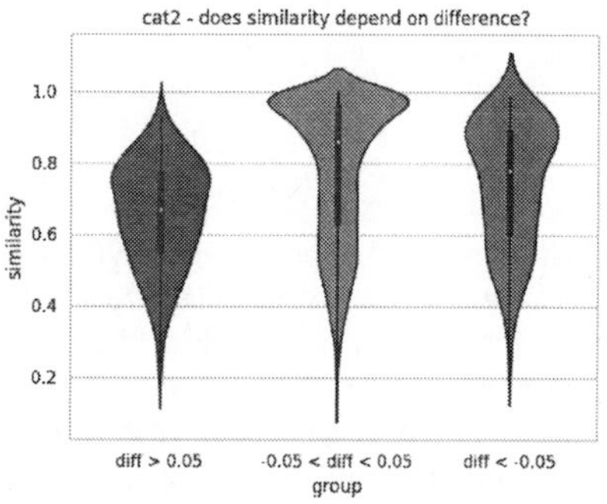

Figure 3: Distribution of average cosine similarities for the three groups of $kappa_j$, showing low, intermediate and high average shifts respectively.

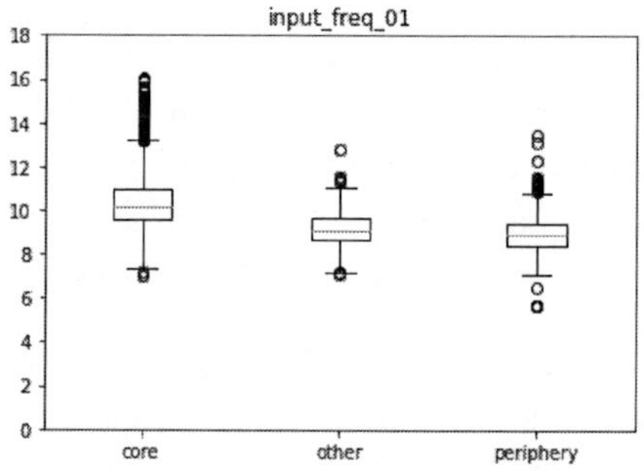

Figure 4: Difference in input frequency between the three groups of constructions: *core* as the ones shared by all speakers, *periphery* as the ones shared by half of the speakers or less, and *other* as the remaining ones.

The three groups show different distributions[3] as shown in Figure 3.

4.2 A population of artificial speakers

Following on Pannitto and Herbelot (2020) experiments, we consider a population of 10 speakers modeled with 10 vanilla character-based LSTMs trained on random samples of the CHILDES corpus (each containing 1 million words).

With this setting, we try to identify the locus of variation among different speakers, under the assumption that some 'core' constructions *must* be shared by all individuals, while others are less important to successful communication.

We restrict the analysis to the constructions to which all 10 speakers have been exposed to through their input (11051 constructions) and create G_{10} as the set of *core constructions* and $G_{\leq 5}$ as the set of *periphery constructions*, i.e. the ones shared by half of the speakers or less. Being trained on random samples taken from the same distribution, the speakers share most of the constructions (9086 out of 11051). However, we expect these numbers to change significantly when the input language varies along more refined sociolinguistic axes.

We also checked, for all speakers, whether the constructions of the *core* group and the constructions of the *periphery* group had significantly different frequencies in the input given to each speaker. As shown in Figure 4, the difference between the three groups are significant despite not appearing as striking as one would expect.

Lastly, we explored the input through $\widetilde{\Lambda_{G_{10}}}$ and $\widetilde{\Lambda_{G_{\leq 5}}}$, as shown in Table 2: both representations (the one obtained through *core* constructions and the one obtained through *periphery* constructions) highlight meaningful patterns in the sentence, but only the former can be considered a grammatical representation shared by the population.

corpus	Core	Periphery
does	AUX	-
n't	n't	-
that	that	PRON
seem	@root	VERB
kind	-	ADV
of	-	-
silly	ADV	ADV

Table 2: A sentence (left column) as it would appear if we restricted to only *core* (middle column) or *periphery* (right column) constructions.

5 Concluding remarks

The nature of linguistic representations is a core issue in linguistic theories of language development. We feel this aspect has been overlooked in the NLMs literature and propose an approach that brings back theoretical insights into the picture. We commit here to the UB constructionist framework, not as an ideal model of human language acquisition, but rather as a set of tools and categories that suffice to explain NLMs' generated language.

Since learning a language largely overlaps with learning to process the input, there must be a relation between processing biases relating to certain types of constructions and the distribution of those constructions in the linguistic input (Christiansen and Chater, 2016a). As experience grounds linguistic knowledge, distributional properties become a key aspect to determine the content of linguistic representations. In this framework, language is not considered as an autonomous cognitive system. Rather, the acquisition of grammar is regarded as any other conceptualization process and knowledge

[3]A Kruskall-Wallis one-way ANOVA was performed and resulted in significant values.

of language emerges from use.

To conclude, the observation of NLMs linguistic abilities would benefit from a constructionist approach. The evaluation can take place at multiple levels and includes properties of the situation described by the linguistic signal, but also properties of the linguistic signal itself. The UB framework may in fact provide useful categories to analyze the statistical properties of artificial language learners, and most importantly allows us to examine the semantic and the syntactic layers in parallel, both in the input received by the learner and in the stochastic output it generates.

References

Colin Bannard, Elena Lieven, and Michael Tomasello. 2009a. Modeling children's early grammatical knowledge. *Proceedings of the National Academy of Sciences*, 106(41):17284–17289.

Colin Bannard, Elena Lieven, and Michael Tomasello. 2009b. Modeling children's early grammatical knowledge. *Proceedings of the National Academy of Sciences of the United States of America*, 106(41):17284–17289.

Michael Barlow and Suzanne Kemmer. 2000. Usage-based models. *Language. Stanford.*

Jeremy K Boyd and Adele E Goldberg. 2009. Input effects within a constructionist framework. *Modern Language Journal*, 93(3):418–429.

Noam Chomsky. 1986. *Knowledge of language: Its nature, origin, and use*. Greenwood Publishing Group.

Morten H Christiansen. 2019. Implicit statistical learning: A tale of two literatures. *Topics in Cognitive Science*, 11(3):468–481.

Morten H Christiansen and Nick Chater. 2016a. *Creating language: Integrating evolution, acquisition, and processing*. MIT Press.

Morten H Christiansen and Nick Chater. 2016b. The Now-or-Never bottleneck: A fundamental constraint on language. *The Behavioral and brain sciences*, 39:e62.

Hannah Cornish, Rick Dale, Simon Kirby, and Morten H Christiansen. 2017. Sequence memory constraints give rise to language-like structure through iterated learning. *PloS one*, 12(1).

Stephen Crain and Paul Pietroski. 2001. Nature, nurture and universal grammar. *Linguistics and philosophy*, 24(2):139–186.

Stephen Crain, Rosalind Thornton, and Keiko Murasugi. 2009. Capturing the evasive passive. *Language acquisition*, 16(2):123–133.

William Croft. 2001. *Radical Construction Grammar: Syntactic Theory in Typological Perspective*. Oxford University Press.

William Croft and D Alan Cruse. 2004. *Cognitive Linguistics*. Cambridge University Press.

Sonja Eisenbeiß. 2009. Generative approaches to language learning. 47(2):273–310.

Katrin Erk. 2012. Vector space models of word meaning and phrase meaning: A survey. *Language and Linguistics Compass*, 6(10):635–653.

Fillmore. 1976. Frame semantics and the nature of language. *Annals of the New York Academy of Sciences.*

Adele E Goldberg. 2003. Constructions: A new theoretical approach to language. *Trends in cognitive sciences*, 7(5):219–224.

Adele E Goldberg. 2006. *Constructions at work: The nature of generalization in language*. Oxford University Press on Demand.

Rebecca L Gómez and LouAnn Gerken. 2000. Infant artificial language learning and language acquisition. *Trends in cognitive sciences*, 4(5):178–186.

Sepp Hochreiter and Jürgen Schmidhuber. 1997. Long short-term memory. *Neural computation*, 9(8):1735–1780.

Jerrold J Katz and Jerry A Fodor. 1963. The structure of a semantic theory. *Language*, 39(2):170–210.

William Labov. 1973. The boundaries of words and their meanings. *New ways of analyzing variation in English.*

Alessandro Lenci. 2008. Distributional semantics in linguistic and cognitive research. *Italian journal of linguistics*, 20(1):1–31.

Alessandro Lenci. 2018. Distributional models of word meaning. *Annual review of Linguistics*, 4:151–171.

David J Lewkowicz, Mark A Schmuckler, and Diane M J Mangalindan. 2018. Learning of hierarchical serial patterns emerges in infancy. *Developmental psychobiology*, 60(3):243–255.

Jeffrey Lidz and Alexander Williams. 2009. Constructions on holiday. 20(1):177–189.

Brian MacWhinney. 2000. *The CHILDES Project: Tools for analyzing talk. Third Edition.* Lawrence Erlbaum Associates.

Montague. 1970. English as a formal language. *Linguaggi nella Societa e nella Tecnica.*

Timothy Osborne, Michael Putnam, and Thomas Groß. 2012. Catenae: Introducing a novel unit of syntactic analysis. *Syntax*, 15(4):354–396.

Ludovica Pannitto and Aurélie Herbelot. 2020. Recurrent babbling: evaluating the acquisition of grammar from limited input data. In *Proceedings of the 24th Conference on Computational Natural Language Learning*, pages 165–176.

Ludovica Pannitto and Aurelie Herbelot. 2022. Can recurrent neural networks validate usage-based theories of grammar acquisition? *Frontiers in Psychology*, 13.

Steven Pinker. 1984. *Language learnability and language development.* Harvard University Press, Cambridge, MA.

Alexa R Romberg and Jenny R Saffran. 2010. Statistical learning and language acquisition. *Wiley Interdisciplinary Reviews: Cognitive Science*, 1(6):906–914.

Neil Smith and Nicholas Allott. 2016. *Chomsky: Ideas and ideals.* Cambridge University Press.

James A Street and Ewa Dąbrowska. 2010. More individual differences in language attainment: How much do adult native speakers of english know about passives and quantifiers? *Lingua. International review of general linguistics. Revue internationale de linguistique generale*, 120(8):2080–2094.

Michael Tomasello. 2003. *Constructing a language: A usage-based theory of language acquisition.* Harvard University Press.

High-dimensional vector spaces can accommodate constructional features quite conveniently

Jussi Karlgren
Numolo
Stockholm, Sweden
jussi@lingvi.st

Abstract

Current language processing tools presuppose input in the form of a sequence of high-dimensional vectors with continuous values. Lexical items can be converted to such vectors with standard methodology and subsequent processing is assumed to handle structural features of the string. Constructional features do typically not fit in that processing pipeline: they are not as clearly sequential, they overlap with other items, and the fact that they are combinations of lexical items obscures their ontological status as observable linguistic items in their own right. Constructional grammar frameworks allow for a more general view on how to understand lexical items and their configurations in a common framework. This paper introduces an approach to accommodate that understanding in a vector symbolic architecture, a processing framework which allows for combinations of continuous vectors and discrete items, convenient for various downstream processing using e.g. neural processing or other tools which expect input in vector form.

1 Continuous and discrete models

Processing models and memory models for knowledge-intensive tasks of many kinds are currently implemented as vector models of various kinds. The latest few generations of implemented natural language processing tools follow this trend, and benefit from the convenient and well-understood processing framework geometric models offer, the seamless incorporation of learning into a continuous model, and the attendant possibility to generalise from a large body of background knowledge to work with a specific task. Results on benchmark tasks has been impressive, and this is gratifying for those of us who have advocated for unsupervised learning, for statistical and probabilistic approaches, and for somewhat neurophysicologically inspired processing architectures.

The most obvious flip side of the impressive results comes with the cost of running such models. The amount of training data required is enormous compared to previous generations of models, the number of parameters to set during training is orders of magnitudes of orders of magnitudes larger, and the expense for appropriate computing infrastructure is prohibitive.

Much of this computing effort appears to be wasteful for those who have an understanding of the linguistic signal. The processing model starts from no understanding of what it is expected to model, is fed chunks of linguistic data with the instruction to pay attention to character sequences (mostly but not always with special attention paid to white space and sentence separators), and eventually will be able to relate the strings it has been fed with to each other in interesting and behaviourally adequate ways.

Previous generations of statistical models have at times experimented with including lexical categories or structural features to enrich the string input, but results have been equivocal and the current generation of natural language processing tools has dispensed with dependency graphs and lexical classes, preferring to infer the operatively effective relations between string elements directly from the data.

2 One can have both

For a linguist, the entire approach causes some frustration. One view of a linguist's job description is to provide the appropriate features for a learning system to pay attention to, and to strive to optimise the convergence of features, categories, and dimensions of variation for a natural language processing system to deliver the best results, the steepest learning curves, and the smallest set of parameters for some set of tasks. The current generation of natural language processing tools do not invite such intervention or such hypothesis testing: indeed,

Proceedings of the First International Workshop on Construction Grammars and NLP (CxGs+NLP, GURT/SyntaxFest 2023), pages 31 - 35

the practice of feature engineering is somewhat frowned upon.

In more general terms, a continuous geometric model has intuitively appealing qualities (even to the extent that the metaphors such a model invites coupled with our understanding about geometry in a physical world can lead our intuitions astray (Karlgren and Kanerva, 2021)): where a symbolic model allows for greater transparency, greater explanatory power, convenient inspectability and editability, and a more direct path to hypothesis testing, a continuous geometric model offers robustness, coverage, and generalisability. And today, by representing linguistic observations as vectors we will have a convenient interface to downstream computation using various past, current, and most likely many future flavours of machine learning.

There is no inherent contradiction between continuous models and discrete elements of study. Words are discrete observations and are routinely represented as vectors in language processing tasks, typically encoded by a shallow neural net which takes local context into account in narrow windows to model syntactic dependencies or slightly larger windows to model topical association. Configurational features such as elements from construction grammars can be represented similarly.

3 The general idea of high-dimensional computation

High-dimensional computation allows for the incorporation of linguistic items, single lexical items, configurational elements, or constituent structures jointly, using simple operations. This framework was first introduced by Plate under the name Holographic Reduced Representation (HRR; Plate, 1991, 2003) and further developed as Multiply–Add–Permute (MAP: Gayler, 1998), Vector Symbolic Architecture (VSA: Gayler, 2004), and Hyperdimensional Computing (Kanerva, 2009). The idea is to encode information in a vector with three simple linear algeabric operations that keep vector dimensionality constant: *vector addition*, *vector multiplication*, and *permutation*. *Addition* of two vectors yields a new vector *similar* to its operand vectors; addition can be used to represent a set. *Multiplication*, coordinate by coordinate, yields a product vector which is *dissimilar* to its operand vectors. *Permutation* takes a single vector, rearranges its coordinates, and produces a vector that is *dissimilar* to the operand. The operations are *invertible*: the operations can be undone and the component vectors retrieved from the result. These operations are based on a well-understood computational algebra, similarly to how most vector models rely on geometry. A vector space together with linear algebraic manipulation operations and geometric access and analysis operations can be used to combine observations into a common vector represtentation systematically, transparently, and explicitly, and for our purposes allows us a convenient way to evaluate the information value of features we expect to be important to understand the linguistic signal.

Random indexing is a high-dimensional computation framework, which assigns randomly generated fixed-dimensional index vectors to observations of interest, to be combined using the above operations. Random indexing traces its roots to Kanerva's Sparse Distributed Memory framework (Kanerva, 1988). A randomly generated index vector is defined to be sparse, i.e. to mostly contain 0s with a small number of 1s and -1s—say 10 non-zero elements in a 1000-dimensional vector—and the characteristics of high-dimensional spaces are such that two such randomly generated vectors will be very close to orthogonal. We assign random index vectors to each linguistic item of interest: single words and constructions alike. If a new previously unencountered item shows up during processing, it can be assigned a new unique index vector without retooling the previously known space of items. In random indexing of linguistic material, addition is used to combine observations that are collocated into a joint vector: an utterance can be represented as the sum of index vectors for every word in it. Permutation can be used to distinguish item occurrences in different roles or different surface forms, to distinguish cases, semantic roles, or head-attribute relations, e.g. This framework will allow us to represent sequences and configurations together with their constituent elements conveniently.

4 Some examples

This section is based on some previously published example implementations and experiments (Karlgren and Kanerva, 2019; Karlgren et al., 2018). Previous work using this approach was used to build general associative lexical resources (Sahlgren et al., 2016) using permutations to differentiate between left hand and right hand context (Sahlgren et al., 2008). This model is a parsimonious method to aggregate cooccurrence statistics and has proven quite useful in practical application, but has today been superseded by large language models that are able to capture longer range dependencies.

This purely lexical model can be enhanced by adding constructional elements, inflectional information, semantic roles, and even contextual extralinguistic information. Sentences such as the ones given in Example (1) both involve fish. This is of course for some purposes a notable observation, but we can add the observation that the fish in question participate in different roles in the sentences. This can be encoded by adding a semantic role label to the *fish* vector, adding a tense and aspect annotation to the main verb or even to all referential expressions to indicate that fish in Sentence (1-b) are agents doing their thing in present progressive in contrast with the fish in Sentence (1-a). What features to represent are up to the hypotheses being considered, and adding spurious features will not confuse the system except adding a slight noise to the resulting vector. The features of interest can be retrieved separately, since the operations used are invertible. The representation of $fish_{agent}$ can be derived from the representation of $fish$ by invoking a permutation specific for agent roles.

(1) a. The fishermen have cured the $[\text{fish}]_{patient}$ by smoking or by salting them in brine.
  b. The $[\text{fish}]_{agent}$ are jumping up like birds now.

(2) a. $fishermen + fishermen_{agent} + cure + fish + fish_{patient} + present-perfect + smoke + salt + brine + ...$
  b. $fish + fish_{agent} + jump + present-progressive + birds + now + ...$

In a series of experiments on a commercial data set of customer reviews we tested the effect of adding amplifiers, negations, and constructional markers for attitudinal expression in addition to lexical features. We represented each sentence in the collection as a vector into which we added the index vector for each term present in it, weighted by inverse frequency. We also added a separate $amplifier$ vector if an amplifier was present; a $negation$ vector if the main verb of the sentence was negated; a number of verbal class vectors $cogitation$, $expression$, $privatesensation$, and some others; separate vectors for each observed tense form in the sentence; vectors for presence of a personal pronoun; vectors for a number of attitudinal classes; and a series of constructional vectors for presence of subclause, presence of auxiliaries, and presence of adverbial constructions. These vectors form a lexical-semantic-constructional space with all features represented jointly. To demonstrate how this space can be queried for features, we represented the Sentence (3-a) separately with only lexical features and with only semantic and constructional features. We then retrieved the most similar sentence from the joint vector space: the lexical vector retrieves Sentence (3-b); the semantic and constructional vector retrieves the more personally expressive utterance with negative sentiment in Sentence (3-c). The original objective of this experimentation was to find attitudinal expressions for certain types of product: here it is useful to show how a large number of features can be used to build a space and then that space can be queried with attention paid to subsets of features.

(3) a. I really did not like the clarinet, I am afraid: it sounded weak!
  b. My sister plays the clarinet.
  c. I'm surrounded by really soft decadent pillows which do not work for me at all.

In a continued set of experiments on attitude analysis we experimented with constructional features and their distribution in a dataset of some one million microblog posts that mention among other things corporate entities. We represented each microblog post as a sum vector of index vectors for individual lexical items; for unique triples of part-of-speech tags—each triple such as $DT - JJ - NN$ or $VBD - RB - RB$ having been assigned its own index vector; for observed tense and aspect for the main verb; for observations of the presence of modal auxiliaries and various adverbs; for semantic role labels for the agent of each clause; for the presence of several categories of amplifiers; and for some extracted configurations for verbs of utterance and cogitation, e.g. $utteranceverb - that$ and other frequent constructions. These features were extracted using the NLTK toolkit (Bird, 2006) and on lexical resources coded using a comprehensive lexically oriented grammatical description of English (Quirk et al., 1985).

Similarly to the Example (3) above, we found, as shown in Example (4) that the resulting representation if only tested for lexical content indicated that the most similar utterance to Sentence (4-a) would be Sentence (4-b) while incorporating the various constructional features Sentence (4-c) was found to be the best match. This we found to be useful for a project on tracking corporate sentiment online (Karlgren et al., 2012). In this case, the agency and animateness of the corporation in question is the significant feature linking the first and the third utterance.

(4) a. <CORPORATION X> announced their intention to move their corporate headquarters to Houston.
b. Houston is rocking, wow <CORPORATION X>!
c. <CORPORATION X> plans to comply with the court order and will provide information to A!

Our examples taken from previous implementations presented here are intended to demonstrate that with very simple additional processing, constructional features can be added to a processing model, allowing the concurrent inclusion of many information sources into one joint representation in a computationally and conceptually habitable way, well supported by established computational practice. These operations are low effort, and can be done selectively to provide a test bench for experimentation to find what the relative effect of constructional features are, given e.g. a classification task or a ranking problem. This information can be selectively retrieved from the vectors as shown in the above examples, but more importantly, they can be used to enrich some given lexical model with constructional features of choice by the operations outlined above. They are not intended to convince the reader of the utility of any specific set of features or of their suitability to some established task—it is the processing model and computational approach that is novel and useful, not our hypotheses about language and its functions.

Such resulting vectors are similar to pre-trained off-the-shelf word embeddings such as are routinely used as input to downstream machine learning models and indeed constructional features can be combined with such word embeddings through the application of addition operations. In general, the current generation of natural language processing tools are agnostic to the content of their input and are able to accommodate even weak signals found in the input. This suggests that a useful validation path to test hypotheses of the effectiveness and usefulness of constructional features is not only to study the end results on benchmark tasks, but the path to get to those results, and to investigate how the model takes the potentially enriched information into account in its training.

5 Take home

This short paper attempts to convince its readers that it is possible to combine lexical and configurational features in a joint vector space model; that combining configurational or constructional features and lexical features in a joint vector space model is a useful and desirable path to investigate the validity of constructional hypotheses; that radical construction grammars provide a theoretical back end to such representations; and that hyperdimensional computing or vector symbolic architectures provide a well-established computational framework for processing such discrete information into a form which can be ingested by today's most popular processing tools. The details of our implementation are not important for this argument but random indexing is a convenient and lightweight approach to combining heterogenous information into a geometric representation.

References

Steven Bird. 2006. NLTK: the natural language toolkit. In *Proceedings of the COLING/ACL 2006 Interactive Presentation Sessions.*

Ross W Gayler. 1998. Multiplicative binding, representation operators & analogy. In D. Gentner, K. J. Holyoak, and B. N. Kokinov, editors, *Advances in analogy research: Integration of theory and data from the cognitive, computational, and neural sciences.* New Bulgarian University.

Ross W Gayler. 2004. Vector symbolic architectures answer Jackendoff's challenges for cognitive neuroscience. *arXiv:cs/0412059.*

Pentti Kanerva. 1988. *Sparse distributed memory.* MIT press.

Pentti Kanerva. 2009. Hyperdimensional computing: An introduction to computing in distributed representation with high-dimensional random vectors. *Cognitive computation*, 1(2).

Jussi Karlgren, Lewis Esposito, Chantal Gratton, and Pentti Kanerva. 2018. Authorship profiling without using topical information: Notebook for PAN at CLEF. In *19th Working Notes of CLEF Conference and Labs of the Evaluation Forum, CLEF 2018, Avignon, France*, volume 2125. CEUR-WS.

Jussi Karlgren and Pentti Kanerva. 2019. High-dimensional distributed semantic spaces for utterances. *Natural Language Engineering*, 25(4).

Jussi Karlgren and Pentti Kanerva. 2021. Semantics in High-Dimensional Space. *Frontiers in Artificial Intelligence*, 4.

Jussi Karlgren, Magnus Sahlgren, Fredrik Olsson, Fredrik Espinoza, and Ola Hamfors. 2012. Usefulness of sentiment analysis. In *Proceedings of the European Conference on Information Retrieval (ECIR).*

Tony Plate. 1991. Holographic Reduced Representations: Convolution Algebra for Compositional Distributed Representations. In *Proceedings of the International Joint Conference on Artificial Intelligence (IJCAI).*

Tony A Plate. 2003. *Holographic Reduced Representation: Distributed representation for cognitive structures.* Number 150 in CSLI Lecture notes. CSLI Publications.

Randolph Quirk, Sidney Greenbaum, Geoffrey Neil Leech, and Jan Svartvik. 1985. A Comprehensive Grammar of the English Language.

Magnus Sahlgren, Amaru Cuba Gyllensten, Fredrik Espinoza, Ola Hamfors, Jussi Karlgren, Fredrik Olsson, Per Persson, Akshay Viswanathan, and Anders Holst. 2016. The Gavagai living lexicon. In *Proceedings of the Tenth International Conference on Language Resources and Evaluation (LREC).*

Magnus Sahlgren, Anders Holst, and Pentti Kanerva. 2008. Permutations as a means to encode order in word space. In *The 30th Annual Meeting of the Cognitive Science Society (CogSci).*

Constructivist Tokenization for English

Allison Fan
Winston Churchill High School
allisonoliviaf@gmail.com

Weiwei Sun
Dept of Computer Science and Technology
University of Cambridge
ws390@cam.ac.uk

Abstract

This paper revisits tokenization from a theoretical perspective, and argues for the necessity of a constructivist approach to tokenization for semantic parsing and modeling language acquisition. We consider two problems: (1) (semi-) automatically converting existing lexicalist annotations, e.g. those of the Penn TreeBank, into constructivist annotations, and (2) automatic tokenization of raw texts. We demonstrate that (1) a heuristic rule-based constructivist tokenizer is able to yield relatively satisfactory accuracy when gold standard Penn TreeBank part-of-speech tags are available, but that some manual annotations are still necessary to obtain gold standard results, and (2) a neural tokenizer is able to provide accurate automatic constructivist tokenization results from raw character sequences. Our research output also includes a set of high-quality morpheme-tokenized corpora, which enable the training of computational models that more closely align with language comprehension and acquisition.

1 Introduction

Although theoretical linguists have been gradually shifting from lexicalism to constructivism, constructivist theories have been barely adapted by computational linguists and psycholinguists. In this paper, we demonstrate the relevance of constructivist approaches to Natural Language Processing (NLP) in the context of tokenization, specifically for English. Though constructivist approaches to text segmentation and treebank annotation have been proposed for some languages such as Hebrew (Tsarfaty and Goldberg, 2008) and Korean (Park, 2017), English tokenization has been viewed as a long-solved problem in NLP. In some NLP tasks, e.g. Neural Machine Translation, it has even been replaced with purely statistics–based approaches, such as Byte Pair Encoding subword tokenization (Sennrich et al., 2016). We, however, argue that existing tokenization methods are not sufficient for at least two subfields — semantic parsing and modeling language acquisition.

We firstly explore the feasibility of (semi-) automatically converting existing lexicalist annotations, such as those in the Penn TreeBank, into constructivist annotations. We demonstrate that simple heuristic rules are able to utilize gold-standard Penn Treebank part of speech tags to produce high-quality constructivist annotations even without manual cleaning, thus substantially increasing efficiency of the constructivist tokenization and tagging process.

Through our rule-based algorithm, we are able to automatically produce a set of silver-standard morpheme-tokenized and tagged corpora from the annotated phrase structure trees of the Penn Treebank (PTB; Marcus et al., 1993) and the CHILDES Treebank (CTB; Pearl and Sprouse, 2013). However, despite the relatively high levels of accuracy of the silver standard corpora, some level of manual annotation is still required to achieve gold standard accuracy.

We then study automatic tokenization for raw, unannotated texts. We built a long short-term memory model (LSTM; Hochreiter and Schmidhuber, 1997) that was able to produce highly accurate tokenization outputs from raw character sequences even when trained with a large portion of silver-standard data. The high performance of our LSTM model is particularly useful in automatically tokenizing texts when previously existing lexicalist annotations are not available.

2 Background–Motivation

2.1 Lexicalist vs Constructivist Approach

There are two main approaches regarding the relationship between morphology and syntax: the lexicalist approach and the constructivist approach. The lexicalist approach was first proposed by Chomsky (1970) and Halle (1973) and states that

Proceedings of the First International Workshop on Construction Grammars and NLP (CxGs+NLP, GURT/SyntaxFest 2023), pages 36 - 40
March 9-12, 2023

there are two separate and distinct components of grammar: the first component, known as the lexicon, in which complex words, or lexical categories, are formed from morphemes, and the second component, known as syntax, in which lexical categories form phrases and sentences. Lexicalism posits that lexical categories are the basic units of syntactic structure, and the smallest elements which can be manipulated by syntactic processes. The other, newer approach to syntax and morphology, known as anti-lexicalism or constructivism, expresses the view that there is no divide between the formation of words and the formation of phrases, and that therefore there is no significant distinction between morphemes and words at the syntactic level. According to constructivism, morphemes are the basic units of syntactic derivation, and semantic composition starts from morphemes rather than words. See Figure 1 for a comparison of syntactic analyses according to different theories.

2.2 Relevance to Modeling Child Language Acquisition

A longitudinal study conducted by Brown (1973) of three First Language (L1) American English speaking children found that there was an approximately consistent order in which the children gradually incorporated morphemes into their speech. Table 1 is Brown's order of morpheme acquisition. The work done by Brown, as well as subsequent research on the order morpheme acquisition, demonstrates the importance of modeling morpheme acquisition. We believe that constructivist annotations are necessary to enable quantitative study in this direction.

2.3 Relevance to Semantic Parsing

The earliest theory that draws on the ideas of constructivism is Distributed Morphology (DM; Halle, 1990; Halle et al., 1993; Halle, 1997; Harley and Noyer, 2003). One key concept in DM is Syntax All the Way Down — morphological elements can be manipulated by syntactic processes as they enter into the same types of constituent structures. Thus, semantic composition initializes from morphemes.

As seen in Figure 1, constructivist tokenization is able to better support semantic parsing, as morphemes, rather than words, correspond to the elementary units of syntactic-semantic composition. For example, in this case, the past tense -ed and the plural -s both convey additional meaning to their

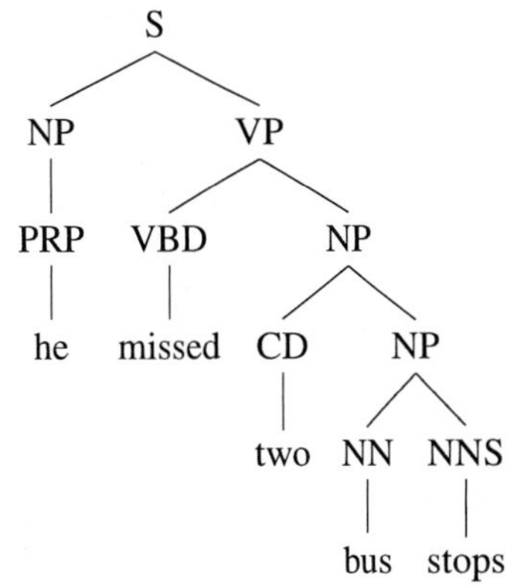

(a) A lexicalist analysis.

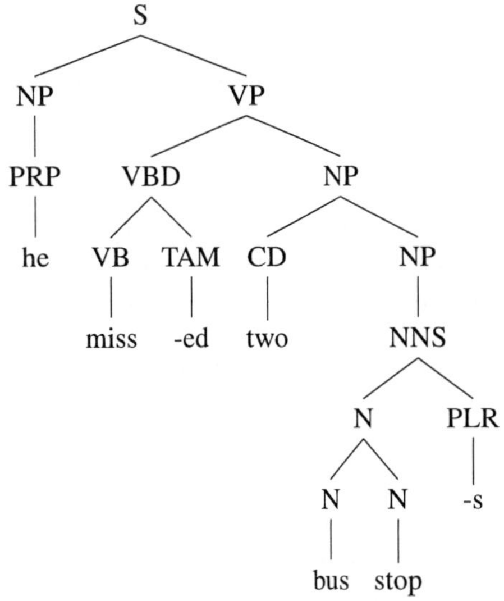

(b) A constructivist analysis.

Figure 1: Contrasting analyses for *he missed two bus stops*. Node labels are practically adapted from PTB annotations.

Rank	Morpheme
1	Present progressive (*-ing*)
2-3	*in, on*
4	Plural (*-s*)
5	Past irregular
6	Possessive (*-'s*)
7	Uncontractible copula (*is, am, are*)
8	Articles (*a, the*)
9	Past regular (*-ed*)
10	Third person singular (*-s*)
11	Third person irregular
12	Uncontractible auxiliary (*is, am, are*)
13	Contractible copula
14	Contractible auxiliary

Table 1: Brown's order of L1 Acquisition of English. Table is from Kwon (2005).

lexical roots that is only able to be distinguished through further parsing to the morpheme level.

3 Rule-Based Tokenization

Dridan and Oepen (2012) presented a rule-based framework for pre-processing text prior to downstream tokenization and demonstrated the effectiveness of a Regular Expression-based approach to tokenization under the lexicalist framework. Inspired by their research, we study the feasibility of introducing a heuristic rule-based tokenizer that works downstream to word-based tokenization to further split PTB-style tokenized and POS-tagged text into functional morphemes, such as the n-categorizer, and lexical roots, following the minimalist theory.

3.1 Data Sources

To gauge our algorithm's accuracy for different types of inputs, our input data sources included both manually annotated gold-standard phrase structure trees as well as unprocessed raw utterance transcripts, detailed as follows:

Penn TreeBank The PTB data inputs consisted of gold-standard annotated phrase structure trees. Since the major parts of PTB have also been annotated with English Resource Semantics (Flickinger, 2000; Flickinger et al., 2014), resulting in DeepBank (Flickinger et al., 2012), the outputs of our system are well aligned to formal semantic annotations.

CHILDES TreeBank CTB is a corpus consisting of manually annotated phrase structure trees derived from child-directed utterance transcriptions in the North American English section of the CHILDES database. The phrase structure tree annotations in the CTB follow the format of PTB, with a few exceptions. CTB provided us with gold-standard child directed speech that more closely resembles the type of language children and infants are exposed to and thus allows us to more accurately model first language acquisition.

CHILDES Raw Texts The final type of input data we used is 'raw', unprocessed and untagged utterances from corpora in the North American English section of the CHILDES database. We separated our raw data inputs into two categories: child-directed speech transcriptions (CDS) and child-produced speech transcriptions (CPS).

3.2 Utilizing PTB POS Tags

Our dataset's tag scheme extracts the PTB-style POS tags and adapts them to label morphemes. We simplify the tags to be a simple POS tag that corresponds with the root of the word (eg VB for verb, N for noun) and an additional tag that marks the function morpheme suffixes of nouns, verbs and adjectives (eg TAM, or tense/aspect/mood for verb function morphemes, PLR for the plural morpheme). It is relatively straightforward to derive labels in regard to cutting-edge Minimalist theories, such as DIV(ide) further.

3.3 Lemmatization

One challenge encountered when tokenizing words into their morphemes was dealing with irregular words, which made it hard to come up with a streamlined set of rules to separate the function morpheme from the lexcial roots of words. Our solution for this issue was to use the WordNet Lemmatizer, which allowed us to get the root forms of nouns, verbs, and adjectives without extraneous morphemes regardless of irregularity. Our algorithm would then add the appropriate functional morphemes to the ends of the words, i.e. *-ed* for past tense verbs, *-s* for plural nouns, based on their original PTB tags.

3.4 Evaluation & Error Analysis

As seen in Table 2, the accuracy of our rule-based system output is largely dependent on the accuracy of the annotations provided in the original input data, as our algorithm bases its tokenization and tagging rules off of the given lexicalist annotations.

	PTB	CTB	CDS	CPS
# tokens	6,069	5,161	3,522	3,588
total # of errors in output	91	51	358	432
# of errors in original	66	29	343	406
# of lemmatization errors	19	12	8	20
# of errors from algorithm	6	10	7	6
% accuracy	97.81	99.01	89.84	87.96

Table 2: Breakdown of errors in the outputs of our rule-based system.

In addition, our algorithm itself introduces very few additional errors. For all four data sources used, the percentage of errors in the output not attributed to annotation errors in the original input data was less than 1% (0.412%, 0.426%, 0.426% and 0.725% for the PTB, CTB, CDS, and CPS data inputs, respectively).

Of the additional errors introduced by our rule-based system, a large portion stemmed from lemmatization. The three types of lemmatization errors observed to occur most frequently include plural nouns not lemmatized to their singular forms, improper lemmatization of present progressive (-ing) verbs, specifically those ending with an *e*, and improper lemmatization of certain irregular verbs that share a spelling with a verb of a different root form, such as *saw*, past tense of *see*, and present tense *saw*, meaning 'to cut'.

However, these cases are very word-specific and, once identified, can easily be fixed through additional, targeted rules to account for these exceptions within the program or through post-processing.

3.5 A Summary of Our Corpora

Gold Data We hand-checked the annotations of approximately **18,340** tokens outputted from our rule-based tokenizer to yield a gold-standard corpus tokenized with the constructivist approach.

# of tokens	Source
5,161	CTB (brown-adam)
3,522	CDS (bloom corpus)
3,588	CPS (bloom corpus)
6,069	PTB (wsj 0001-0018)

Table 3: Token counts, excluding punctuation, of our gold-standard corpora.

Silver Data We also used our rule-based tokenizer to automatically produce silver standard data from annotated CTB & PTB phrase structure trees. The accuracy of our silver-standard data is approximately 99% and 98% for the CTB and PTB respectively, as shown by the evaluation in Table 2.

# of tokens	Source
99,636	CTB (brown-adam)
274,606	CTB (brown-sarah)
108,189	CTB (hslld-hv1-mt)
30,717	PTB (wsj 00)

Table 4: Token counts, excluding punctuation, of our silver-standard corpora.

Bronze Data We also used our rule-based tokenizer to automatically produce bronze standard data from CHILDES raw texts. The accuracy of our silver-standard data is approximately 89% as shown by the evaluation in Table 2.

# of tokens	Source
176,700	CDS (bloom corpus)
126,286	CPS (bloom corpus)

Table 5: Token counts, excluding punctuation, of our bronze-standard corpora.

4 Neural Tokenisation

To fully automate tokenization from raw text inputs, we train a LSTM model with our manually cleaned gold-standard data as well as large-scale silver-standard data derived from the PTB and CTB phrase structure trees using our rule-based system. Our tokenizer is based on character labeling, in which the B(egin), I(nside), and O(utside) labels are used to encode the positional information of each character in an input sentence in regard to its position in its respective token. Experiments indicate that LSTM, together with our data, are effective in building a high performing constructivist tokenizer, which obtained an average accuracy of over 99%.

5 Conclusion and Future Work

This project demonstrated that automatic constructivist tokenization is feasible and can achieve high levels of accuracy, despite the complexity when going beyond words to morphemes. Although one might still need to manually clean resulting corpora to achieve gold standard accuracy, our rule-based tokenizer is able to substantially increase the efficiency of producing constructivist corpora. We also demonstrated that the use of deep learning, such as LSTM models, can be a promising means of building a tokenizer. It is particularly useful in situations where the complexities / irregularity of a language become too difficult or cumbersome to codify into a rule based algorithm.

In future research, it would be interesting to explore how these two types of constructivist tokenizers perform in more complex, morpheme-heavy languages, such as Turkish. Another area of potential future research is to explore ways to enrich the corpora we produced in this project by adding syntactic and semantic annotations. The new corpora we produced will enable the next phase of research of building computational language acquisition models based on Constructivism. Our corpora will also allow future research in developing new Natural Language Understanding systems.

References

Roger Brown. 1973. Development of the first language in the human species. *American Psychologist*, 28(2):97–106.

N Chomsky. 1970. Remarks on nominalization. ra jacobs & ps rosembaum (eds.), readings in english transformational grammar. *Waltham Mass.*

Rebecca Dridan and Stephan Oepen. 2012. Tokenization: Returning to a long solved problem — a survey, contrastive experiment, recommendations, and toolkit —. In *Proceedings of the 50th Annual Meeting of the Association for Computational Linguistics (Volume 2: Short Papers)*, pages 378–382, Jeju Island, Korea. Association for Computational Linguistics.

Dan Flickinger. 2000. On building a more efficient grammar by exploiting types. *Natural Language Engineering*, 6(1):15–28.

Dan Flickinger, Emily M. Bender, and Stephan Oepen. 2014. Towards an encyclopedia of compositional semantics: Documenting the interface of the English Resource Grammar. In *Proceedings of the Ninth International Conference on Language Resources and Evaluation (LREC-2014)*, pages 875–881. European Language Resources Association (ELRA).

Daniel Flickinger, Yi Zhang, and Valia Kordoni. 2012. Deepbank: A dynamically annotated treebank of the wall street journal. In *Proceedings of the Eleventh International Workshop on Treebanks and Linguistic Theories*, pages 85–96.

Morris Halle. 1973. Prolegomena to a theory of word formation. *Linguistic inquiry*, 4(1):3–16.

Morris Halle. 1990. An approach to morphology. In *North East Linguistics Society*, volume 20, page 12.

Morris Halle. 1997. Distributed morphology: Impoverishment and fission. *MITWPL*, 30:425–449.

Morris Halle, Alec Marantz, Kenneth Hale, and Samuel Jay Keyser. 1993. Distributed morphology and the pieces of inflection. *1993*, pages 111–176.

Heidi Harley and Rolf Noyer. 2003. Distributed morphology. *The Second Glot International State-of-the-Article Book*, page 463–496.

Sepp Hochreiter and Jürgen Schmidhuber. 1997. Long Short-Term Memory. *Neural Comput.*, 9(8):1735–1780.

Eun-Young Kwon. 2005. The "natural order" of morpheme acquisition: A historical survey and discussion of three putative determinants.

Mitchell P. Marcus, Beatrice Santorini, and Mary Ann Marcinkiewicz. 1993. Building a large annotated corpus of English: The Penn Treebank. *Computational Linguistics*, 19(2):313–330.

Jungyeul Park. 2017. Segmentation granularity in dependency representations for korean. In *International Conference on Dependency Linguistics*.

Lisa Pearl and Jon Sprouse. 2013. Syntactic islands and learning biases: Combining experimental syntax and computational modeling to investigate the language acquisition problem. *Language Acquisition*, 20(1):23–68.

Rico Sennrich, Barry Haddow, and Alexandra Birch. 2016. Neural machine translation of rare words with subword units. In *Proceedings of the 54th Annual Meeting of the Association for Computational Linguistics (Volume 1: Long Papers)*, pages 1715–1725, Berlin, Germany. Association for Computational Linguistics.

Reut Tsarfaty and Yoav Goldberg. 2008. Word-based or morpheme-based? annotation strategies for modern hebrew clitics. In *LREC*.

Fluid Construction Grammar: State of the Art and Future Outlook

Katrien Beuls[1] and **Paul Van Eecke**[2,3,4]
[1]Faculté d'informatique, Université de Namur, rue Grandgagnage 21, B-5000 Namur
[2]Artificial Intelligence Laboratory, Vrije Universiteit Brussel, Pleinlaan 2, B-1050 Brussels
[3]KU Leuven, Faculty of Arts, Blijde Inkomststraat 21, B-3000 Leuven
[4]KU Leuven, imec research group itec, Etienne Sabbelaan 51, B-8500 Kortrijk
katrien.beuls@unamur.be
paul@ai.vub.ac.be

Abstract

Fluid Construction Grammar (FCG) is a computational framework that provides a formalism for representing construction grammars and a processing engine that supports construction-based language comprehension and production. FCG is conceived as a computational operationalisation of the basic tenets of construction grammar. It thereby aims to establish more solid foundations for constructionist theories of language, while expanding their application potential in the fields of artificial intelligence and natural language understanding. This paper aims to provide a brief introduction to the FCG research programme, reflecting on what has been achieved so far and identifying key challenges for the future.

1 Introduction

Fluid Construction Grammar (FCG[1]) (Steels and De Beule, 2006; Steels, 2011, 2017; van Trijp et al., 2022) is a computational framework that aims to operationalise the foundational principles underlying constructionist approaches to language. On a high level, the FCG framework serves two main purposes. On the one hand, it aims to provide a solid methodological basis for studying the emergence, evolution, acquisition and processing of language from a construction grammar perspective, through a standardised formalisation and a tractable computational operationalisation. On the other hand, it aims to facilitate the building of intelligent agents that are capable of communicating with humans and each other through languages that exhibit the robustness, flexibility and adaptivity of human languages.

In this paper, we aim to provide a brief introduction to the FCG research programme, highlighting its relevance in the field of linguistics on the one hand, and in the fields of artificial intelligence and natural language understanding on the other. We start by situating the FCG framework within the field of construction grammar (Section 2) and then lay out in a step-by-step manner how FCG provides a faithful computational operationalisation of the basic tenets of construction grammar (Section 3). We then discuss how constructions are learned as compositional generalisations over recurring syntactico-semantic patterns (Section 4) and proceed with an overview of applications that integrate FCG technologies (Section 5). Finally, we consider a number of key challenges and opportunities for future computational construction grammar research and conclude that the automatic learning of large-scale, usage-based construction grammars that support both language comprehension and production is a promising and timely research direction that is now well within reach (Section 6).

2 Situating Fluid Construction Grammar

Over the last four decades, the linguistic community has become increasingly more interested in constructionist approaches to language, as witnessed by the increased presence of talks, tutorials, courses and workshops at international conferences and schools (van Trijp et al., 2022). The term 'constructionist approaches to language' (Goldberg, 2003) is used to refer to a variety of theoretical frameworks, which all share a number of key foundational principles. These principles, as laid out by among others Fillmore (1988), Goldberg (1995), Kay and Fillmore (1999) and Croft (2001), and which are commonly referred to as the *basic tenets of construction grammar*, are summarised by van Trijp et al. (2022) as follows:

1. **All linguistic knowledge is captured in the form of constructions**. Constructions (cxns for short) are defined as form-meaning pairings that facilitate the comprehension and production of linguistic utterances. Comprehension corresponds to the process of mapping

[1] https://fcg-net.org

Proceedings of the First International Workshop on Construction Grammars and NLP (CxGs+NLP, GURT/SyntaxFest 2023), pages 41 - 50
March 9-12, 2023 ©2023 Association for Computational Linguistics

from an utterance to its meaning representation, while production corresponds to the inverse process of mapping from a meaning representation to an utterance that expresses it. All linguistic phenomena, whether they are traditionally seen as regular, irregular or idiomatic, are considered to be of equal interest. The same formal machinery is used to handle all phenomena.

2. **There exists a lexicon-grammar continuum, with no distinction between "words" and "grammar rules"**. Each construction is situated somewhere on this continuum. Constructions can range from entirely idiomatic expressions, over partially productive patterns, to entirely abstract schemata. Examples of these types of constructions are respectively (i) the BREAK-A-LEG-CXN, which constitutes a holistic pairing between the utterance "*break a leg!*" and the meaning of wishing an addressee good luck, (ii) the X-TAKE-Y-FOR-GRANTED-CXN, which includes variable slots for the agent and the undergoer, and expresses that the former does not value the latter, and (iii) the RESULTATIVE-CXN in "*the Tasmanian tiger was hunted to extinction*", which expresses that the Tasmanian tiger was extinct as a result of hunting.

3. **Constructions can contain information from all levels of linguistic analysis**. Construction grammar does not make an a priori distinction between the different layers of traditional linguistic analysis, such as phonetics, phonology, morphology, syntax, semantics and pragmatics. Constructions can, but do not need to, include information from any of these layers at the same time, as long as they constitute a mapping between some aspects of meaning and some aspects of form. It is entirely open what the form side and the meaning side of a construction can contain. For example, the form side typically includes phonetic, phonological, morphological, syntactic or multimodal information, while the meaning side typically includes semantic and/or pragmatic information.

4. **Construction grammars are dynamic systems, of which the constructions and their entrenchment are in constant flux**. Constructions always represent the linguistic knowledge of an individual language user. Constructions are acquired and change over time. They can be more or less entrenched as they are used more or less frequently and successfully in communication.

Constructionist theories of language have explicitly or implicitly built on these basic tenets since the 1980s, with initial formalisations being inspired by phrase structure grammars (Fillmore, 1988). Later, when the Lakovian/Goldbergian branch of construction grammar, often referred to as *cognitive construction grammar*, became predominant (Lakoff, 1987; Goldberg, 1995), the focus on formalisation gradually faded into the background. As is justifiable for an emerging field of research, the focus was more on the conceptual clarification of the loosely defined innovative ideas, rather than on the construction of a solid methodological framework (cf. Langacker, 1987, p. 1 and 42-45). However, the absence of such a framework led to the criticism that construction grammar was often not more than "*a set of insightful but untestable ideas*" (Bod, 2009, p. 2–3). Initial efforts to establish such a framework in the early 2000s gave rise to the emergence of the field of computational construction grammar, with Embodied Construction Grammar (ECG) (Bergen and Chang, 2005; Feldman et al., 2009), Sign-Based Construction Grammar (SBCG) (Sag, 2012; Van Eynde, 2016) and Fluid Construction Grammar (Steels and De Beule, 2006; Steels, 2011; van Trijp et al., 2022) being the most advanced projects in this area.

Computational operationalisations of construction grammar have four main objectives. First of all, they are important for verifying the internal consistency of construction grammar theories, which is impossible to do by hand for larger grammars. Second, they facilitate the large-scale empirical validation of these theories on corpora of language use. Third, they can serve as a standard for exchange and collaboration between construction grammar researchers. Finally, they make it possible to exploit construction grammar insights and analyses for the purpose of building language technology applications.

3 Operationalising Construction Grammar

We will now briefly discuss how the basic tenets of construction grammar can be computationally operationalised. We will focus solely on how this is achieved in the framework of Fluid Construction Grammar. For an introduction into the FCG system itself, including the syntax and semantics of the formalism, we refer the reader to Chapter 3 of Van Eecke (2018).

3.1 All linguistic knowledge is captured in the form of constructions

It is clear from the basic tenets of construction grammar that constructions are by definition pairings between (aspects of) form and (aspects of) meaning. However, the theory is less clear about what counts as form and what counts as meaning. In FCG, we approach this question from a communication perspective, starting from the role of constructions in language comprehension and production. We define form as the result of the language production process and as the starting point of the language comprehension process. Likewise, we define meaning as the result of the language comprehension process and as the starting point of the language production process. In other terms, form comprises all that is externalised by a speaker and observed by a listener. Meaning is then all that is expressed by a speaker and reconstructed by a listener. Typically, form comprises linguistic features that traditionally belong to the domains of phonetics, phonology, morphology, syntax and multi-modality, while meaning typically encompasses linguistic features that traditionally belong to the domains of semantics and pragmatics. Operationally defining form and meaning in this way excellently fits the constructionist perspective on language, as it starts from the role of form and meaning in linguistic communication. Not only is the distinction purposeful, it is also clear-cut and avoids other, more problematic, distinctions between the traditional levels of linguistic analysis.

FCG defines a dedicated data structure for representing constructions, which formalises form-meaning mappings in a way that is adequate for constructional language processing. FCG operationalises constructional language processing as a state-space search process, in which constructions can add linguistic information to a transient feature structure (see Bleys et al., 2011; Van Eecke and Beuls, 2017). The skeleton of FCG's construction data structure is shown in Figure 1. On the highest level, the information captured by a construction is structured in two parts, separated by a horizontal arrow. The right-hand side holds the preconditions

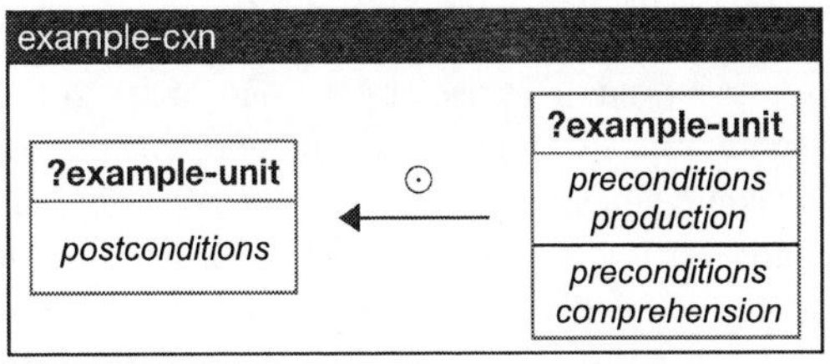

Figure 1: The skeleton of FCG's construction data structure.

for the construction to apply, and the left-hand side holds the information that the construction contributes during its application. The preconditions are divided into two sets, one set for comprehension written below a horizontal line and another set for production written above it. The application of a construction proceeds in two phases. First, the preconditions for the direction of processing are matched against the transient structure using a subset unification algorithm that checks whether these preconditions are compatible with the transient structure. If so, the postconditions are merged into the transient structure through another unification process (Steels and De Beule, 2006; Sierra Santibáñez, 2012), along with the preconditions of the other direction of processing. Solving a comprehension or production problem consists then in finding a sequence of constructions that adequately maps an utterance to its meaning representation (in comprehension) or a meaning representation to an utterance that expresses it (in production).

FCG does not impose any specific features to be included in a construction, which means that the nature, use and names of features and their values is entirely up to the grammar designer or learning system.

3.2 There exists a lexicon-grammar continuum

FCG's construction data structure supports the constructionist view that there is no clear-cut distinction between "words" and "grammar rules". Constructions can capture form-meaning patterns of arbitrary size and degree of abstraction. This means that they can cover units that would traditionally be called phonemes, morphemes or words, but also larger units that range from idiomatic expressions over partially instantiated patterns to entirely abstract schemata. Constructions can thus include features encoding low-level material such as sounds/strings or meaning predicates, along with features that encode more abstract information, for example through the use of grammatical categories. Importantly, all constructions are represented using the same data structure and there is no formal distinction between constructions covering lexemes (sometimes called lexical constructions) and those covering larger, more abstract patterns (sometimes called grammatical constructions). Constructions do not assume any symmetry between their form pole and their meaning pole, not in terms of complexity, nor in terms of compositionality. For example, complex or compositional forms can correspond to atomic meaning predicates and complex semantic structures can correspond to atomic or non-compositional forms.

All information captured by constructions is expressed through the use of feature structures, of which the features and values are open-ended. As such, a construction can include features expressing constraints on the word order of its constituent parts and features that represent hierarchical structures. However, the complete or partial specification of word order patterns is inherently optional, and constructions do not necessarily correspond to tree-building operations (van Trijp, 2016).

3.3 Constructions can contain information from all levels of linguistic analysis

FCG operationalises constructional language processing through general mechanisms, in particular as a state-space search process in which the preconditions and postconditions of its operators (i.e. the constructions) are feature structures that are matched and merged through first-order syntactic unification algorithms (Steels and De Beule, 2006; Sierra Santibáñez, 2012; Van Eecke, 2018). This allows the system to process feature structures consisting of arbitrary symbols, which do not even need to be declared beforehand. The range of features and values that can be used is thus open-ended and there is no restriction on the kind of information that the feature structures can represent. Indeed, the symbols carry the meaning associated to them by the grammar engineer or learning system, and have no meaning to the FCG system itself apart from their occurrences in the feature structures. Consequently, both the preconditions and the postconditions of a construction can contain features encoding information on any or all levels of traditional linguistic analysis.

3.4 Construction grammars are dynamic systems

FCG considers grammars, i.e. inventories of constructions, to represent the linguistic knowledge of an individual, autonomous agent. It assumes that the grammars are learnt and evolve over time, adapting to changes in the environment and communicative needs of the agent. Constructions hold a score, which reflects their entrenchment in the grammar. During language comprehension and production, constructions with a higher entrenchment score are preferred over constructions with a lower score. While different experiments might implement the use of entrenchment scores differently, the general idea is that the scores of constructions are updated according to their successful or unsuccessful use in communication. Constructions that are frequently used successfully become more entrenched, while constructions that are used unsuccessfully become less entrenched until they might eventually disappear from the grammar. The fact that features and their possible values do not need to be declared beforehand (see 3.3) ensures that new constructions carrying new features can be dynamically added to the grammar should the need arise.

4 Learning Construction Grammars

Now that we have established computational representations for constructions, as well as processing mechanisms that use these constructions for operationalising language comprehension and production, we can approach the question of where these constructions originate and how they are shaped by the communicative needs of their hosts. Again, we start from theoretical and empirical work in usage-based linguistics with the aim of building mechanistic models that computationally operationalise the theoretical insights that were obtained and the empirical evidence that was gathered, in order to support communication in artificial agents.

Usage-based theories of language acquisition describe two main cognitive processes involved in the acquisition of language through communicative interactions: *intention reading* and *pattern finding* (Tomasello, 2003). Intention reading is the process through which listeners hypothesize about the intended meaning of an observed utterance, by reasoning about the situation in which this utterance was formulated. For example, when a child observes the utterance "more-milk?" and receives more milk at the same time, the child can hypothesise that the meaning of this utterance is that an additional portion of this thirst-quenching white liquid will be served. Pattern finding is then the generalisation process through which abstract patterns can be distilled. For example, if the same child then observes the utterance "more-mash?" in a situation where it is served an additional portion of this delicious soft mass, it can generalise to the pattern "more-X?" with the meaning of being served an additional portion of something. At the same time, it can infer that "milk" and "mash" respectively refer to this thirst-quenching white liquid and this delicious soft mass.

The processes of intention reading and pattern finding yield pairings between meaning and form and therefore, by definition, constructions. Initially, a child, or an intelligent agent in our case, cannot do more than store holistic mappings between observed utterances and their (hypothesised) meanings. Indeed, these holophrastic constructions are at this point not further decomposable, as the learner has no information on whether and how specific parts of their meaning might correspond to specific parts of their form. Later, when similar, yet not identical utterances are observed in similar, yet not identical situations, more general item-based constructions can be created, through generalisation over the compositional parts of the form-meaning pairings. The item-based constructions then capture the relations between these variable elements along with any non-compositional aspects of the original form-meaning mappings. Over the course of increasingly more communicative interactions, these generalisations lead to increasingly more abstract constructions. At some point, the constructions adequately reflect the compositional and non-compositional aspects of the language, and the construction inventory of the learner stabilises.

As intention reading hypothesises about the intended meaning underlying an observed utterance in a particular situation, it can yield a hypothesis that might hold in that situation but not in others. Consequently, generalisation over these suboptimal hypotheses might lead to more abstract constructions that are suboptimal as well. It is here that the entrenchment dynamics described in the previous section come into play. Over time, constructions that are used more frequently and successfully in communication become more entrenched. At the same time, suboptimal constructions, which often lead to communicative failure, become less entrenched until they eventually disappear from the construction inventory of the learner. After a sufficient number of communicative interactions, the construction inventory stabilises on a set of generally applicable constructions that cover the learner's communicative needs.

The process of language acquisition through intention reading and pattern finding is operationalised in Fluid Construction Grammar through a meta-layer learning architecture that supports (i) the composition of meaning representations based on the situation (intention reading) and (ii) the generalisation over form-meaning mappings of various degrees of abstraction (pattern finding) (Van Eecke and Beuls, 2017; Van Eecke, 2018; Nevens et al., 2022; Doumen et al., 2023). An example of such a generalisation operation, taken from the experiment described in Nevens et al. (2022) is shown in Figure 2. In this figure, a learner agent observes the utterance "*how many cylinders are there?*" in a 3D scene of geometrical figures, but cannot understand it, as the utterance is currently not covered by the constructions in its construction inventory. The learner agent receives feedback in the form of the answer to the question ("*one*"). Starting from this answer, it can then construct a meaning hypothesis. In this case, the agent hypothesises that the utterance "*how many cylinders are there?*" corresponds to the meaning of segmenting the scene, activating the cylinder prototype, using that prototype to filter the segmented scene for cylinders and counting the items in the filtered set. Indeed, upon execution, this procedural semantic representation leads to the answer "*one*" in this scene. The result of the intention reading operation is shown in Subfigure A of Figure 2.

The agent then identifies a construction in its construction inventory that is minimally different from this pairing between the observed utterance and its hypothesised meaning, namely the holophrastic HOW-MANY-SPHERES-ARE-THERE-?-CXN shown in Subfigure B. This previously acquired construction maps between the utterance "*how many spheres are there?*" and the meaning of segmenting the scene, activating the sphere prototype, using that prototype to filter the segmented scene for spheres and counting the items in the filtered set. Based on this previously acquired construction, the observed utterance and its hypothesised meaning, the agent creates a new item-based

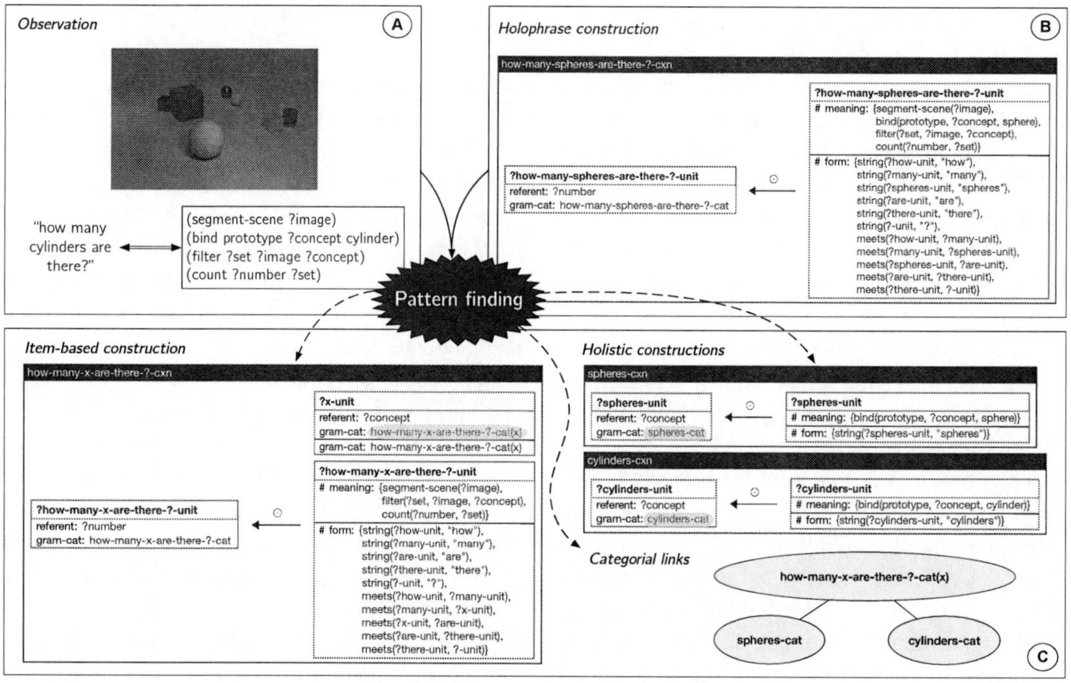

Figure 2: Example of a pattern finding operation that generalises over the observed utterance "*how many cylinders are there?*" paired with its hypothesized meaning (A) and an existing holophrase construction HOW-MANY-SPHERES-ARE-THERE-?-CXN (B). It thereby expands the construction inventory with a new item-based construction HOW-MANY-X-ARE-THERE-?-CXN, two new holistic constructions CYLINDERS-CXN and SPHERES-CXN, and two new categorial links that capture how these constructions can be combined (C).

construction along with two new holistic constructions, as shown in Subfigure C. The item-based construction maps between the form "*how many X are there?*", with X being a variable unit, and its meaning representation of segmenting the scene, filtering the segmented scene for the prototype specified by the variable unit and counting the items in the filtered set. The lexical constructions respectively map between the forms "*cylinders*" and "*spheres*" and the meaning representations of activating the cylinder prototype and activating the sphere prototype. Along with these three constructions, also two categorial links are learnt, which capture the way in which the holistic constructions can combine with the item-based construction. The constructions and categorial links that were acquired are bidirectional and can now be used by the agent for language comprehension and production.

The mechanisms of intention reading and pattern finding are combined with the entrenchment dynamics introduced above. New constructions and categorial links are introduced with a given initial entrenchment score. This score is increased if a construction or categorial link was used in a successful communicative interaction. The score is decreased if it was used in an unsuccessful communicative interaction, or if it was not used but could have been used (i.e. it was a competitor to a successful solution). If the score reaches a specified bottom threshold, the construction or categorial link is removed. These evolutionary dynamics of rewarding and punishing constructions and categorial links ensure that communicatively adequate constructions survive, while inadequate or suboptimal constructions disappear. Not only does this make the system robust against the introduction of inadequate constructions, for example due to bad hypotheses resulting from intention reading, it also ensures that the construction inventory eventually stabilises on the most generally applicable constructions. These are the most abstract constructions possible, i.e. those that are not compositional and can therefore not be further generalised over.

Figure 3, adopted from Nevens et al. (2022), shows the typical dynamics of an experiment in which a construction grammar is learnt through intention reading and pattern finding. The x-axis corresponds to the time dimension, expressed here

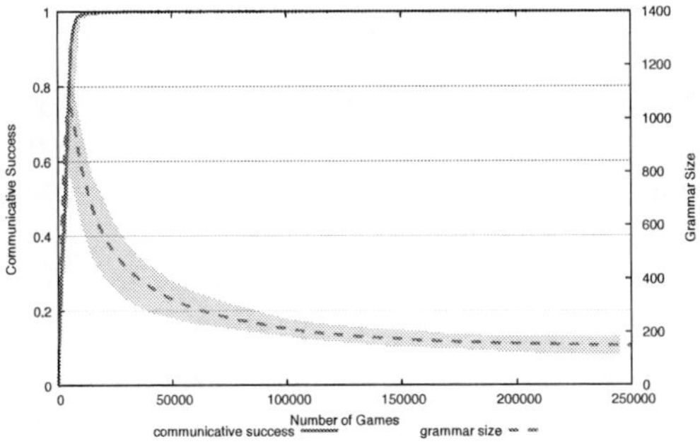

Figure 3: Typical dynamics of an experiment in which a construction grammar is acquired by an autonomous agent through the mechanisms of intention reading and syntactico-semantic pattern finding during communicative interactions. Figure adopted from Nevens et al. (2022).

in terms of the number of communicative interactions in which an agent has participated. The y-axis shows the average communicative success (green line) and the number of construction in the construction inventory of the agent (yellow line) over time. The communicative success starts at 0, as the agent starts without any constructions in its construction inventory. As more and more interactions take place, the communicative success rises to 1, which means that every communicative interaction is successful. The number of constructions in the construction inventory of the agent starts at 0 as well, and then rapidly grows to over 1000. It then starts to decrease, as a result of the entrenchment dynamics, and stabilises somewhere between 150 and 200. During this process, constructions capturing communicatively inadequate form-meaning mappings, as well as form-meaning mappings that are also captured by more generally applicable constructions, disappear from the grammar.

The example discussed in this section is meant to illustrate how an inventory of constructions can be learnt in a usage-based fashion through syntactico-semantic generalisation operations, and how the construction inventory of an agent is shaped by past successes and failure in communication. The exact mechanisms through which the intention reading and pattern finding processes are operationalised, along with the a precise definition of the entrenchment dynamics, fall outside the scope of this paper, although we happily refer the interested reader to publications such as Van Eecke and Beuls (2018) and Nevens et al. (2022).

5 Applications of FCG

Fluid Construction Grammar was originally developed to be used as the language processing component in experiments on the emergence and evolution of language (see e.g. Steels, 2004; van Trijp, 2008; Pauw and Hilferty, 2012; Beuls and Steels, 2013; Spranger, 2016; Cornudella Gaya et al., 2016; Nevens et al., 2019b). As such, it is designed to represent the emergent linguistic knowledge of autonomous agents, as well as to use this knowledge for language comprehension and production. The fact that FCG is rooted in such experiments is reflected in a number of important design choices.

First of all, FCG focusses on representations of linguistic knowledge that are adequate for both language comprehension and production. Second, it provides good support for grounded language processing, for example by providing the possibility to use procedural semantic representations (Woods, 1968; Winograd, 1972; Spranger et al., 2010) and procedural attachment in the constructions (Bundy and Wallen, 1984; Van Eecke, 2018). Third, it focusses on the data-efficient learning of constructions, whereby as much linguistic knowledge as possible is extracted from individual communicative interactions. Fourth, it uses transparent and human-interpretable representations. Finally, it is designed to represent and process ever-evolving grammars, in which new constructions can dynamically be added and in which adequacy of constructions can evolve as changes in the environment or task take place.

While experiments on the emergence and evolution of languages in populations of autonomous agents through task-based communicative interactions are the most prominent application domain for FCG, the design properties mentioned above also make it an attractive framework for a wider range of applications. A first series of applications tackles typical NLP/NLU benchmarks that focus on grounded language processing on the one hand, and on the integration of language processing and reasoning on the other. Typical examples of such tasks are visual question answering (VQA) and visual dialogue, in which the task consists in answering a series of questions about a given image. FCG is then used as a semantic parsing module, which maps from questions to executable queries (Nevens et al., 2019a). The main advantage of the use of FCG in such applications, as compared to the use of neural approaches, is that it provides a transparent and explainable model that can be learnt efficiently (Nevens et al., 2022). Interactive demonstrations of the use of FCG in NLP/NLU systems are provided at the following links respectively for VQA[2] and visual dialogue[3].

A second series of applications makes use of FCG to support the analysis of opinion dynamics expressed in online (social) media. In particular, FCG is used in such applications to extract semantic frames from textual data, such as newspaper articles and comments, subreddits, and parliamentary speeches. Concrete examples are the Penelope Climate Change Opinion Observatory[4] and the Penelope Opinion Facilitator[5]. The opinion observatory (Willaert et al., 2020, 2022) aims to provide social science researchers with a low-barrier tool for studying opinion landscapes expressed in a wide range of digital sources. The opinion facilitator (Willaert et al., 2021) aims to provide a reading instrument for the general public that automatically interlinks news articles based on the expression of similar or opposing views. Both tools focus on opinions expressed in the context of the climate change debate and thereby emphasise the detection and extraction of causal frames (Beuls et al., 2021).

A final series of applications makes use of FCG to support linguistic research. Apart from the obvious advantages that a computational construction grammar implementation brings to the construction grammarian, including the automatic verification and empirical validation of construction grammars, FCG can also serve as the basis for methodological tools supporting usage-based linguistic research. An example of such a tool is the CCxG Explorer[6], which enables usage-based linguists to search for corpus examples that instantiate a semantic structure of interest using any morpho-syntactic realisation. In this way, they can find examples of morpho-syntactic phenomena without the need to identify these phenomena beforehand as is required with other tools.

[2]https://ehai.ai.vub.ac.be/demos/visual-question-answering

[3]https://ehai.ai.vub.ac.be/demos/visual-dialog

[4]https://penelope.vub.be/observatories/climate-change-opinion-observatory

[5]https://penelope.vub.be/opinion-facilitator

[6]https://ehai.ai.vub.ac.be/ccxg-explorer/

6 Conclusion and Outlook

The primary objective of this paper was to provide a brief introduction to the Fluid Construction Grammar research programme, reflecting on what has been achieved so far and identifying key challenges for the future. Let us start by reflecting on the achievements. First of all, we now have at our disposal a computational framework that provides a faithful formalisation and computational operationalisation of the basic tenets of construction grammar. This framework can be used to represent linguistic knowledge in the form of constructions and to use these constructions for language comprehension and production purposes. We also have a basic theory of how constructions can be acquired in a usage-based fashion through syntactico-semantic generalisation processes. Finally, the application potential of FCG has been demonstrated extensively in experiments on emergent languages and on a smaller scale in a number of proof-of-concept language technology applications.

While the last decade has undeniably witnessed major advances in the FCG framework and research programme, even more fascinating challenges and exciting opportunities lie ahead of us now. A first challenge concerns the scaling of constructionist approaches to language on both the theoretical and the computational level, in particular when it comes to modelling the systemic relations between hundreds of thousands of constructions. A second challenge concerns the further development of syntactico-semantic learning operators. This includes for example the design of pattern finding operators that can more elegantly handle linguistic phenomena related to grammatical agreement, more general algorithms for generalising over semantic structures, and techniques that can find minimal differences between speech signals rather than strings. A third challenge resides in converting the recent advances achieved in the domain of learning large-scale FCG grammars into powerful language technology applications. A final challenge concerns the abstraction of FCG's learning mechanisms into an accessible toolbox for end-users. This toolbox would enable AI and NLP engineers to equip intelligent agents with the ability to acquire communicatively adequate grammars during situated task-oriented interactions.

In sum, we strongly believe that the future of computational construction grammar looks brighter than ever and that hugely exciting times lie ahead.

Acknowledgements

We would like to express our gratitude to the multi-talented team of researchers that have contributed to the FCG research programme in the past, and to the current team who ensures that the future of computational construction grammar looks brighter than ever: Luc Steels, Remi van Trijp, Jens Nevens, Tom Willaert, Lara Verheyen, Jonas Doumen, Jérôme Botoko Ekila, Veronica Schmalz, Liesbet De Vos, Alexane Jouglar and Jeroen Van Soest. The research reported on in this paper was financed by the Research Foundation Flanders (FWO) through a postdoctoral grant awarded to Paul Van Eecke (75929) and the European Union's Horizon 2020 research and innovation programme under grant agreement no. 951846 (MUHAI - `https://www.muhai.org`).

References

Benjamin Bergen and Nancy Chang. 2005. Embodied Construction Grammar in simulation-based language understanding. In Mirjam Fried and Jan-Ola Östman, editors, *Construction Grammars: Cognitive Grounding and Theoretical Extensions*, pages 147–190. John Benjamins, Amsterdam.

Katrien Beuls and Luc Steels. 2013. Agent-based models of strategies for the emergence and evolution of grammatical agreement. *PloS One*, 8(3):e58960.

Katrien Beuls, Paul Van Eecke, and Vanja Sophie Cangalovic. 2021. A computational construction grammar approach to semantic frame extraction. *Linguistics Vanguard*, 7(1):20180015.

Joris Bleys, Kevin Stadler, and Joachim De Beule. 2011. Search in linguistic processing. In Luc Steels, editor, *Design Patterns in Fluid Construction Grammar*, pages 149–179. John Benjamins, Amsterdam.

Rens Bod. 2009. Constructions at work or at rest? *Cognitive Linguistics*, 20(1):129–134.

Alan Bundy and Lincoln Wallen. 1984. Procedural attachment. In *Catalogue of Artificial Intelligence Tools*, pages 98–99. Springer.

Miquel Cornudella Gaya, Thierry Poibeau, and Remi van Trijp. 2016. The role of intrinsic motivation in artificial language emergence: a case study on colour. In *Proceedings of COLING 2016, the 26th International Conference on Computational Linguistics: Technical Papers*, pages 1646–1656.

William Croft. 2001. *Radical construction grammar: Syntactic theory in typological perspective*. Oxford University Press, Oxford.

Jonas Doumen, Katrien Beuls, and Paul Van Eecke. 2023. Modelling language acquisition through syntactico-semantic pattern finding. In *Findings of the Association for Computational Linguistics: EACL 2023*. Forthcoming.

Jerome Feldman, Ellen Dodge, and John Bryant. 2009. Embodied Construction Grammar. In Bernd Heine and Heiko Narrog, editors, *The Oxford Handbook of Linguistic Analysis*, pages 121–146. Oxford University Press, Oxford.

Charles J Fillmore. 1988. The mechanisms of "construction grammar". In *Annual Meeting of the Berkeley Linguistics Society*, volume 14, pages 35–55.

Adele Goldberg. 1995. *Constructions: A construction grammar approach to argument structure*. University of Chicago Press, Chicago.

Adele Goldberg. 2003. Constructions: A new theoretical approach to language. *Trends in Cognitive Sciences*, 7(5):219–224.

Paul Kay and Charles Fillmore. 1999. Grammatical constructions and linguistic generalizations: The what's x doing y? construction. *Language*, 75(1):1–33.

George Lakoff. 1987. *Women, fire, and dangerous things: What categories reveal about the mind*. University of Chicago Press.

Ronald W Langacker. 1987. *Foundations of cognitive grammar: Theoretical prerequisites*, volume 1. Stanford University Press, Stanford.

Jens Nevens, Jonas Doumen, Paul Van Eecke, and Katrien Beuls. 2022. Language acquisition through intention reading and pattern finding. In *Proceedings of the 29th International Conference on Computational Linguistics*, pages 15–25, Gyeongju, Republic of Korea. International Committee on Computational Linguistics.

Jens Nevens, Paul Van Eecke, and Katrien Beuls. 2019a. Computational construction grammar for visual question answering. *Linguistics Vanguard*, 5(1):20180070.

Jens Nevens, Paul Van Eecke, and Katrien Beuls. 2019b. A practical guide to studying emergent communication through grounded language games. In *AISB Language Learning for Artificial Agents Symposium*, pages 1–8.

Simon Pauw and Joseph Hilferty. 2012. The emergence of quantifiers. volume 3, pages 277–304. John Benjamins, Amsterdam.

Ivan A. Sag. 2012. Sign-based construction grammar: An informal synopsis. In Hans C. Boas and Ivan A. Sag, editors, *Sign-based construction grammar*, pages 69–202. CSLI Publications/Center for the Study of Language and Information, Stanford.

Josefina Sierra Santibáñez. 2012. A logic programming approach to parsing and production in Fluid Construction Grammar. In Luc Steels, editor, *Computational Issues in Fluid Construction Grammar*, volume 7249 of *Lecture Notes in Computer Science*, pages 239–255. Springer, Berlin.

Michael Spranger. 2016. *The evolution of grounded spatial language*. Language Science Press, Berlin.

Michael Spranger, Simon Pauw, and Martin Loetzsch. 2010. Open-ended semantics co-evolving with spatial language. In *Evolution of Language. The Proceedings of the 10th International Conference (EVOLANGX)*, pages 297–304. World Scientific.

Luc Steels. 2004. Constructivist development of grounded construction grammar. In *Proceedings of the 42nd Annual Meeting of the Association for Computational Linguistics (ACL-04)*, pages 9–16.

Luc Steels, editor. 2011. *Design patterns in Fluid Construction Grammar*. John Benjamins, Amsterdam.

Luc Steels. 2017. Basics of Fluid Construction Grammar. *Constructions and Frames*, 9(2):178–225.

Luc Steels and Joachim De Beule. 2006. Unify and merge in fluid construction grammar. In *Symbol Grounding and Beyond*, pages 197–223, Berlin, Heidelberg. Springer.

Luc Steels and Joachim De Beule. 2006. Unify and merge in Fluid Construction Grammar. In *International Workshop on Emergence and Evolution of Linguistic Communication*, pages 197–223. Springer.

Luc Steels and Joachim De Beule. 2006. A (very) brief introduction to Fluid Construction Grammar. In *Proceedings of the Third Workshop on Scalable Natural Language Understanding*, pages 73–80, New York.

Michael Tomasello. 2003. *Constructing a Language: A Usage-Based Theory of Language Acquisition*. Harvard University Press, Harvard.

Paul Van Eecke. 2018. *Generalisation and specialisation operators for computational construction grammar and their application in evolutionary linguistics Research*. Ph.D. thesis, Vrije Universiteit Brussel, Brussels: VUB Press.

Paul Van Eecke and Katrien Beuls. 2017. Metalayer problem solving for computational construction grammar. In *The 2017 AAAI Spring Symposium Series*, pages 258–265, Palo Alto, Ca. AAAI Press.

Paul Van Eecke and Katrien Beuls. 2018. Exploring the creative potential of computational construction grammar. *Zeitschrift für Anglistik und Amerikanistik*, 66(3):341–355.

Frank Van Eynde. 2016. Sign-based construction grammar: A guided tour. *Journal of Linguistics*, 52(1):194–217.

Remi van Trijp. 2008. The emergence of semantic roles in fluid construction grammar. In *The Evolution Of Language*, pages 346–353. World Scientific.

Remi van Trijp. 2016. Chopping down the syntax tree: What constructions can do instead. *Belgian Journal of Linguistics*, 30(1):15–38.

Remi van Trijp, Katrien Beuls, and Paul Van Eecke. 2022. The FCG editor: An innovative environment for engineering computational construction grammars. *PLOS ONE*, 17(6):1–27.

Tom Willaert, Sven Banisch, Paul Van Eecke, and Katrien Beuls. 2022. Tracking causal relations in the news: data, tools, and models for the analysis of argumentative statements in online media. *Digital Scholarship in the Humanities*. Fqab107.

Tom Willaert, Paul Van Eecke, Katrien Beuls, and Luc Steels. 2020. Building social media observatories for monitoring online opinion dynamics. *Social Media + Society*, 6(2):2056305119898778.

Tom Willaert, Paul Van Eecke, Jeroen Van Soest, and Katrien Beuls. 2021. An opinion facilitator for online news media. *Frontiers in Big Data*, 4:46.

Terry Winograd. 1972. Understanding natural language. *Cognitive Psychology*, 3(1):1–191.

William A. Woods. 1968. Procedural semantics for a question-answering machine. In *Proceedings of the December 9-11, 1968, Fall Joint Computer Conference, Part I*, pages 457–471, New York, NY, USA.

An Argument Structure Construction Treebank

Kristopher Kyle and Hakyung Sung
Learner Corpus Research and Applied Data Science Lab
Linguistics Department, University of Oregon
https://lcr-ads-lab.github.io/LCR-ADS-Home/
{kkyle2, hsung}@uoregon.edu

Abstract

In this paper we introduce a freely available treebank that includes argument structure construction (ASC) annotation. We then use the treebank to train probabilistic annotation models that rely on verb lemmas and/ or syntactic frames. We also use the treebank data to train a highly accurate transformer-based annotation model (F1 = 91.8%). Future directions for the development of the treebank and annotation models are discussed.

1 Introduction

In cognitive linguistics, a construction represents a form-meaning pair. In English, for example, the verb form *laughed* prototypically represents a particular action in the past wherein an entity expresses joy, mirth, or scorn "with a chuckle or explosive vocal sound" (Merriam-Webster, n.d.). Constructions exist at all levels of language (e.g., morphological, lexical, syntactic/argument structure, etc.; Goldberg, 2003). Therefore, while we can analyze *laughed* as a particular form-meaning pair, we can also consider the morphological level, wherein the form *laughed* represents a schematic past-tense construction denoting an event that occurred in the past (laugh_{verb} + $\textit{-ed}_{past}$). Constructions also exist at the syntactic/lexicogrammatical level, wherein a verb and its argument structure constitute a form that corresponds to a propositional meaning (e.g., Diessel, 2004; Fillmore, Kay, & O'Connor, 1988; Goldberg, 1995; 2003; 2006; Jackendoff, 2002). These constructions are referred to as argument structure constructions (ASCs). For example, $\textit{they}_{agent}$ $\textit{laughed}_{verb}$ represents an intransitive ASC, and $\textit{they}_{agent}$ $\textit{laughed}_{verb}$ $\textit{him}_{theme}$ $\textit{[out of the room]}_{goal}$ represents a caused-motion construction. Research has suggested that ASCs are psycholinguisticly real and that both the schematic argument structure (e.g., *agent-verb-theme-goal)* and the verb that fills them (e.g., *laugh*) contribute to sentence meaning (e.g., Bencini & Goldberg, 2000; Gries & Wulff, 2005).

ASCs and Language Learning: Analyzing the relationship between ASC use and productive language development and proficiency has been an increasingly important area of investigation in both first (L1) and second (L2) language learning research (e.g., Clark, 1996; Diessel, 2013; Ellis, 2002; Ellis & Ferreira-Junior, 2009a,b; Hwang & Kim, 2022; Kyle, 2016; Kyle & Crossley, 2017; Kyle et al., 2021; Ninio, 1999; Tomasello & Brooks, 1998). Research suggests that individuals first learn fixed form-meaning pairs that occur frequently in their language experiences. Through more [and varied] language experiences, individuals learn that some pieces of a fixed for-meaning-pair is schematic (e.g., the verb slot). They then tend to overgeneralize the items that can fill a particular slot. Through even more language experiences, they tune their linguistic system to the particular items that tend to occur in a particular slot in a particular construction (see, e.g., Ellis, 2002; Ninio, 1999; Tomasello & Brooks, 1998). For later development (at least in L2 contexts), research has shown that more advanced users tend to use a wider range of ASCs (e.g., Hwang & Kim, 2022) and verb-ASC combinations (e.g., Ellis & Ferreira-Junior, 2009a,b) and (on average) more strongly associated verb-ASC combinations (Kyle, 2016; Kyle & Crossley, 2017).

Extracting ASCs from Corpora: An important issue in studies that analyze the characteristics of ASC use is the method used to identify ASCs and their verbs. Many studies use a manual approach to identify ASCs. While this is appropriate for small-scale studies that measure input directly and/or investigate a limited set of ASCs (e.g., Goldberg et al., 2004; Ellis & Ferreira-Junior, 2009a,b) such an approach puts practical limits the amount of data

Proceedings of the First International Workshop on Construction Grammars and NLP (CxGs+NLP, GURT/SyntaxFest 2023), pages 51 - 62
March 9-12, 2023 ©2023 Association for Computational Linguistics

that can be analyzed. Given the increase in availability of large datasets of learner data (e.g., Blanchard et al., 2013; Granger et al., 2009; Ishikawa, 2013) and the increased use of reference corpora as a representation of language experiences (e.g., Römer et al., 2014), automatic methods of ASC extraction have been proposed. These have primarily included either the use of syntactic frames as ASCs (e.g., O'Donnell & Ellis, 2010; Kyle, 2016; Römer et al., 2014) or rule-based systems that rely on syntactic frames and explicit lexical information (Hwang & Kim, 2022). To date, however, no approaches have used machine-learning techniques to predict ASCs directly, primarily because no ASC treebank is currently available.

Contributions of this study: In this study, we build on previous related projects such as PropBank (Palmer et al., 2005), FrameNet (Fillmore et al., 2003), VerbNet (Schuler, 2005) and Universal Propositions (Akbik et al., 2015) to create a publicly available treebank of ASCs. We also leverage machine learning algorithms to create a publicly available automated ASC annotation model.

2 Extracting ASCs from Natural Language Data

ASCs have been extracted from corpora for a range of research purposes. These include (among others), investigating alternation (e.g., dative alternation in English; e.g, Gries & Wulff, 2009; Romain, 2022), verb-construction contingencies (e.g., Ellis & Ferreira-Junior, 2009a,b; Kyle, 2016; Kyle & Crossley, 2017), the validity of using corpus data to represent the mental construction of L1 and L2 users (e.g., Römer et al., 2014), and investigating language proficiency and/or development (e.g., Hwang & Kim, 2022; Kyle & Crossley, 2017; Kyle et al., 2021).

2.1 Manual approaches

The default method of ASC extraction has been manual and/or semi-automated annotation of particular ASC structures. This usually involves pre-selecting candidate verb forms and then determining whether each use of the verb form represents a particular construction. For example, Ellis and Ferreira-Junior (2009a, b) annotated a corpus of L1/L2 interview data (Perdue, 1993) for three construction types (verb-locative, verb-object-locative, and double object constructions) using a list of verbs and a follow up manual analysis. Similar procedures have been used in a number of other studies (e.g., Gries & Wulff, 2009; Romain, 2022) While this approach can achieve high accuracies, the manual nature of searches practically limits how much data can be examined. Furthermore, if the goal is to comprehensively examine the relationship between verbs and ASCs (which is the case in some studies), all verbs (and their constructions) in a corpus must be examined.

2.2 Syntactic frame as construction approach

As the availability of large corpora of language use increased and the use of dependency representations gained traction in the field of natural language processing, some scholars began to use dependency-based syntactic frames to identify constructions (e.g., O'Donnell & Ellis, 2010; Kyle, 2016; Kyle & Crossley, 2017). For example, the syntactic frame *subject-verb-object$_{indirect}$-object$_{direct}$* can be used to reliably identify ditransitive constructions. O'Donnell & Ellis (2010) used a dependency-parsed version of the BNC (Andersen et al., 2008) to preliminarily extract constructions for the purposes of examining verb-construction contingencies. Ellis and colleagues used a related approach to explore the relationship between corpus contingencies and online choices in verb-preposition-object constructions (e.g., Römer et al., 2014). However, the relatively low accuracy of the RASP parser (F1 = .763 averaged annotation accuracy) limited the types and specificity of the constructions that could be reliably examined.

As dependency parsers increased in accuracy (and speed) with the introduction of neural-net models (e.g., F1 = .896; Chen & Manning, 2014) and transformer models (e.g., F1 = .951; Honnibal et al., 2020) some researchers (e.g., Kyle, 2016; Kyle & Crossley, 2017; Kyle et al., 2021) explored the contingency of dependency-based syntactic frames and verbs in large corpora such as the Corpus of Contemporary American English (Davies, 2009). These contingencies were then successfully used to model differences in language use across L2 proficiency levels.

While the syntactic frame approach has been useful in a number of contexts, syntactic frames do not directly represent ASCs in all cases. Multiple dependency-based syntactic frames can map onto a single ASC and conversely a single syntactic frame may represent multiple ASCs depending on the context. For example, *subject-verb-object-oblique*$_{prep\_on}$ can represent both a simple transitive construction (*I*$_{subject}$ *found*$_{verb}$ *this*$_{object}$ *[on a bulletin board]*$_{oblique}$) or a caused-motion construction (*I*$_{subject}$ *put*$_{verb}$ *it*$_{object}$ *[on my hand]*$_{oblique}$).

2.3 Rule-based approach

Another approach uses a set of rules written over a dependency representation to identify particular ASCs. For example, Hwang & Kim (2022) identified 11 ASC types (e.g., caused-motion, ditransitive) using a manually derived rule-based system that relies on dependency-based syntactic frames and some lexical items. Although they do not report accuracy on a by-ASC basis, they report an overall F1 score of .82. While this approach represents an interesting preliminary step in identifying particular ASCs, it is not clear how well it can generalize to unseen structures and/or lexical items.

2.4 Other potential approaches

When we convey meaning via a particular form of ASC, a verb interacts with the arguments in the construction. Semantically, the arguments in the construction relate to abstract meanings such as *agent, patient, theme, goal, result,* etc. (Fillmore, 1968; Palmer, Gildea, & Xue, 2010), which are called semantic roles. Semantic roles help encode the general senses that are basic to human experience (Scene Encoding Hypothesis, Goldberg, 1995; Kay & Fillmore, 1999), which in turn are useful for classifying ASCs.

As previously noted, a limitation of the syntactic frame approach is that functional grammatical labels (e.g., subject, direct object, oblique) are not fine-grained enough to determine the semantic role of an argument. Although some preliminary work has been done in the area of automatic semantic role labeling (e.g., Gardner et al., 2018; Shi & Jin, 2019), current state of the art models are not accurate enough to make this a feasible option (though this may change in the future). However, treebanks with manually-annotated semantic role labels present a helpful starting point for a treebank of ASCs.

2.5 Machine-learning approaches

In order for machine-learning models to be used to create automatic ASC annotation models, treebanks that include ASC information are needed. Although some previous work has been done on specific ASC types, such as caused-motion constructions (Hwang, 2014; Hwang et al., 2010), to our knowledge there are currently no publicly available treebanks that are annotated for ASCs. Additionally, although some previous work has trained models to identify a specific ASC type (e.g., Hwang et al., 2010, 2015), there have been no machine-learning based models that annotate a wider range of ASCs. In this study we address these gaps by introducing a publicly available treebank annotated for ASCs. We then introduce a series of automatic ASC annotation models, including a highly accurate transformer-based model.

3 Method

3.1 Creating an ASC treebank

For this project, we used the English portion of the Universal Propositions project (Akbik et al., 2015), which represents a merge of the Universal Dependencies version of the English Web Treebank (EWT; Bies et al., 2012; Silveira et al., 2014) and PropBank (Palmer et al., 2005). The EWT corpus includes sentences sampled from five web registers, including blogs, newsgroups, emails, reviews, and Yahoo! Answers.

We used a semiautomatic approach to annotating the ASC treebank. For each sentence in the training section of the EWT, we first extracted the large-grained argument structures using the default PropBank semantic role labels (e.g., *ARG0-Verbsense-ARG1*). We then converted the large-grained arguments to fine-grained semantic role frames (e.g., *agent-Verb-theme*) using relation mappings from the PropBank frame files (Palmer et al., 2005), which also draw on information in FrameNet (Fillmore et al., 2003) and VerbNet (Schuler, 2005). After a discussion of ASC categorization between the authors that included co-annotation of 100 sentences, the second author (a PhD student with a specialization in construction grammar) manually assigned an ASC to each semantic role frame that occurred at least 5 times in the corpus (n = 355) based on the semantics of the frame and its typical use in the treebank sentences. For example, the semantic role frame *theme-Verb-attribute* was annotated as an attributive construction and *agent-Verb-theme* was annotated as a transitive simple construction. In some cases, the corpus analysis indicated that particular semantic role frames could represent

ASC	Most frequent verbs	Total Freq	Train	Dev	Test
TRAN_S	*have, do, say*	12,431	9,965	1,213	1,253
ATTR	*be, seem, look*	6,004	4,723	648	633
INTRAN_S	*go, work, come*	2,754	2,200	289	265
PASSIVE	*attach, do, call*	1,818	1,481	167	170
INTRAN_MOT	*go, come, get*	1,098	915	88	95
TRAN_RES	*let, make, get*	977	795	90	92
CAUS_MOT	*take, put, send*	675	546	64	65
DITRAN	*give, tell, ask*	534	448	40	46
INTRAN_RES	*become, go, come*	146	121	9	16
Total		**26,437**	**21,194**	**2,608**	**2,635**

Table 1: ASC Representation in Treebank

multiple ASCs. This most often occurred in cases where a fine-grained semantic role for a particular argument of a particular verb was unavailable in PropBank, leading to an underspecified semantic role frame. In these cases, the use of each semantic role frame + verb combination that occurred at least twice in the treebank was checked and each was assigned an ASC. Particularly ambiguous cases were resolved through discussions with the first author. As a final step, we conducted spot checks which led to a small number of corrections. This approach resulted in the categorization of 94.1% of the ASCs in the treebank. Any sentences that included uncategorized ASCs were omitted from further analysis.

In order to evaluate the quality of the semi-automated annotation process, the Authors independently annotated a random sample of 100 sentences from the ASC treebank. The 100 sentences included 189 ASC tokens. The results demonstrated substantial agreement between annotators (*kappa* = .773; *simple agreement rate* = 84.1%; Landis & Koch, 1977). The Authors then adjudicated the annotations until perfect agreement was reached. The annotations generated by the semi-automated process demonstrated excellent agreement with the adjudicated scores (*kappa* = .884, *simple agreement rate* = 92.1%).

In total, 26,437 ASC instances were annotated and included in the analysis (see Table 1 for a summary of the distribution of ASCs in each section of the treebank). The ASC Treebank is freely available at https://github.com/LCR-ADS-Lab/ASC-Treebank and https://osf.io/ncjx8/?view_only=163c81a90eec44fb9ee317ff6fa4d4a6).

3.2 ASCs represented

Though there are many commonalities across ASC types that are investigated, there is currently no definitive set of ASCs that should be included in an ASC tag set, and there are varying levels of specificity that could be represented (e.g., Hwang et al., 2010; 2015). The current study drew on a range of previous literature (e.g., Biber et al., 1999; Goldberg, 1995, 2006; Hwang & Kim, 2022). The nine ASC types included in this study represent an attempt to balance specificity and semantic generalization. Note that all examples in the following subsections come from the training section of the treebank.

3.2.1 Attributive construction

The attributive (ATTR) ASC includes two arguments, namely a *theme* and an *attribute*. The *attribute* is prototypically represented by a noun (e.g., *[it]$_{theme}$ was [an evolution]$_{attribute}$*), an adjective (*[I]$_{theme}$ am [sure]$_{attribute}$*), or a prepositional phrase (*[your dog]$_{theme}$ ... is [in the same room]$_{attribute}$*; Biber et al., 1999). Most commonly, the copular verb *be* is used in this construction.

3.2.2 Intransitive constructions

Intransitive constructions typically include a single argument but can include two arguments if the construction denotes more than a simple action, such as a movement or a state change of a subject argument. We subcategorize intransitive constructions into simple, motion, and resultative ASCs.

Intransitive simple: The intransitive simple (INTRAN_S) ASC includes a single argument and typically denotes either what an *agent* does (e.g., *[I]$_{agent}$ am working from our Hong Kong office*) or what happens to a *theme* (e.g., *[Martin's box]$_{theme}$ is working wonderfully*)".

Intransitive motion: The intransitive motion (INTRAN_MOT) ASC involves two arguments including a *mover/theme* and a *path* (Goldberg, 1995). The path is typically denoted via an adverbial particle (e.g., *[The morbidity rate]$_{theme}$ is going [up]$_{ARGM\text{-}DIR}$*) or a prepositional phrase (e.g., *[I]$_{theme}$ went [across the bay]$_{goal}$*).

Intransitive resultative: The intransitive resultative (INTRAN_RES) ASC involves two arguments, including a *patient* and a *result*. The construction denotes a patient changing state (e.g., *[The spine]$_{patient}$ will become [flexible]$_{result}$*).

3.2.3 Simple transitive construction

The simple transitive construction (TRAN_S) includes two arguments that describe an action done by a subject argument to an object argument. The simple transitive ASC prototypically includes an *agent* and a *theme/patient*. The *theme/patient* generally represents an entity that is affected by the action denoted by the verb (Biber et al., 1999; e.g., *[They]$_{agent}$ are targeting [ambulances]$_{theme}$*). The simple transitive can also denote mental activities (e.g., *[I]$_{agent}$ thought [the US government was looking for me]$_{theme}$*) and states (e.g., *[I]$_{experiencer}$ love [my gym]$_{stimulus}$*). The simple transitive is also inclusive of communication activities such as speaking or writing (e.g., *[He]$_{agent}$ claimed [that they have the means to stage]$_{topic}$*).

3.2.4 Ditransitive Construction

The ditransitive construction (DITRAN) prototypically includes three arguments (e.g., *agent, recipient,* and *theme*). It evokes the notion of literal or metaphorical transfer (e.g., *[You]$_{agent}$ feed [your rabbits]$_{recipient}$ [non-veg items]$_{theme}$*). The ditransitive construction is inclusive of the transfer of a topic during communication (e.g., *[I]$_{agent}$ told [the little girl]$_{recipient}$ [that she would have to accompany me to school]$_{topic}$*).

3.2.5 Complex Transitive Constructions

Complex transitive constructions include three arguments that describe either a movement or a change in state of an object argument caused by an action of a subject argument. We subcategorize these into caused-motion and transitive resultative constructions as outlined below.

Caused-motion: The caused-motion (CAUS_MOT) ASC includes an *agent* that causes a *theme* to move along a path designated by a directional phrase (Goldberg, 1999). Semantically, caused-motion ASCs are inclusive of both direct causation (e.g., *[I]$_{agent}$ took [it]$_{theme}$ [there]$_{destination}$*) and indirect causation (e.g., *[The body]$_{agent}$ brings [stability]$_{theme}$ [to the region]$_{goal}$*).

Transitive resultative: The transitive resultative (TRAN_RES) prototypically includes an *agent*, a *patient/theme* and a *result* wherein the *agent* causes the *patient/theme* to become the *result* (e.g., ... *[the vessel]$_{agent}$ changed [its name]$_{patient}$ at sea to [Horizon]$_{result}$*). We also include verb-particle constructions wherein the paired particle has a figurative meaning of the resultative state (e.g., *[No preacher]$_{agent}$ has ever blown [himself]$_{theme}$ [up]$_{C\text{-}V}$*).

3.2.6 Passive Constructions

Passive (PASSIVE) contains short passive (a form without an expressed agent in *by*-phrase; e.g., *[You]$_{theme}$ are invited$_{_Vpassive}$ to join with members of the forum*) and long passive (with an expressed agent; e.g., *coined$_{_Vpassive}$ [by Bill Gates]$_{agent}$ to represent the company* (Biber et al., 1999). This also includes past participle pre-modifiers (e.g., *overlooked*$_{\_\text{Vpassive}}$ *[problem]$_{theme}$*) and post-modifiers (e.g., *She guided me through a very difficult period dealing with a family member's suicide, coupled$_{_Vpassive}$ with elder abuse*).

3.2.7 Annotation scheme summary

In total, the corpus is annotated for nine ASC types. Multiple, overlapping ASCs may be present in a particular utterance. For example, a clausal argument of an ASC will represent an additional ASC as in [*But the best way is [to use coupons*]$_{TRAN\_S}$]$_{ATTR}$.

3.2.8 Model Training and Evaluation

We trained three probabilistic models and a transformer model based on RoBERTa (Liu et al., 2019) embeddings. The probabilistic models served two purposes. The first purpose was theoretical in nature (e.g., how well can we predict an ASC based on its verb versus its syntactic frame) and the second was as a set of linguistically-informed baseline models. A transformer model was also used because these models are particularly well suited for the task of ASC identification given that they use a high-featured vector space representation of the context to predict the category of a section of text. The probabilistic models presumed that main verb heads of argument structure constructions were pre-identified (which is relatively trivial using a part of speech tagger and a dependency parser), while the transformer model evaluated all tokens and identified whether a token was the head of an ASC, and which ASC was represented by the token. As such, the annotation task for the probabilistic models was less demanding than the annotation task for the transformer model.

Model 1 (Verb lemmas): The first model calculated the probability that a particular verb lemma token would occur in a particular ASC. While it is likely that better results would be achieved using verb senses instead of verb lemmas, automated verb sense disambiguation is not currently sufficiently accurate to make this approach generalizable for data outside of PropBank. Each main verb lemma that represented the head of an ASC was annotated as the most probable ASC for that verb. For example, in the training data, the verb lemma *put* was most likely to occur in the CAUS_MOT construction, though it also occurred in the TRAN_S and TRAN_RES constructions. Any verb in the development or test set that was not represented in the training data was assigned the most frequent ASC in the training data (TRAN_S).

Model 2 (Syntactic frames): The second model calculated the probability that a particular syntactic frame token would represent an ASC. Drawing on previous research (e.g., Kyle, 2016; Kyle & Crossley, 2017; Kyle et al., 2021; O'Donnell & Ellis, 2010), syntactic frames were operationalized based on the functional grammatical labels included in the dependency representation. In this case, dependency representations followed Universal Dependencies (UD; Nivre et al., 2020). Copular constructions were adapted slightly to allow the copular verb to represent the head of copular constructions. Following previous research (e.g., Kyle & Crossley, 2017; Römer et al., 2014), concrete realizations of prepositions were included in the syntactic frames, and auxiliary verbs were excluded. For example, the syntactic frame *subject_verb_object_on-oblique*, most commonly represented the TRAN_S ASC (e.g., … *[you]$_{nsubj}$ have [a bunch of stuff]$_{object}$ [on your plate]$_{obl}$*), though it also represented the CAUS_MOT ASC (e.g., *[It]$_{nsubj}$ put [hair]$_{obj}$ [on my chest]$_{obl}$*). Any syntactic frames in the development or test set that were not represented in the training data were assigned the most frequent ASC in the training data (TRAN_S).

Model 3 (Verb lemma + Syntactic frames): The third model calculated the probability that a particular verb lemma + syntactic frame combination token would represent a particular ASC. As a concrete example, while the verb *put* occurs in multiple ASCs, and the syntactic frame *subject_verb_object_on-oblique* represents at least two ASCs, in the training data the combination of *put + subject_verb_object_on-oblique* represented a single ASC (CAUS_MOT). This model used three back-offs. If the verb lemma + syntactic frame was not represented in the training data, the syntactic frame probabilities were used, followed by the verb lemma probabilities and, as a last resort, the most common tag in the training data (TRAN_S).

ASC	**Freq**	**lemma model**	**syntactic frame model**	**lemma + syntactic frame model**	**transformer model**
TRAN_S	1,253	0.821	0.824	0.897	**0.938**
ATTR	633	**0.982**	0.884	0.972	**0.982**
INTRAN_S	265	0.373	0.617	0.713	**0.859**
PASSIVE	170	0.283	0.799	0.809	**0.862**
INTRAN_MOT	95	0.522	0.258	0.540	**0.769**
TRAN_RES	92	0.397	0.723	0.756	**0.798**
CAUS_MOT	65	0.301	0.524	0.557	**0.742**
DITRAN	46	0.536	0.747	0.825	**0.905**
INTRAN_RES	16	0.519	0.105	0.640	**0.759**
Weighted Average		0.735	0.779	0.862	**0.918**

Table 2: F1 scores for each model (test set)

ASC	P	R	F1
TRAN_S	0.927	0.949	0.938
ATTR	0.989	0.975	0.982
INTRAN_S	0.884	0.837	0.859
PASSIVE	0.878	0.847	0.862
INTRAN_MOT	0.750	0.789	0.769
TRAN_RES	0.802	0.793	0.798
CAUS_MOT	0.731	0.754	0.742
DITRAN	0.878	0.935	0.905
INTRAN_RES	0.846	0.688	0.759
Weighted Average	0.917	0.920	0.918

Table 3: Transformer model results in terms of precision, recall, and F1

Model 4 (Transformer model): The fourth model used RoBERTa embeddings to predict whether a word represented the head of a particular ASC. Unlike Models 1-3, which classified an ASC based on a pre-identified main verb, syntactic frame, or verb + syntactic frame combination, Model 4 evaluated each word in a sentence and determined a) whether the word represented the head of an ASC (i.e., was a main verb) and if so, b) the ASC represented by that verb in the sentence. Models were trained using the transformer-based single-class named entities model in Spacy (version 3.4; Honnibal et al., 2020). Models were developed using the training set data, fine-tuned using the development set data, and finally evaluated on the test set data.

4 Results

The results indicated that all models performed well above the simple baseline accuracy (F1 = .307 when all ASCs are tagged as TRAN_S). The transformer model achieved the highest overall classification accuracy (F1 = .918), followed by the verb lemma + syntactic frame model, the syntactic frame model, and the verb lemma model. With regard to individual ASC types, the transformer model also achieved the highest F1 score for each of the 9 ASCs represented in the treebank (inclusive of a tie with the lemma model for the ATTR ASC). The results for the four models (F1 scores) are summarized in Table 2. The full results (precision, recall, and F1 for each ASC type) for the transformer model are included in Table 3.

5 Discussion

In this study, we introduce a treebank with ASC annotations and an automated ASC annotation model. Below, we discuss features of and future directions for the corpus and the prediction models. We also discuss future directions with regard to applied research using the model.

5.1 ASC Treebank

To our knowledge, the ASC Treebank represents the first publicly available and open-source treebank annotated for ASC types. In total, the ASC treebank currently includes 30,664 annotated ASCs across 9 ASC types. When sentences that include uncategorized ASCs are excluded, 26,437 ASCs annotations are represented.

5.1.1 ASC representation

Although some ASCs are well-represented in the treebank (e.g., TRAN_S, ATTR, and INTRAN_S), others are underrepresented (e.g., CAUS_MOT, DITRAN, INTRAN_RES, and TRAN_RES). Instances of the INTRAN_RES ASC, for example, comprises only 0.5% of ASCs instances in the treebank. While this may be representative of the registers included in the EWT (i.e., blogs, newsgroups, emails, reviews, and Yahoo! Answers) the distribution may not be representative of other registers. Regardless, very low representation of INTRAN_RES likely contributed to lower annotation accuracy for this ASC. Future treebank development should include a focus on including more instances of underrepresented ASC types.

5.1.2 Register representation

It is well known that natural language processing models work better on in-domain texts (i.e., texts that share register features) than on out of domain texts (e.g., McClosky et al., 2006). Although the EWT treebank was a convenient context in which to build an ASC treebank, some researchers will be interested in extracting and analyzing texts from registers other than those represented by the EWT. Future treebank development should therefore include a focus on increasing register coverage. Ideally, this would involve adding manual annotations to other publicly available corpora, such as written and spoken L2 corpora that are annotated for universal dependencies (e.g., Berzak et al., 2016; Kyle et al., 2022).

5.1.3 Improved annotation and treebank coverage

The inclusion of verb senses and semantic role labels from Propbank, FrameNet, and VerbNet allowed for the efficient annotation of a relatively large number of ASCs. In total 30,664 (94.1%) of the ASCs in the treebank could be identified using a relatively small set (n = 355) of semantic frame to ASC mappings (plus some verb + semantic frame specific mappings). However, 5.9% of the ASCs in the treebank remain uncategorized. Future treebank development should include a focus on manually annotating the remaining uncategorized ASCs.

One limitation to the approach of using semantic frame (and verb + semantic frame) to ASC mappings is that some semantic role frames in ProbBank (even when augmented with information from VerbNet and FrameNet) may correspond to multiple ASCs. In the EWT data, this was relatively common when one or more elements in semantic frames were underspecified (e.g., *agent-Verb-**ARG2***). In many cases, ambiguous cases could be addressed by looking at how each semantic frame was used in context with a particular verb. However, in some cases, even seemingly unambiguous semantic frames and/or verb sense + semantic frame combinations could be mapped to multiple ASCs. For example, the verb sense *go.08* when used in the semantic frames *(experiencer-)Verb-result* prototypically represents the INTRAN_RES ASC (e.g., *the company went bankrupt*). However, in the EWT, this combination also includes a very few instances that are not representative of the INTRAN_RES ASC, such as *go on your computer*. The small-scale accuracy analysis (100-sentences; 189 ASCs) suggested that agreement was high between the ASC annotations produced by the semi-automated process used in this study and the adjudicated gold-standard ACS annotations (*kappa* = .884; *simple agreement rate* = 92.1%). Although this agreement was higher than between two expert annotators, there is certainly room for improving the quality of the ASC annotations in the treebank. Future treebank development should therefore include a focus on providing additional quality checks and edits in the treebank.

5.2 Prediction models

In this study, three probabilistic models focused on verbs and/or syntactic frames and one transformer model was trained and tested. All models performed well above baseline accuracy. Below we provide a summary of the strengths and weakness of each model, followed by a concrete example of the performance of the most accurate model (transformer model).

5.2.1 Verb lemma model

The verb lemma model (precision = 0.742, recall = 0.758, F1 = 0.735) performed better than baseline, but less well than the other models. Unsurprisingly, the verb lemma model performed well when identifying ATTR (precision = 0.987, recall = .973, F1 = .982), given that the copular verb *be* is very strongly associated with ATTR. The verb model also performed reasonably well when identifying the TRAN_S ASC (precision = 0.755, recall = .900, F1 = .821), but did not perform well (F1 < .600) when identifying other ASCs. These results provide some support for the notion that verbs are not the only (and not necessarily the primary) determinant of the meaning of a sentence/clause (e.g., Bencini & Goldberg, 2000).

5.2.2 Syntactic frame model

The syntactic frame model (precision = 0.793, recall = 0.784, F1 = 0.779) performed better than the verb lemma model, but less well than the remaining two models. The syntactic frame model performed reasonably well (F1 > .700) when annotating 5 of the 9 ASCs (e.g., ATTR, TRAN_S, DITRAN) but performed less well with other four, and in particular those with ambiguous dependency structures (e.g., INTRAN_RES and CAUSE_MOT). These results suggest that although syntactic frames derived from dependency representations are helpful in the identification of some ASCs, dependency syntactic frames should likely not be equated with ASCs.

5.2.3 Verb lemma + syntactic frame model

Unsurprisingly, the verb lemma + syntactic frame model performed much better (precision = 0.866, recall = 0.863, F1 = 0.862) than the models that relied on verb lemmas or syntactic frames only. The model performed reasonably well (F1 > .700) when annotating 6 of the 9 ASCs, but performed less well when annotating CAUS_MOT, INTRAN_MOT, and INTRAN_RES. These structures were particularly difficult to annotate accurately because ambiguity can only be resolved by determining (in the case of CAUS_MOT and INTRAN_RES) whether a predicate phrase such as a prepositional phrase represents a *goal/path/source* or has a different function. While ambiguities can sometimes be resolved by the preposition used, this is not always the case (leading to low annotation accuracies). This provides further support for the distinction between syntactic frames and ASCs and the need for treebanks annotated for features beyond syntactic dependency representations.

5.2.4 Transformer model

The best performing model was the transformer model (precision = 0.917, recall = 0.920, F1 = 0.918). Unlike the probabilistic models, all ASCs were annotated with an F1 > 0.740. Three ASCs (TRAN_S, ATTR, and DITRAN) were annotated with an F1 > .900. Two more ASCs (INTRAN_S and PASSIVE) were annotated with an F1 > 0.850. These results suggest that transformer models, which rely on a highly-featured vector space representation of a word's context, are particularly well-suited for the automated annotation of ASCs. While these results represent a high degree of accuracy in automated ASC identification, there are still important improvements to be made with regard to the annotation of structures that are less well represented in the ASC treebank (e.g., INTRAN_RES and CAUS_MOT). Future research should focus on improving annotation of these features through model optimization techniques such as oversampling and the addition of sentences to the treebank that include underrepresented ASCs.

5.2.5 Concrete example

To demonstrate the performance of the transformer model in concrete terms, we used the transformer model to identify ASCs in the 16 sentences used in Bencini & Goldberg (2000). In the study, four verbs (*get*, *slice*, *throw, and took*) were each used in four ASCs (TRAN_S, DITRAN, CAUS_MOT, and TRAN_RES). The transformer model from this current study accurately classified all instances of the TRAN_S ASC (*Anita threw the hammer.*, *Michelle got the book*, *Barbara sliced the bread*, and *Audrey took the watch*), the DITRAN ASC (*Chris threw Linda the pencil*, *Beth got Liz an invitation*, *Jennifer sliced Terry an apple*, and *Paula took Sue a message*), and the CAUS_MOT ASC (*Pat threw the keys on the roof*, *Laura got the ball into the net*, *Meg sliced the ham onto the plate*, and *Kim took the rose into the house*). However, the model struggled to classify the TRANS_RES ASCs, and only classified two of the four correctly (*Dana got the mattress inflated* and *Nancy sliced the tire open*). The other two TRAN_RES instances (*Lyn threw the box apart* and *Rachel took the wall down*) were classified as CAUS_MOT, suggesting that more (and more diverse) instances of the TRAN_RES ASC are needed in future iterations of the treebank.

5.3 Applications for future research in linguistics

Previous corpus-based studies of language development and/or proficiency have typically either used manual/semi-automatic approaches to the identification of ASCs (e.g., Ellis & Ferreira-Junior, 2009a; Goldberg et al., 2004). Such approaches are resource intensive and, in most cases, lead to the analysis of a relatively small dataset and/or a limited number of ASCs. Some researchers have leveraged advances in dependency annotation to identify ASCs in larger corpora of both highly proficient language users and language learners using verb + syntactic frame combinations (e.g., Hwang & Kim, 2022; Kyle, 2016; Kyle & Crossley, 2017). The results of this study suggest that while verb + syntactic frames can be used to identify ASCs with a reasonable degree of accuracy (F1 = .862), the transformer-based annotation model introduced in this study is both more accurate overall (F1 = .918) and more stable across ASC types. Future research should investigate the application of the model introduced in this study to corpus-based studies of language learning and in areas such as automatic essay scoring and feedback. This research should include the replication of previous studies that have used less accurate methods of identifying ASCs (e.g., Hwang & Kim, 2022; Kyle & Crossley, 2017).

6 Conclusion

In this study, we introduce publicly available and open-source treebank annotated with ASCs. We also present a highly accurate ASC annotation model, which performs much better (F1 = 0.918) than previously reported rule-based systems (F1 = 0.820; Hwang & Kim, 2021). While improvements can be made with regard to the size and representativeness of the treebank, the results of this study suggest that future treebank annotation efforts would be beneficial to researchers interested in examining ASC use at scale.

References

Akbik, A., Chiticariu, L., Danilevsky, M., Li, Y., Vaithyanathan, S., & Zhu, H. (2015, July). Generating high quality proposition banks for multilingual semantic role labeling. In *Proceedings of the 53rd Annual Meeting of the Association for Computational Linguistics and the 7th International Joint Conference on Natural Language Processing (Volume 1),* 397-407.

Andersen, Ø. E., Nioche, J., Briscoe, T., & Carroll, J. A. (2008). The BNC parsed with RASP4UIMA. *Proceedings of the Sixth International Language Resources and Evaluation (LREC08)*, 28-30.

Bencini, G. M., & Goldberg, A. E. (2000). The contribution of argument structure constructions to sentence meaning. *Journal of Memory and Language*, *43*(4), 640-651.

Berzak, Y., Kenney, J., Spadine, C., Wang, J. X., Lam, L., Mori, K. S., Garza, S., & Katz, B. (2016). Universal dependencies for learner English. In *Proceedings of the 54th Annual Meeting of the Association for Computational Linguistics*, 737-746.

Biber, D., Johansson, S., Leech, G., Conrad, S., Finegan, E., & Quirk, R. (1999). *Longman grammar of spoken and written English* (Vol. 2). London: Longman.

Bies, A., Mott, J., Warner, C., & Kulick, S. (2012). English web treebank. *Linguistic Data Consortium, Philadelphia, PA.*

Blanchard, D., Tetreault, J., Higgins, D., Cahill, A., & Chodorow, M. (2013). TOEFL11: A corpus of non-native English. *ETS Research Report Series*, *2013*(2), i-15.

Chen, D., & Manning, C. D. (2014). A fast and accurate dependency parser using neural networks. In *Proceedings of the 2014 conference on empirical methods in natural language processing (EMNLP)*, 740-750.

Clark, H. H. (1996). *Using language*. Cambridge university press.

Ninio, A. (1999). Pathbreaking verbs in syntactic development and the question of prototypical transitivity. *Journal of child language*, *26*(3), 619-653.

Davies, M. (2009). The 385+ million word Corpus of Contemporary American English (1990–2008+): Design, architecture, and linguistic insights. *International Journal of Corpus Linguistics, 14*(2), 159–190. https:// doi.org/10.1075/ijcl.14.2.02dav.

Diessel, H. (2004). *The acquisition of complex sentences*. Cambridge University Press.

Diessel, H. (2013). Construction grammar and first language acquisition. *The Oxford handbook of construction grammar*, *347*, 364.

Ellis, N. C. (2002). Frequency effects in language processing: A review with implications for theories of implicit and explicit language acquisition. *Studies in second language acquisition*, *24*(2), 143-188.

Ellis, N. C., & Ferreira-Junior, F. (2009a). Constructions and their acquisition: Islands and the distinctiveness of their occupancy. *Annual Review of Cognitive Linguistics*, *7*(1), 188-221.

Ellis, N. C., & Ferreira–Junior, F. (2009b). Construction learning as a function of frequency, frequency distribution, and function. *The Modern language journal*, *93*(3), 370-385.

Fillmore, C. J. (1968). The case for case. In E. Bach & R. T. Harms. (Eds.), *Universals in linguistic theory,* 1-88.

Fillmore, C. J., Johnson, C. R., & Petruck, M. R. (2003). Background to Framenet. *International journal of lexicography*, *16*(3), 235-250.

Fillmore, C. J., Kay, P., & O'connor, M. C. (1988). Regularity and idiomaticity in grammatical constructions: The case of let alone. *Language*, *64*(3), 501-538.

Gardner, M., Grus, J., Neumann, M., Tafjord, O., Dasigi, P., Liu, N., Peters, M., Schmitz, Mi., & Zettlemoyer, L. (2018). Allennlp: A deep semantic natural language processing platform. In *Proceedings of Workshop for NLP Open Source Software (NLP-OSS)*, 1-6.

Goldberg, A. E. (1995). *Constructions: A construction grammar approach to argument structure*. University of Chicago Press.

Goldberg, A. E. (2003). Constructions: A new theoretical approach to language. *Trends in cognitive sciences*, 7(5), 219-224.

Goldberg, A. E. (2006). *Constructions at work: The nature of generalization in language*. Oxford University Press on Demand.

Goldberg, A. E., Casenhiser, D. M., & Sethuraman, N. (2004). Learning argument structure generalizations. *Cognitive Linguistics*, *15*(3), 289-316.

Granger, S., Dagneaux, E., Meunier, F., & Paquot, M. (Eds.). (2009). *International corpus of learner English* (Vol. 2). Louvain-la-Neuve: Presses universitaires de Louvain.

Gries, S. T., & Wulff, S. (2005). Do foreign language learners also have constructions?. *Annual Review of Cognitive Linguistics*, *3*(1), 182-200.

Gries, S. T., & Wulff, S. (2009). Psycholinguistic and corpus-linguistic evidence for L2 constructions. *Annual Review of Cognitive Linguistics*, *7*(1), 163-186.

Hwang, J. D. (2014). Identification and representation of caused motion constructions (Doctoral dissertation). University of Colorado at Boulder.

Hwang, H., & Kim, H. (2022). Automatic Analysis of Constructional Diversity as a Predictor of EFL Students' Writing Proficiency. *Applied Linguistics*.

Hwang, J. D., Nielsen, R., & Palmer, M. (2010). Towards a domain independent semantics: Enhancing semantic representation with construction grammar. In *Proceedings of the NAACL HLT Workshop on Extracting and Using Constructions in Computational Linguistics*, 1-8.

Hwang, J. D., & Palmer, M. (2015). Identification of caused motion construction. In *Proceedings of the Fourth Joint Conference on Lexical and Computational Semantics*, 51-60.

Honnibal, M., Montani, I., Van Landeghem, S., & Boyd, A. (2020). spaCy: Industrial-strength Natural Language Processing in Python.

Ishikawa, S. I. (2013). The ICNALE and sophisticated contrastive interlanguage analysis of Asian learners of English. *Learner corpus studies in Asia and the world*, *1*(1), 91-118.

Jackendoff, R. (2002). *Foundations of language*. Oxford University Press.

Kay, P., & Fillmore, C. J. (1999). Grammatical constructions and linguistic generalizations: The What's X doing Y? construction. *Language, 75*(1), 1–33.

Kyle, K. (2016). Measuring syntactic development in L2 writing: Fine grained indices of syntactic complexity and usage-based indices of syntactic sophistication. (Doctoral dissertation). Georgia State University.

Kyle, K., & Crossley, S. (2017). Assessing syntactic sophistication in L2 writing: A usage-based approach. *Language Testing*, *34*(4), 513-535.

Kyle, K., Crossley, S., & Verspoor, M. (2021). Measuring longitudinal writing development using indices of syntactic complexity and sophistication. *Studies in Second Language Acquisition, 43*(4), 781–812.

Kyle, K., Eguchi, M., Miller, A., & Sither, T. (2022). A Dependency Treebank of Spoken Second Language English. In *Proceedings of the 17th Workshop on Innovative Use of NLP for Building Educational Applications*, 39-45.

Landis, J. R., & Koch, G. G. (1977). An application of hierarchical kappa-type statistics in the assessment of majority agreement among multiple observers. *Biometrics*, 363-374.

Merriam-Webster. (n.d.). Laugh. In *Merriam-Webste.com dictionary.* Retrieved November 10, 2022.

McClosky, D., Charniak, E., & Johnson, M. (2006). Reranking and self-training for parser adaptation. In *Proceedings of the 21st International Conference on Computational Linguistics and 44th Annual Meeting of the Association for Computational Linguistics*, 337-344.

Nivre, J., Marneffe, M.-C. de, Ginter, F., Hajic, J., Manning, C. D., Pyysalo, S., Schuster, S., Tyers, F., & Zeman, D. (2020). Universal Dependencies v2: An Evergrowing Multilingual Treebank Collection. In *Proceedings of the Twelfth Language Resources and Evaluation Conference*, 4034–4043.

Ninio, A. (1999). Pathbreaking verbs in syntactic development and the question of prototypical transitivity. *Journal of child language*, *26*(3), 619-653.

O'Donnell, M. B., & Ellis, N. C. (2010). Towards an inventory of English verb argument constructions. In *Proceedings of the NAACL HLT Workshop on Extracting and Using Constructions in Computational Linguistics,* 9–16.

Palmer, M., Gildea, D., & Kingsbury, P. (2005). The proposition bank: An annotated corpus of semantic roles. *Computational linguistics*, *31*(1), 71-106.

Palmer, M., Gildea, D., & Xue, N. (2010). Semantic role labeling. *Synthesis Lectures on Human Language Technologies*, *3*(1), 1-103.

Perdue, C. (Ed.). (1993). *Adult language acquisition: Crosslinguistic perspectives*. Cambridge: Cambridge University Press.

Romain, L. (2022). Putting the argument back into argument structure constructions. *Cognitive Linguistics, 33*(1), 35-64.

Römer, U., Roberson, A., O'Donnell, M. B., & Ellis, N. C. (2014). Linking learner corpus and experimental data in studying second language learners' knowledge of verb-argument constructions. *ICAME Journal*, *38*(1), 115–135.

Schuler, K. K. (2005). *VerbNet: A broad-coverage, comprehensive verb lexicon*. University of Pennsylvania.

Shi, P., & Lin, J. (2019). Simple bert models for relation extraction and semantic role labeling. *arXiv:1904.05255*.

Silveira, N., Dozat, T., De Marneffe, M.-C., Bowman, S., Connor, M., Bauer, J., & Manning, C. (2014). A Gold Standard Dependency Corpus for English. In *Proceedings of the Ninth International Conference on Language Resources and Evaluation (LREC'14)*, 2897–2904.

Tomasello, M., & Brooks, P. J. (1998). Young children's earliest transitive and intransitive constructions. *Cognitive Linguistics, 9*(4), 379–395.

Investigating Stylistic Profiles for the Task of Empathy Classification in Medical Narrative Essays

Priyanka Dey
Computer Science Department
University of Illinois, Urbana-Champaign
pdey3@illinois.edu

Roxana Girju
Department of Linguistics,
Computer Science Department,
Beckman Institute,
University of Illinois, Urbana-Champaign
girju@illinois.edu

Abstract

One important aspect of language is how speakers generate utterances and texts to convey their intended meanings. In this paper, we bring various aspects of the Construction Grammar (CxG) and the Systemic Functional Grammar (SFG) theories in a deep learning computational framework to model empathic language. Our corpus consists of 440 essays written by premed students as narrated simulated patient–doctor interactions. We start with baseline classifiers (state-of-the-art recurrent neural networks and transformer models). Then, we enrich these models with a set of linguistic constructions proving the importance of this novel approach to the task of empathy classification for this dataset. Our results indicate the potential of such constructions to contribute to the overall empathy profile of first-person narrative essays.

1 Introduction

Much of our everyday experience is shaped and defined by actions and events, thoughts and perceptions which can be accounted for in different ways in the system of language. The grammatical choices we make when writing an essay (i.e., pronoun use, active or passive verb phrases, sentence construction) differ from those we use to email someone, or those we utter in a keynote speech. "Word choice and sentence structure are an expression of the way we attend to the words of others, the way we position ourselves in relation to others" (Micciche, 2004). Such choices allow us to compare not only the various options available in the grammar, but also what is expressed in discourse with what is suppressed (Menéndez, 2017).

Given the great variability in the modes of expression of languages, the search for an adequate design of grammar has long motivated research in linguistic theory. One such approach is CxG (Kay and et al., 1999; Goldberg, 1995; Fillmore et al., 2006) which prioritizes the role of constructions, conventional form-meaning pairs, in the continuum between lexis and syntax (Van Valin, 2007). As such, these constructions form a structured inventory of speakers' knowledge of the conventions of their language (Langacker, 1987).

Another particular grammatical facility for capturing experience in language is Halliday's system of transitivity as part of the Systemic Functional Grammar (SFG) (Halliday, 1994; Halliday et al., 2014), a theory of language centred around the notion of language function. SFG pays great attention to how speakers generate utterances and texts to convey their intended meanings. This can make our writing effective, but also give the audience a sense of our own personality. However, unlike CxG, Halliday's system of transitivity describes the way in which the world of our experience is divided by grammar into a 'manageable set of process types' (Halliday et al., 2014) each offering not only a form-meaning mapping, but also a range of stylistic options for the construal of any given experience through language. In stylistics, researchers have used this model to uncover and study the grammatical patterns through which texts can enact a particular ideology, or an individual's distinctive 'mind style' of language (Fowler, 1996).

The idea of 'style as choice' in Halliday's transitivity system can be best understood as experiential strategies (like avoiding material processes or repeating passive voice constructions) such as those identified as contributing to a reduced sense of awareness, intentionality or control in the human agent responsible (Fowler, 2013; Simpson and Canning, 2014). Such an individual is often said to appear 'helpless' and 'detached' (Halliday, 2019; Simpson, 2003), or 'disembodied' (Hoover, 2004). Take for instance, construction choices like 'I reassured her' vs. 'She was reassured', or "I greeted her upon entrance" vs. "The nurse greeted her upon entrance" vs. "She was greeted upon entrance" – which show the degree of agency and

Proceedings of the First International Workshop on Construction Grammars and NLP (CxGs+NLP, GURT/SyntaxFest 2023), pages 63 - 74
March 9-12, 2023 ©2023 Association for Computational Linguistics

intended involvement on the part of the agent in the action. Such linguistic choices often occur together in stylistic profiling exercises to showcase the techniques contributing to 'passivity', or the degree of suppression of agency and power in characterisation (Kies, 1992).

In this paper, we try to bring CxG and SFG closer together in the study of discourse level construction of arguments for the analysis of empathic content of narrative essays. Specifically, inspired by research in critical discourse analysis, we are taking a step further to show ways in which such construction choices can manipulate (and even reduce) the attention we give to the agency and moral responsibility of individuals (Jeffries, 2017; Van Dijk, 2017). Specifically, such form-meaning-style mappings can be used to capture the point of view as an aspect of narrative organization and the perspective through which a story is told, the way the characters are portrayed in terms of their understanding of the processes they are involved in, as well as their own participation in the story. In this respect, "narratives seem necessary for empathy [..] they give us access to contexts that are broader than our own contexts and that allow us to understand a broad variety of situations" (Gallagher, 2012). They provide a form/structure that allows us to frame an understanding of others, together with a learned set of skills and practical knowledge that shapes our understanding of what we and others are experiencing.

Drawing on Halliday's transitivity framework rooted in Systemic Functional Linguistics, this paper attempts to reveal the (dis)engaged style of empathic student essays from a semantic-grammatical point of view. Specifically, we want to investigate how certain types of processes (i.e., verbs) and constructions (i.e., passive voice) function to cast the essay writers (as main protagonists and agents) as perhaps rather ineffectual, passive, and detached observers of the events around them and of the patient's emotional states.

We take a narrative approach to empathy and explore the experiences of premed students at a large university by analysing their self-reflective writing portfolios consisting of a corpus of first-person essays written by them as narrated simulated patient-doctor interactions. The corpus has been previously annotated and organized (Shi et al., 2021; Michalski and Girju, 2022) following established practices and theoretical conceptualizations in psychology (Cuff et al., 2016; Eisenberg et al., 2006; Rameson et al., 2012). Computationally, we introduce a set of informative baseline experiments using state-of-the-art recurrent neural networks and transformer models for classifying the various forms of empathy. As initial experiments show relatively low scores, we measure the presence of several grammatical structures, leveraging Halliday's theory of transitivity, and its correlation with the essays' overall empathy scores. We apply this framework to state-of- the-art and representative neural network models and show significant improvement in the empathy classification task for this dataset. Although previous research suggests that narrative-based interventions tend to be effective education-based methods, it is less clear what are some of the linguistic mechanisms through which narratives achieve such an effect, especially applied to empathy, which is another contribution of this research.

2 Related Work

In spite of its increasing theoretical and practical interest, empathy research in computational linguistics has been relatively sparse and limited to empathy recognition, empathetic response generation, or empathic language analysis in counselling sessions. Investigations of empathy as it relates to clinical practice have received even less attention given the inherent data and privacy concerns.

Most of the research on empathy detection has focused on spoken conversations or interactions, some in online platforms (e.g. (Pérez-Rosas et al., 2017; Khanpour et al., 2017; Otterbacher et al., 2017; Sharma et al., 2021; Hosseini and Caragea, 2021), very little on narrative genre (Buechel et al., 2018; Wambsganss et al., 2021), and even less in clinical settings. Buechel et al. (2018) used crowdsourced workers to self-report their empathy and distress levels and to write empathic reactions to news stories. Wambsganss et al. (2021) built a text corpus of student peer reviews collected from a German business innovation class annotated for cognitive and affective empathy levels. Using Batson's Empathic Concern-Personal Distress Scale (Batson et al., 1987), Buechel et al. (2018) have focused only on negative empathy instances (i.e., pain and sadness "by witnessing another person's suffering"). However, empathy is not always negative (Fan et al., 2011). A dataset reflecting empahatic language should ideally allow for expressions of empathy that encompass a variety of emotions, and even distinguish between sympathy and empathy.[1]

Following a multimodal approach to empathy prediction, R. M. Frankel (2000) and Cordella and Musgrave (2009) identify sequential patterns of empathy in video-recorded exchanges between medical graduates and cancer patients. Sharma et al. (2020) analyzed the discourse of conversations in online peer-to-peer support platforms. Novice writers were trained to improve low-empathy responses and provided writers with adequate feedback on how to recognize and interpret others' feelings or experiences. In follow-up research, they performed a set of experiments (Sharma et al., 2021) whose results seemed to indicate that empathic written discourse should be coherent, specific to the conversation at hand, and lexically diverse.

To our knowledge, no previous research has investigated the contribution of grammatical constructions like Halliday's transitivity system to the task of empathy detection in any genre, let alone in clinical education.[2]

3 Self-reflective Narrative Essays in Medical Training

Simulation-based education (SBE) is an important and accepted practice of teaching, educating, training, and coaching health-care professionals in simulated environments (Bearman et al., 2019). Four decades-worth of SBE research has shown that "simulation technology, used under the right conditions ... can have large and sustained effects on knowledge and skill acquisition and maintenance among medical learners" (McGaghie et al., 2014). In fact, simulation-based education, an umbrella term that covers a very broad spectrum of learning activities from communication skill role-playing to teamwork simulations, is known to contribute to shaping experiences in undergraduate and postgraduate medical, nursing and other health education. In all these activities, learners contextually enact a task which evokes a real-world situation allowing them to undertake it as if it were real, even though they know it is not (Dieckmann et al., 2007; Bearman, 2003).

Personal narratives and storytelling can be viewed as central to social existence (Bruner, 1991), as stories of lived experience (Van Manen, 2016), or as a way in which one constructs notions of self (Ezzy, 1998). In this research, we focus on self-reflective narratives written by premed students given a simulated scenario. Simulation is strongly based on our first-person experiences since it relies on resources that are available to the simulator. In a simulation process, the writer puts themselves in the other's situation and asks "what would I do if I were in that situation?" Perspective taking is crucial for fostering affective abilities, enabling writers to imagine and learn about the emotions of others and to share them, too. As empathy is other-directed (De Vignemont and Jacob, 2012; Gallagher, 2012), this means that we, as narrators, are open to the experience and the life of the other, in their context, as we can understand it. Some evidence shows that we can take such reliance on narrative resources to open up the process toward a more enriched and non-simulationist narrative practice (i.e., real doctor-patients interactions in clinical context) (Gallagher, 2012).

This study's intervention was designed as a written assignment in which premed students were asked to consider a hypothetical scenario where they took the role of a physician breaking the news of an unfavorable diagnosis of high blood cholesterol to a middle-aged patient[3]. They were instructed to recount (using first person voice) the hypothetical doctor-patient interaction where they explained the diagnosis and prescribed medical treatment to the patient using layman terms and language they believed would comfort as well as persuade the hypothetical patient to adhere to their prescription. Prior to writing, students completed a standard empathic training reading assignment (Baile et al., 2000). They received the following prompt instructions and scenario information.[4]

Prompt Instructions: Imagine yourself as a physician breaking bad news to a patient. Describe the dialogue between the patient and you, as their primary care physician. In your own words, write an essay reporting your recollection of the interaction as it happened (write in past tense). Think of how you would break this news if you were in this scenario in real life. In your essay, you should be reflecting on (1) how the patient felt during this scenario and (2) how you responded to your patient's

[1] Some studies don't seem to differentiate between sympathy and empathy (Rashkin et al., 2018; Lin et al., 2019).

[2] Besides our own research (Shi et al., 2021; Michalski and Girju, 2022; Dey and Girju, 2022; Girju and Girju, 2022).

[3] The patient was referred to as Betty, initially. Later in the data collection, students could also identify the patient as John.

[4] All data collected for this study adheres to the approved Institutional Review Board protocol.

questions in the scenario below.

Scenario: Betty is 32 years old, has a spouse, and two young children (age 3 and 5). You became Betty's general practitioner last year. Betty has no family history of heart disease. In the past 6 months, she has begun experiencing left-side chest pain. Betty's bloodwork has revealed that her cholesterol is dangerously high. Betty will require statin therapy and may benefit from a healthier diet and exercise.

With the students' consent, we collected a corpus of 774 essays over a period of one academic year (Shi et al., 2021). Following a thorough annotation process, annotators (undergraduate and graduate students in psychology and social work)[5] labeled a subset of 440 randomly selected essays at sentences level following established practices in psychology (Cuff et al., 2016; Eisenberg et al., 2006; Rameson et al., 2012). The labels are: *cognitive empathy* (the drive and ability to identify and understand another's emotional or mental states; e.g., "She looked tired"); *affective empathy* (the capacity to experience an appropriate emotion in response to another's emotional or mental state; e.g.: "I felt the pain"); and *prosocial behavior* (a response to having identified the perspective of another with the intention of acting upon the other's mental and/or emotional state; e.g.: "I reassured her this was the best way"). Everything else was "no empathy". The six paid undergraduate students were trained on the task and instructed to annotate the data. Two meta-annotators, paid graduate students with prior experience with the task, reviewed the work of the annotators and updated the annotation guidelines at regular intervals, in an iterative loop process after each batch of essays[6]. The meta-annotators reached a Cohen's kappa of 0.82, a good level of agreement. Disagreed cases were discussed and mitigated. At the end, all the essays were re-annotated per the most up-to-date guidelines.

In this paper, we collapsed all the affective, cognitive, and prosocial empathy labels into one *Empathy Language* label – since we are interested here only in emphatic vs. non-empathic sentences. After integrating the annotations and storing the data for efficient search (Michalski and Girju, 2022), our corpus consisted of 10,120 data points (i.e., sentences) highlighted or not with empathy. Each essay was also rated by our annotators with a score on a scale from 1-5 (one being the lowest) to reflect overall empathy content at essay level.

4 Constructions and Stylistic Profiles in Empathic Narrative Essays

In CxG, constructions can vary in size and complexity – i.e., morphemes, words, idioms, phrases, sentences. In this paper, we focus mainly on simple sentence-level constructions[7], which, since we work with English, are typically of the form S V [O], where S is the subject, V is the verb, and O is the object (e.g., a thing, a location, an attribute). For instance, "Betty took my hand" matches the construction S V O with the semantics <Agent Predicate Goal>. SFG and CxG give the same semantic analysis, modulo some terminological differences (Lin and Peng, 2006). Specifically, they agree that the sentence above describes a process (or a predicate), which involves two participant roles providing the same linking relationship between the semantic and the syntactic structures: an Actor (or Agent) / Subject, and a Goal (Patient) / Object.

We start by checking whether the subject of a sentence consists of a human or a non-human agent. After identifying the grammatical subjects in the dataset's sentences with the Python Spacy package, we manually checked the list of human agents (the five most frequent being *I* (24.56%), *She* (5.76%), *Betty* (18.43%), *John* (6.24%), *Patient* (4.86%)).[8]

Halliday's transitivity model describes the way in which the world of our experience can be divided by grammar into a manageable set of process types, the most basic of which are: *material processes* (external actions or events in the world around us; e.g., verbs like "write", "walk", "kick") and *mental processes* (internal events; e.g., verbs of thinking, feeling, perceiving). We first identify sentences containing material and mental processes by extracting the verbs in each sentence (Table 1). About 75% of the dataset contains such processes, with material processes appearing more frequently than mental ones (by a small margin: 0.9%).

Inspired by the success of Halliday's transitivity system on cognitive effects of linguistic constructions in literary texts (Nuttall, 2019), we also examine a set of construction choices which seem

[5]The students were hired based on previous experience with similar projects in social work and psychology.

[6]10 essays per week

[7]We also consider constructions at word level - i.e., verbs.

[8]Other subjects: *Nurse*, *Doctor*, *Family*, *Children*, *Wife*, *Husband*, and *Spouse*

to co-occur in texts as material and mental actions or events. In our quest of understanding empathy expression in student narrative essays, we want to test if such contributions lead to a reduced sense of intentionality, awareness or control for the agentive individual represented (i.e., the essay writer in the role of the doctor), and thus, identifying the stylistic profile of the narrative. Specifically, these constructions are: *Human Actor + Process (HA+P); Body Part + Process (BP+P); Other Inanimate Actor + Process (IA+P); Goal + Process (G+P)* (see Table 1). We identify HA+P to be the most common construction within our dataset, appearing in just less than half of the sentences (49.82%). The remaining constructions are much rarer with G+P being the least frequent (12.54%).

Drawing from (Langacker, 1987), Nuttall (2019) also notes that these experiences can vary in force-dynamic (energetic) quality and thus sentences exhibiting an energetic tone are linked with 'high' transitivity and those with lower or static energy can be linked to 'low' transitivity. In order to identify energetic sentences, we leverage the IBM Watson Tone Analyzer API (Yin et al., 2017) which assesses the emotions, social propensities, and language styles of a sentence. We denote sentences containing high extroversion and high confidence (values > 0.8) as energetic. Sentences with low scores are marked as static. 61.77% of the sentences exhibit a static tone, energetic tone being less frequent.

In SFG, active and passive voice plays an important role as well. Nuttall (2019) shows that, in some genres, text indicating a lower degree of agentive control tends to use more passive voice constructions. As this is also relevant to our task, we test whether voice contributes indeed to a reduced sense of intentionality, awareness or control for the Agent (in particular the essay writer playing the doctor's role) and how these features correlate with the overall empathy score at essay level. Using an in-house grammatical-role extraction tool developed on top of Spacy's dependency parser, we find that 66% of sentences use active voice and 34% passive voice.[9] 77.92% of active-voice sentences exhibit human actor subjects and only 22.08% include non-human actors. Similarly for passive voice, the majority (83.09%) of sentences had human actors. Comparing frequencies of active and passive voice across various essay empathy score ranges (Figure 1), we notice that higher empathy essays (scores >3) seem to rely more on active voice (65-70% of the sentences in active voice) as opposed to lower empathy essays (scores < 3) which have less than 65% of sentences in active voice.

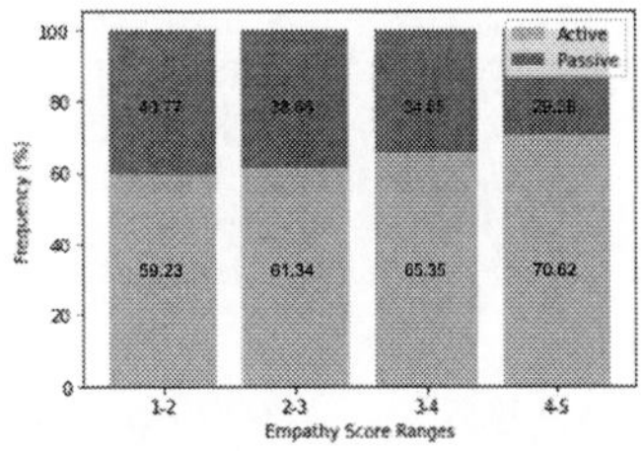

Figure 1: Frequency distribution (%) of voice in essays for various overall empathy score ranges

Stylistic research has also shown (Nuttall, 2019) the importance of movement of body parts as non-human agents. We, too, parsed sentences for the use of body parts, i.e. *eyes*, *arms*, *head* and curated a list based on anatomical terminology as defined by wiktionary.org (2022) resulting in about 18.61% of the dataset sentences (statistics for top 5 most common bodyparts are in Table 2).

Table 1 summarize all the identified constructions and stylistic features discussed in this section.

5 Empathy Classification Task

Our ultimate goal is to build an informed and performant classifier able to determine the degree of empathetic content of a medical essay overall and at sentence level. Taking advantage of form-meaning-style mappings in the language system, in this paper, we built and test a number of state-of-the-art classifiers enriched with varied constructions and stylistic features (Table 1) which are described next.

5.1 Identification of Sentence Themes

In medical training, students learn not only how to diagnose and treat patients' medical conditions, but also how to witness the patient's illness experience. In fact, in practical interactions with patients, they often switch between these positions: empathizing with the patient's situation (i.e., witnessing what it is like for the patient), and providing medical care (i.e., understanding what they need medically).

As such, we wanted to capture the distribution of such emphatic content and medical information in

[9]The active/passive voice ratio varies per genre (Strunk Jr and White, 2007). Note that in a sentence using passive voice, the subject is acted upon, which shows the main character's degree of detachment, which is of interest here.

Feature	Frequency	Definition	Example
Active	62.12%	the subject of the sentence is the one doing the action expressed by the verb	"I watched as the patient slowly sat down in the chair."
Passive	37.88%	the subject is the person or thing acted on or affected by the verb's action	"The patient I just had an appointment with is named Betty."
Material	37.39%	external actions or events in the world around us	"The nurse had already retrieved the bloodwork reports and handed them to me before I entered the room."
Mental	36.49%	events/feelings expressed by a user	" 'I can imagine that you have several questions, so I am happy to answer any questions or clear any doubts you might have.' I said to her. "
HA+P	49.82%	consists of a human actor and a material/mental process	"I calmly started explaining the treatment options."
BP+P	15.85%	consists of a non-human actor related to body parts in material/mental process	"Her shoulders started shaking when she heard the news, and I could tell she would need some time to process the news."
IE+P	18.34%	consists of an inanimate actor in material/mental process	"The file was already in the room when I arrived."
G+P	12.54%	consists of the passivisation of material/mental process and deletion of actor	"The effects of her lifestyle had already started to affect her physical strength."
Energetic	38.23%	e.g., high extroversion and confidence	"I could see Betty fidgeting with her fingers as she began to process the news."
Static	61.77%	e.g., low extroversion and confidence	"The nurse brought in the file quickly."

Table 1: Our set of SFG's transitivity constructions with their distribution and examples. Note that the total distribution should not add to 100%, as these are not mutually exclusive features.

Body Part	POS Used	Frequency	Example
Eye	subject, indirect object, prepositional object	42.96%	"I saw in her eyes tears forming as she realized the gravity of the issue at hand."
Hand	subject, prepositional object, indirect object, direct object	16.14%	"John began clasping his hands."
Head	direct object, indirect object	8.60%	"John shook his head as he sat down across from me."
Shoulder	subject, prepositional object, direct object	5.47%	"The patient shrugged his shoulders."
Body	subject, prepositional object, direct object	4.99%	"The vitals showed that the patient's body was not in its healthiest form."

Table 2: Most common body parts in the empathy essay dataset

our narrative essays of hypothetical doctor-patient interactions. Specifically, we looked at recurring topics within sentences and identified the following themes in our dataset at the sentence level: *Medical Procedural Information; Empathetic Language; Both* (Medical and Empathetic Language); and *Neither*. Sentences referring to *Medical Procedural Information* were identified based on keyword matching following established medical term vocabulary generated from Dr. Kavita Ganesan's work on clinical concepts (Ganesan et al., 2016). Sentences containing *Empathetic Language* were already annotated manually by our annotators for each essay at the sentence level (see Section 3). Sentences containing both medical procedural info and empathetic content were marked as *Both*, while remaining sentences are marked as *Neither*. Table 3 shows these categories, their definitions, examples and counts per category (10,120 sentences overall). We also give examples of two essays highlighted with these themes in the Appendix (Section 7).

In the next sections we present the classification results of various multi-class machine learning models (for each of the 4 themes: *Medical Procedural Information*, *Empathetic Language*, *Both*, and *Neither*).

5.2 Baseline Models and Analysis

In evaluating several state-of-the-art machine learning algorithms, we started with two representative baseline models: support vector machines (SVM) and logistic regression (logR). As we are interested in observing the performance of deep learning methods, we also experiment with long-short term memory (LSTM) (Hochreiter and Schmidhuber, 1997), bidirectional long-short term memory (bi-LSTM) (Graves and Schmidhuber, 2005), and convolutional neural network (CNN) (Kim, 2014) models; additionally, we use the transformer models BERT (Devlin et al., 2018) and roBERTa.

Theme	Freq.	Example
Medical Procedural Information	37.39%	"The patient's vitals showed that his body was not healthy and it was necessary to make some diet and lifestyle changes."
Empathetic Language	36.49%	"I noticed Betty looked confused and so I tried to reassure her we would do everything possible to make the changes in her lifestyle."
Both	21.28%	"I knew the statin treatment could be difficult, so I wanted to make sure Betty felt comfortable and understood the procedure."
Neither	4.84%	"The file was left on the counter, and I picked it up before going in to see Betty."

Table 3: Examples and distribution of identified themes in sentences

Classifier	Medical Procedural Information			Empathetic Language			Both			Neither		
	Prec.	Rec.	F1	Prec.	Rec.	F1	Prec.	Rec.	F1	Prec.	Rec.	F1
SVM	0.70	0.68	0.69	0.52	0.61	0.56	0.49	0.47	0.48	0.78	0.39	0.51
LogR	0.62	0.67	0.64	0.49	0.54	0.51	0.51	0.53	0.52	0.68	0.61	0.64
LSTM	0.64	0.69	0.67	0.51	0.54	0.52	0.59	0.53	0.56	0.66	0.61	0.63
biLSTM	0.65	0.7	0.68	0.51	0.54	0.52	0.56	0.53	0.54	0.68	0.62	0.65
CNN	0.70	0.71	0.70	0.52	0.54	0.53	0.64	0.53	0.57	0.71	0.63	0.66
BERT	0.69	0.72	0.70	0.55	0.61	0.58	0.57	0.63	0.60	0.68	0.65	0.66
constructionBERT	0.71	0.73	0.72	0.64	0.67	0.65	0.76	0.58	0.66	0.78	0.72	0.75
constructionBERT-*Voice:Active*	0.71	0.73	0.72	0.58	0.63	0.65	0.64	0.64	0.62	0.77	0.72	0.74
constructionBERT-*Voice:Passive*	0.71	0.73	0.72	0.65	0.67	0.66	0.76	0.61	0.67	0.78	0.72	0.75
constructionBERT-*Process:Material*	0.70	0.72	0.71	0.61	0.65	0.63	0.68	0.58	0.63	0.78	0.72	0.75
constructionBERT-*Process:Mental*	0.70	0.72	0.71	0.59	0.63	0.61	0.66	0.58	0.62	0.78	0.71	0.74
constructionBERT-*HA+P*	0.69	0.72	0.70	0.59	0.64	0.62	0.66	0.58	0.62	0.68	0.69	0.68
constructionBERT-*BP+P*	0.71	0.73	0.72	0.55	0.64	0.59	0.61	0.63	0.62	0.71	0.72	0.71
constructionBERT-*IE+P*	0.70	0.73	0.71	0.61	0.64	0.62	0.73	0.57	0.64	0.76	0.72	0.74
constructionBERT-*G+P*	0.71	0.73	0.72	0.64	0.66	0.65	0.74	0.56	0.64	0.78	0.72	0.75
constructionBERT-*Tone:Energetic*	0.71	0.73	0.72	0.58	0.62	0.60	0.66	0.57	0.61	0.78	0.72	0.75
constructionBERT-*Tone:Static*	0.71	0.73	0.72	0.64	0.62	0.63	0.71	0.58	0.64	0.78	0.73	0.75

Table 4: Precision, recall and F1 scores of all baseline classifiers on the imbalanced test dataset: 770 *Medical Procedural Information*, 722 *Empathetic Language*, 433 *Both*, 98 *Neither* sentences

As we are performing sentence classification, our features are unigrams (single words). For the logistic regression models, we used a L2 regularization and for the SVM models, a linear kernel function. We initialized the embedding layers in our neural models (LSTM, bi-LSTM, CNN) with GloVe embeddings since the expression of empathy involves larger units than words, and embeddings are known to better capture contextual information. We further decided to apply an attention layer to these models to learn patterns that may improve the classification. For the transformer BERT and roBERTa models, we use the default embeddings and apply a dropout layer with probability 0.4 which helps to regularize the model; we use a linear output layer and apply a sigmoid on the outputs. For each type of theme, we reserve an 80/20 training/test ratio, with 5-fold cross validation. As our dataset is imbalanced, we report the precision, recall, and F1-score (harmonic mean of the precision and recall) as shown in Table 4.

We observe that the classification of *Empathetic Language* is particularly difficult. The best model is the transformer BERT model which achieves an F-1 score of 0.58. On the other hand, sentences with *Medical Procedural Information* are much easier to identify with most classifiers achieving an F-1 score above 0.65. Sentences labeled *Both* are increasingly difficult (best classifier score of 0.6 F-1). Classification scores for sentences containing *Neither* fall just short of scores from *Medical Procedural Information* sentences.

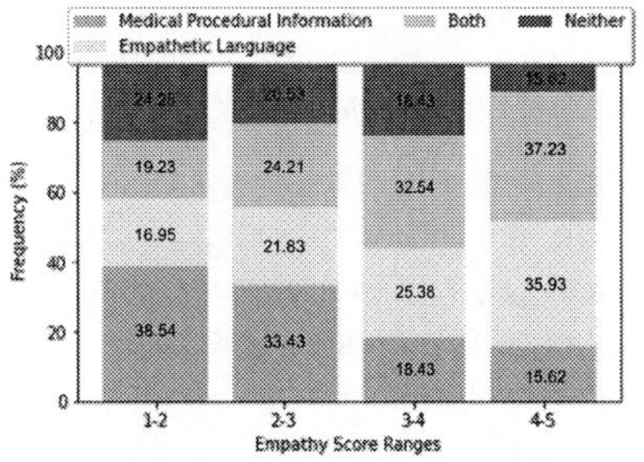

Figure 2: Frequency distribution (%) of themes in essays for various empathy score ranges

To better understand how these themes correlate with the overall empathy score at essay level, we compare frequencies and distribution of each theme for various essay empathy score ranges (Figure 2) across the entire dataset. High empathy essays (scores >3) tend to show a large amount of *Empathetic Language* and *Both*, while low empathy essays (scores < 3) seem to favor *Medical Procedural Information* language.

Heatmaps of Medical Narrative Essays. It is also interesting to visually analyze the distribution of these themes in the layout of the narrative essays. Thus, for each essay, we highlight the sentences containing each theme and generate heat maps that might highlight high theme concentrations. We standardized the format of each essay to an A4 paper,[10] generating a 42 x 14 matrix. [11] For each essay and position – i.e., (row, column) – we note the occurrence of each theme. We then build a heat map from these counts, thus generating 3 heatmaps, one for each theme along the following overall empathy score ranges: (1-2), (2-3), (3-4), and (4-5) (Figure 3).

The heatmaps for theme *Medical Procedural Information* for low empathy score essays show darker colors (purple) indicating a higher frequency of use at the beginning and middle of the essay. Lighter colors (orange and yellow) showcasing lower concentrations of the theme seems to be more prevalent in higher empathy score essays. *Empathetic Language* tends to increase in coverage (i.e., darker color portions) from low to high-score empathy essays, with a preference toward the end of the essay.[12] *Both* themes seem to concentrate, specifically towards the top and middle of the essays for high empathy scores (darker colors). Low empathy essays also show some shades of purple (i.e. some concentration) towards the bottom and lower third of the essays.

5.3 Incorporating Halliday Features into the Theme Classifier

In this section, we seek to improve our sentence theme classifier by incorporating the constructions and stylistic features identified in Section 4. For each sentence, we append a Boolean value indicating whether each feature is present in the given sentence – e.g., if a sentence is in active voice (feature *Active* is 1; feature *Passive* is 0); if the sentence contains a HA+P (feature value is 1), and so on.

[10]Times New Roman, size 12: 42 lines of 14 words each

[11]We generated a separate heatmap (size: 81 x 14) for 24 essays since these were much longer and didn't fit on a standard A4 paper. These showed similar position patterns.

[12]A closer look indicates that students who wrote low-empathy essays showed a tendency to use some emotional language in the last paragraph - which appeared rather rushed and forced.

Since in our baseline experiments the BERT model gave the best results across all 4 themes, we extend it here with all the features (construction-BERT) and report new scores (see bottom part of Table 4). Indeed, the inclusion of these features yields better performance, with a large increase for most of our themes including, *Empathetic Language*, *Both*, and *Neither*, and smaller performance increases in *Medical Procedural Information*.

Leave-one-out feature contribution experiments (see bottom of Table 4) show that removing *Voice: Active* and *Voice: Passive* slightly decreases performance in *Empathetic Language* and *Both* (with *Voice: Active* providing the highest decrease).

Removing *Processes* also shows a fair decrease in all themes except *Neither* which shows no change in performance. A deeper analysis indicates that *Processes: Material* helps with *Medical Procedural Information* but hurts performance on *Empathetic Language*.

The constructions *HA+P* and *BP+P* are most important for classification; the removal of *BP+P* yields the lowest F-1 score measure for detecting empathy. This shows the doctor (i.e., the student writer) paid particular attention to the patient's emotional state (thus showing empathy). Body parts in this type of discourse are particularly associated with non-verbal emotional language, which is highly indicative of empathy. *HA+P* is also an important feature for the theme *Neither*. Removal of *IE+P* gives a slight decrease in performance, while *G+P* has almost no effect on the classification results. Finally, the *Tone: Energetic* and *Tone: Static* features (constructionBERT-*Tone*) show to be important for the themes *Medical Procedural Information*, *Empathetic Language*, and *Both*. For *Tone: Energetic*, there is a 0.02 decrease in F-1 for medical procedural information, and a 0.05 for *Empathetic Language* and *Both*. For *Tone: Static*, we observe a decrease in performance for *Empathetic Language* by 0.02 and *Both* by 0.01.

With our binary classification task, we see similar patterns as constructionBERT-Tone yields much lower performances. The energetic and static tones yield 0.004 and 0.01 increases in F-1 scores for *Medical Procedural Information* and *Empathetic Language*. Our analysis also showed that G+P (Goal+Process), Processes (Mental and Material), and HA+P (Human Actor+Process) were also increasingly important for score improvements.

Interested in directly comparing the *Medical Pro-*

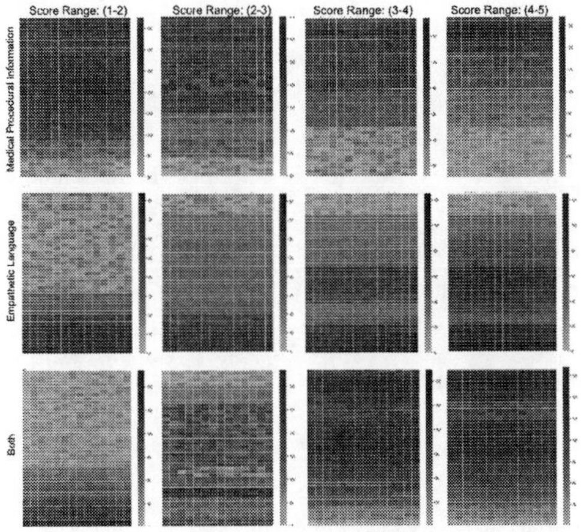

Figure 3: Heatmaps for themes in sentences of narrative essays across all overall empathy score ranges: Row#1 shows heatmaps for *Medical Procedural Information*; Row#2 for *Empathetic Language*; Row#3 for *Both*. Dark colors (purple) indicate that many essays exhibit the theme in the respective position of the essay. Light colors (yellow) indicate a small number of essays have occurrences of the theme for the given position.

cedural Information and *Empathetic Language* sentences, we further built a binary version of the simple BERT model, and another of constructionBERT, and found these tasks to be slightly easier. The binary BERT model achieved an F-1 score of 0.75 for *Medical Procedural Information* and a 0.62 for *Empathetic Language*. After adding the generated features (i.e., the binary constructionBERT), we see a small increase in F-1 scores (+0.01 for *Medical Procedural Information* and +0.03 for *Empathetic Language*).

Overall, the results of the effects of transitivity features on meaning, perceived agency and involvement of the Agent are in line with those obtained for literary genre texts by Nuttall (2019) through manual inspection. More specifically, the stylistic choices given by such linguistic constructions seem to be good indicators of the degree of perceived agency an Agent has in relation to others and the environment, as tested here for the empathy task on our dataset. In research on stylistics, the set and usage of such stylistic constructions and features in a text is known as the stylistic profile of the text. Encouraged by the correlations between Halliday's features with our essay level empathy scores, we would like to extrapolate and maintain that a set of rich stylistic constructions (like those tested in this research) can ultimately lead to informative **Empathy Profiles** – essay level form-meaning-style structures that can give an indication of the degree of social and empathetic detachment of the doctor toward the patient. Of course, while more research is needed in this direction, we believe we showed here the potential of such an approach to the task of empathy detection classification overall, and to clinical context in particular.

6 Conclusions

Medical education incorporates guided self-reflective practices that show how important it is for students to develop an awareness of the emotional and relational aspects of the clinical encounter with their patients (Warmington, 2019). The way people identify themselves and perform in particular roles and in relation to others brings together a specific set of values, attitudes, and competencies that can be supported through ongoing self-reflection. Such interactions can be captured in language via constructions as part of CxG and Halliday's transitivity system.

In this paper, we bring various aspects of these theories in a deep learning computational framework to model empathetic language in a corpus of essays written by premed students as narrated simulated patient–doctor interactions. We start with baseline classifiers (state-of-the-art recurrent neural networks and transformer models). Then, we enrich these models with a set of linguistic constructions proving the importance of this novel approach to the task of empathy classification for this dataset. Our results indicate the potential of such constructions to contribute to the overall empathy profile of first-person narrative essays.

References

Walter F Baile, Robert Buckman, Renato Lenzi, Gary Glober, Estela A Beale, and Andrzej P Kudelka. 2000. Spikes—a six-step protocol for delivering bad news: application to the patient with cancer.

C Daniel Batson, Jim Fultz, and Patricia A Schoenrade. 1987. Distress and empathy: Two qualitatively distinct vicarious emotions with different motivational consequences. *Journal of personality*, 55(1):19–39.

Margaret Bearman. 2003. Is virtual the same as real? medical students' experiences of a virtual patient. *Academic Medicine*, 78(5):538–545.

Margaret Bearman, Jennene Greenhill, and Debra Nestel. 2019. The power of simulation: a large-scale narrative analysis of learners' experiences. *Medical education*, 53(4):369–379.

Jerome Bruner. 1991. The narrative construction of reality. *Critical inquiry*, 18(1):1–21.

Sven Buechel, Anneke Buffone, Barry Slaff, Lyle Ungar, and Joao Sedoc. 2018. Modeling empathy and distress in reaction to news stories. *arXiv preprint arXiv:1808.10399*.

M. Cordella and S. Musgrave. 2009. Oral communication skills of international medical graduates: Assessing empathy in discourse. *Communication and Medicine*, 6(2):129–142.

Benjamin MP Cuff, Sarah J Brown, Laura Taylor, and Douglas J Howat. 2016. Empathy: A review of the concept. *Emotion review*, 8(2):144–153.

Frédérique De Vignemont and Pierre Jacob. 2012. What is it like to feel another's pain? *Philosophy of science*, 79(2):295–316.

Jacob Devlin, Ming-Wei Chang, Kenton Lee, and Kristina Toutanova. 2018. Bert: Pre-training of deep bidirectional transformers for language understanding. *arXiv preprint arXiv:1810.04805*.

Priyanka Dey and Roxana Girju. 2022. Enriching deep learning with frame semantics for empathy classification in medical narrative essays. In *Proceedings of the 2022 Workshop on Health Text Mining and Information Analysis (LouHI) collocated with the Conference on Empirical Methods in Natural Language Processing (EMNLP)*, hybrid. Association for Computational Linguistics.

Peter Dieckmann, David Gaba, and Marcus Rall. 2007. Deepening the theoretical foundations of patient simulation as social practice. *Simulation in Healthcare*, 2(3):183–193.

Nancy Eisenberg, Richard A Fabes, and Tracy L Spinrad. 2006. Prosocial development. In *Volume III. Social, Emotional, and Personality Development*. John Wiley & Sons, Inc.

Douglas Ezzy. 1998. Theorizing narrative identity: Symbolic interactionism and hermeneutics. *Sociological quarterly*, 39(2):239–252.

Y. Fan, Duncan NW, de Greck M, and Northoff G. 2011. Is there a core neural network in empathy? an fmri based quantitative meta-analysis. *Neuroscience Biobehavioral Review*, 35(3):903–911.

Charles J Fillmore, Paul Kay, and Laura A Michaelis. 2006. *Construction grammar*. Center for the Study of Language and Information.

Roger Fowler. 1996. *Linguistic Criticism*. Oxford: Oxford University Press, 2nd edition.

Roger Fowler. 2013. *Linguistics and Novel*. Routledge.

Shaun Gallagher. 2012. Empathy, simulation, and narrative. *Science in Context*, 25(3):355–381.

Kavita Ganesan, Shane Lloyd, and Vikren Sarkar. 2016. Discovering related clinical concepts using large amounts of clinical notes. *Biomed Eng Comput Biol*, 7(Suppl 2):27–33. Becb-suppl.2-2016-027[PII], 27656096[pmid].

Roxana Girju and Marina Girju. 2022. Design considerations for an NLP-driven empathy and emotion interface for clinician training via telemedicine. In *Proceedings of the Second Workshop on Bridging Human–Computer Interaction and Natural Language Processing*, pages 21–27, Seattle, Washington. Association for Computational Linguistics.

Adele Goldberg. 1995. Constructions: a construction grammar approach to argument structure. *Chicago: The University of Chicago*.

Alex Graves and Jürgen Schmidhuber. 2005. Framewise phoneme classification with bidirectional lstm and other neural network architectures. *Neural networks*, 18(5-6):602–610.

Michael AK Halliday. 1994. An introduction to functional grammar, london: Edward arnold.———& ruqaiya hasan. 1976. *Cohesion in English. London & New York: Longman. SHELL NOUNS*, 131.

Michael AK Halliday. 2019. Linguistic function and literary style: an inquiry into the language of william golding's' the inheritors'. In *Essays in modern stylistics*, pages 325–360. Routledge.

Michael Alexander Kirkwood Halliday, Christian MIM Matthiessen, Michael Halliday, and Christian Matthiessen. 2014. *An introduction to functional grammar*. Routledge.

Sepp Hochreiter and Jürgen Schmidhuber. 1997. Long short-term memory. *Neural computation*, 9(8):1735–1780.

David L Hoover. 2004. Altered texts, altered worlds, altered styles. *Language and Literature*, 13(2):99–118.

Mahshid Hosseini and Cornelia Caragea. 2021. Distilling knowledge for empathy detection. In *Findings of the Association for Computational Linguistics: EMNLP 2021*, pages 3713–3724, Punta Cana, Dominican Republic. Association for Computational Linguistics.

Lesley Jeffries. 2017. *Critical stylistics: The power of English*. Bloomsbury Publishing.

Paul Kay and et al. 1999. Grammatical constructions and linguistic generalizations: the what's x doing y? construction. *Language*, 75(1):1–33.

Hamed Khanpour, Cornelia Caragea, and Prakhar Biyani. 2017. Identifying empathetic messages in online health communities. In *Proceedings of the Eighth International Joint Conference on Natural Language Processing (Volume 2: Short Papers)*, pages 246–251.

Daniel Kies. 1992. The uses of passivity: suppressing agency in nineteen eighty-four. *Advances in systemic linguistics: Recent theory and practice*, pages 229–250.

Yoon Kim. 2014. Convolutional neural networks for sentence classification.

Ronald W Langacker. 1987. *Foundations of cognitive grammar: Theoretical prerequisites*, volume 1. Stanford university press.

FY Lin and AX Peng. 2006. Systemic functional grammar and construction grammar. In *Presented during the 33rd International Systemic Functional Congress*, pages 331–347.

Zhaojiang Lin, Andrea Madotto, Jamin Shin, Peng Xu, and Pascale Fung. 2019. Moel: Mixture of empathetic listeners. *arXiv preprint arXiv:1908.07687*.

William C McGaghie, Saul B Issenberg, Jeffrey H Barsuk, and Diane B Wayne. 2014. A critical review of simulation-based mastery learning with translational outcomes. *Medical education*, 48(4):375–385.

Enrique Menéndez. 2017. Christopher hart: Discourse, grammar and ideology. *Pragmática Sociocultural/Sociocultural Pragmatics*, 5(2):259–262.

Laura R Micciche. 2004. Making a case for rhetorical grammar. *College Composition and Communication*, pages 716–737.

Martin Michalski and Roxana Girju. 2022. An empathy account of premed students' narrative essays. *OSF Preprints*.

Louise Nuttall. 2019. Transitivity, agency, mind style: What's the lowest common denominator? *Language and Literature*, 28(2):159–179.

Jahna Otterbacher, Chee Siang Ang, Marina Litvak, and David Atkins. 2017. Show me you care: Trait empathy, linguistic style, and mimicry on facebook. *ACM Transactions on Internet Technology (TOIT)*, 17(1):1–22.

Verónica Pérez-Rosas, Rada Mihalcea, Kenneth Resnicow, Satinder Singh, and Lawrence An. 2017. Understanding and predicting empathic behavior in counseling therapy. In *Proceedings of the 55th Annual Meeting of the Association for Computational Linguistics (Volume 1: Long Papers)*, pages 1426–1435.

R. M. Frankel. 2000. *The (socio) linguistic turn in physician-patient communication research*. Georgetown University Press, Boston, MA.

Lian T Rameson, Sylvia A Morelli, and Matthew D Lieberman. 2012. The neural correlates of empathy: experience, automaticity, and prosocial behavior. *Journal of cognitive neuroscience*, 24(1):235–245.

Hannah Rashkin, Eric Michael Smith, Margaret Li, and Y-Lan Boureau. 2018. Towards empathetic open-domain conversation models: A new benchmark and dataset. *arXiv preprint arXiv:1811.00207*.

Ashish Sharma, Inna W Lin, Adam S Miner, David C Atkins, and Tim Althoff. 2021. Towards facilitating empathic conversations in online mental health support: A reinforcement learning approach. In *Proceedings of the Web Conference 2021*, pages 194–205.

Ashish Sharma, Adam Miner, David Atkins, and Tim Althoff. 2020. A computational approach to understanding empathy expressed in text-based mental health support. In *Proceedings of the 2020 Conference on Empirical Methods in Natural Language Processing (EMNLP)*, pages 5263–5276, Online. Association for Computational Linguistics.

Shuju Shi, Yinglun Sun, Jose Zavala, Jeffrey Moore, and Roxana Girju. 2021. Modeling clinical empathy in narrative essays. In *2021 IEEE 15th International Conference on Semantic Computing (ICSC)*, pages 215–220.

Paul Simpson. 2003. *Language, ideology and point of view*. Routledge.

Paul Simpson and Patricia Canning. 2014. Action and event. In *The Cambridge handbook of stylistics*, pages 281–299. Cambridge University Press.

William Strunk Jr and Elwyn Brooks White. 2007. *The Elements of Style Illustrated*. Penguin.

Teun A Van Dijk. 2017. *Discourse and power*. Bloomsbury Publishing.

Max Van Manen. 2016. *Researching lived experience: Human science for an action sensitive pedagogy*. Routledge.

Robert D Van Valin. 2007. Adele e. goldberg, constructions at work: the nature of generalization in language. oxford: Oxford university press, 2006. pp. vii+ 280. *Journal of Linguistics*, 43(1):234–240.

Thiemo Wambsganss, Christina Niklaus, Matthias Söllner, Siegfried Handschuh, and Jan Marco Leimeister. 2021. Supporting cognitive and emotional empathic writing of students. *arXiv preprint arXiv:2105.14815*.

Sally G Warmington. 2019. *Storytelling encounters as medical education: crafting relational identity*. Routledge.

wiktionary.org. 2022. Appendix:visual dictionary/human body - body parts. [Online; accessed 29-October-2022].

Peifeng Yin, Zhe Liu, Anbang Xu, and Taiga Nakamura. 2017. Tone analyzer for online customer service: An unsupervised model with interfered training. In *Proceedings of the 2017 ACM on Conference on Information and Knowledge Management*, CIKM '17, page 1887–1895, New York, NY, USA. Association for Computing Machinery.

7 Appendix

Figure 4 shows two examples of essays, one with low empathy and one with high empathy, highlighted with the themes: *Medical Procedural Information* (cyan), *Empathetic Language* (yellow), and *Both* (green). *Neither* sentences are not highlighted. It is interesting to see that in Essay (a), the sentences mentioning diet and exercise were not identified as *Medical Procedural Information* given that they were not found in Dr. Kavita Ganesan's work on clinical concepts (Ganesan et al., 2016).

Betty is 32 years old, has a spouse, and two young children (age 3 and 5). Betty has no family history of heart disease. In the past 6 months, Betty has begun experiencing left-side chest pain. Betty's bloodwork has revealed that her cholesterol is dangerously high. Betty will require statin therapy and may benefit from a healthier diet and exercise.

I asked what medical concerns that she has or any past medical history. I confirmed with her that concerns are valid and that the chest pain is something I am concerned about also. I told her that the blood work panel that was performed confirmed her concern. I asked her what she knows about her latest blood cholesterol levels history. I informed her that the cholesterol levels have reached an actionable level and we will need to decide which plan will be the best plan to implement. I asked her what she knows about LDL and HDL and how they work and what affects each of them. I explained which parts she did not quite understand on her level of need. I explained about the change in diet and exercise that will be an important part of the plan moving forward. I explained how the other part of the plan will include the use of statins as a means of lowering the LDL levels in her body. I explained the side effects of statins in how type 2 diabetes may be one possible side effect. I explained that once on the cholesterol drug that she should keep taking them because it is keeping an important balance in the body's cholesterol levels. I explained the symptoms that she could experience with drugs that should be reported to me immediately and if there are any other concerns that she should call me with those concerns. She seemed receptive to the treatment plan. I will follow-up with her in a month to evaluate the progress and review her bloodwork. She will have a consult for diet planning within a week.

(a) Example of Essay with Empathy Score: 1

What a whirlwind that was. Everything was a surprise; the diagnosis, her reaction, her response. Heck, even my response was a bit startling. High cholesterol? But how? She has no history of this kind of thing and at such a young age too. I mean, the chest pain is a clear sign, but even that is surprising to see in a woman like Betty. It's terrible knowing that I had to tell someone that not only did they have a condition that could kill them, but it also was their fault too. I understand Betty's reaction; anyone in her situation would've thrown a tantrum. I just hated experiencing that, but I guess it's a part of the job description. After she calmed down, I told her that she could call her husband to inform him of the situation, but before calling, I figured it was a good idea to go over the next steps.

The treatment that was prescribed to Betty is called Statin Therapy. What the statin does is block the enzyme HMG CoA Reductase that is essentially what makes cholesterol. This reduces the amount of cholesterol produced in the liver. Of course, most patients don't care much for how the treatments work unless they have to do something, so naturally, Betty was more concerned with the idea of eating healthy and exercising.

I'm sure in the back of her mind, she knew that those two things would be somewhat required, but like any person who is comfortable in their lifestyle, she fought the changes. "Is there any other way?" she said. I could tell she was distraught over this idea that she had to choose between comfort and health. I find it easiest to soothe the patient by going over the plan in small steps. It's also helpful to show them the benefits in the long-term and the final goal. She seemed reluctant at first, but I think by the end of our conversation, I was able to coax her into believing that this is a good thing for her. It's good to note that it's always positive to identify these conditions as early as possible, so, at the very least, I can say with confidence that I'm glad Betty came in.

(b) Example of Essay with Empathy Score: 5

Figure 4: Two Sample Essays from the Dataset Highlighted by Sentence Themes

UMR annotation of Chinese Verb compounds and related constructions

Haibo Sun[†], Yifan Zhu[*], Jin Zhao[◇], Nianwen Xue[‡]
Brandeis University
{ hsun[†],zhuyifan[*],jinzhao[◇],xuen[‡]}@brandeis.edu

Abstract

This paper discusses the challenges of annotating the predicate-argument structure of Chinese verb compounds in Uniform Meaning Representation (UMR), a recent meaning representation framework that extends Abstract Meaning Representation (AMR) to cross-linguistic settings. The key issue is to decide whether to annotate the argument structure of a verb compound as a whole, or to annotate the argument structure of their component verbs as well as the relations between them. We examine different types of Chinese verb compounds, and propose how to annotate them based on the principle of compositionality, level of grammaticalization, and productivity of component verbs. We propose a solution to the practical problem of having to define the semantic roles for Chinese verb compounds that are quite open-ended by separating compositional verb compounds from verb compounds that are non-compositional or have grammaticalized verb components. For compositional verb compounds, instead of annotating the argument structure of the verb compound as a whole, we annotate the argument structure of the component verbs as well as the semantic relations between them as creating an exhaustive list of such verb compounds is infeasible. Verb compounds with grammaticalized verb components also tend to be productive and we represent grammaticalized verb compounds as either attributes of the primary verb or as relations.

1 Introduction

Uniform Meaning Representation (UMR) (Gysel et al., 2021) is a meaning representation designed to annotate the semantic content of a text and it pairs a sentence-level representation with a document-level representation. Its sentence-level representation adopts the predicate-argument structure backbone of Abstract Meaning Representation (AMR) (Banarescu et al., 2013) but extends it to cross-linguistic settings by providing shared concepts and relations that can be applied cross-linguistically, particularly to morphologically complex low-resource languages. UMR also adds a document-level representation that captures linguistic phenomena such as coreference as well as temporal (Zhang and Xue, 2018; Yao et al., 2020) and modal dependencies (Vigus et al., 2019) that potentially go beyond sentence boundaries .

For the predicate-argument structure annotation, UMR is flexible in allowing the use of both generic semantic roles such as agent, theme, patient and predicate-specific roles, a practice popularized by the proposition bank approach to semantic role labeling (Palmer et al., 2005; Xue and Palmer, 2009). The predicate-specific roles in the propbanks are defined in *frame files* that have entries for each predicate in a language. For each sense of a predicate, a set of *core* roles are assigned unique numerical IDs that are prefixed by *Arg*. For instance, the non-polysemous English verb "sink" has the following roles:

Arg0: causer of sinking
Arg1: thing sinking
Arg2: extent
Arg3: start point
Arg4: end point, destination
Arg5: instrument

These roles can then be used to annotate instances of "sink", where not all arguments of sink may be realized:

(1) The enemy sank the ship.
```
(s / sink-01
    :Arg0 (e / enemy)
    :Arg1 (s2 / ship
        :ref-number Singular)
    :aspect Performance)
```


Proceedings of the First International Workshop on Construction Grammars and NLP (CxGs+NLP, GURT/SyntaxFest 2023), pages 75 - 84
March 9-12, 2023 ©2023 Association for Computational Linguistics

For languages like Chinese where compounding is a robust word formation process (Packard, 2000), the predicate-specific approach of semantic role annotation in UMR provides both opportunities and challenges. For verb compounds that consist of verbs that each have their own argument structure, they can be represented in a straightforward manner in UMR, as shown in (2), where each component verb 哭 [ku, "cry"][1] and 湿 [shi, "wet"] has its own argument structure, and the semantic relation between them is one of *:cause-of*, indicating the former is the cause of the latter.

(2) 他 把 手帕 哭-湿 了
he ACC handkerchief cry-wet PF

"He cried so much that his handkerchief is wet."[2]

```
(x4a / 哭-01[ku, "cry"]
      :Arg0 (i / individual-person
            :ref-person 3rd
            :ref-number Singular)
      :cause-of (x4b / 湿-01[shi, "wet"]
                 :Arg0 (x3 / 手帕 [shou-pa,
                              "handkerchief"]))
      :aspect Performance)
```

The challenge, however, is that Chinese verb compounds involve various degrees of grammaticalization and idiomaticity, and it is not always appropriate to treat component verbs in a compound as separate predicates that each have their argument structures. In order for there to be consistent annotation, there needs to be a set of criteria that the annotator follows when determining which verb compounds should be treated holistically as having a single argument structure and which should have separate predicate-argument structures for their component verbs.

In this paper, we will examine different types of verb compounds and propose how we will annotate them in UMR. When deciding if a verb compound needs to have the argument structure of their component verbs annotated, we consider idiomaticity (or non-compositionality), levels of grammaticalization, and productivity. For instance, when a verb compound becomes highly idiomatic and its meaning as a whole cannot be predicted from their component verbs, it no longer makes sense to annotate the predicate-argument structure of the component verbs. Similarly, when a component verb in a verb compound is highly grammaticalized and its lexical content is semantically "bleached", there is less value in annotating the predicate-argument structure of this component verb, and it is more appropriate to treat them as attributes for the primary predicates or as relations between the primary predicates and one of its arguments.

When examining these verb compounds, we will classify them into broad categories based on syntactic and semantic relations between their component verbs, as they have been standardly done in linguistic annotation work (Xue et al., 2005). Here we focus on verb compounds that consist of two verbs, in the form of V_1 and V_2. They include resultative (VR) and directional verb (VD) compounds, subordinating compounds (VSB) in which the first verb modifies the second verb, coordinating compounds (VCD) in which the verbs either happen sequentially or have an equal status, and verb compounds that have the second verb as a copula verb (VCP). We will also examine the UMR annotation of light verb constructions that are similar in form but not content to verb compounds.

The rest of the paper is organized as follows. In Section 2, we examine different types of verb compounds and show how they are treated in UMR. In Section 3, we discuss how to annotate related verb constructions in UMR. We discuss related work in Section 4, and conclude in Section 5.

2 Types of verb compounds

In this section we examine different types of verb compounds, and show how we plan to annotate them in UMR.

2.1 Resultative verb compounds

Resultative verb compounds are a type of verb compounds that have been discussed extensively in linguistic literature (Thompson, 1973; Lu, 1977; Li, 1990; Packard, 2000). In general, resultative verb compounds are in the form of V_1 and V_2 where V_2 is broadly considered to be the result of V_1. As we will show, however, the semantic relation between the two component verbs tends to be quite diverse and is not always strictly

[1]Throughout the paper, the pinyin and translation in square brackets are not part of the UMR annotation and are merely provided for readability

[2]The glossing abbreviations used in this paper are: PF: perfective aspect, PRG: progressive aspect, EXP: experiential aspect, CL: classifier, ACC: accusative case marker

one of cause and result. Similarly, there is also quite a bit of variability in the argument structure of each component verb. In addition, the meaning of some resultative verb compounds cannot be predicted from their component verbs, and they are thus non-compositional, in which case the argument structure as a whole should be annotated. In other cases, one of their component verbs are grammaticalized to a certain degree. When this happens, it also makes sense to annotate the argument structure of the verb compound as a whole rather than the argument structure of each component verb.

2.1.1 Compositional Resultative Compounds

When resultative verb compounds are compositional, the argument structure of the component verbs is annotated. This is illustrated in (3), where the athlete's running lead to her shoes being broken. V_1 跑 [pao, "running"] is the cause, and V_2 坏 [huai, "break"] is the result. In UMR, this relation is labeled as **:cause-of** indicating that the first predicate is the cause of the second predicate, or conversely, the second predicate is the result of the first predicate.

(3) 运动员 跑坏 了 鞋 。
Athlete run-break PF shoe .

"The athlete broke (her/his) shoes because of running."

```
(x2b / 跑-01 [pao, "running"]
      :Arg0 (x1 / 运动员 [ yundongyuan,
                  "athlete"]
      :cause-of (x2a / 坏-01[huai, "break"]
                  :Arg0 (x4 / 鞋 [xie, "shoe"])))
```

By annotating the argument structure of the component verbs, we obviate the need to create a frame file for the verb compound as a whole, in addition to those for the component verbs. However, the annotator needs a reliable compositionality test to determine if this verb compound is compositional. We can test the compositionality of this verb compound by paraphrasing this sentence as ''运动员 ["athlete"] 跑 ["run"]'' , and ''鞋子 ["shoe"] 坏 ["break"] 了 [PF]''. If the component verbs ''跑 ["run"]'' and ''坏 ["break"]'' have the same meaning in the paraphrase as they do in the verb compound, then we know this verb compound is compositional. Otherwise it is not.

Another compositional verb compound example is provided in (4):

(4) 他 买-亏 了 这 衣服
he buy-loss PF this clothes

"He bought this dress at a loss."

```
(x2a / 买-01[mai, "buy"]
      :Arg0 (i / individual-person
                  :ref-person 3rd
                  :ref-number Singular)
      :Arg1 (x5 / 衣服 [yifu, "clothes"]
                  :mod (x4 / 这 [zhe, "this"]))
      :cause-of (x2b / 亏-01[kui, "at a loss"]
                  :Arg0 i )
      :aspect Performance)
```

This example means that the person bought clothes at a time when the price of the clothes was high, and he thus suffered a loss in the sense that he could have bought them when the price was lower. In this case, the buying event is straightly speaking not the "cause" of the loss. It is the timing of the buying event that caused the loss. The net consequence is that he suffered the loss. The UMR does not make such fine-grained distinctions, and **:cause-of** is still used to annotate the relation between the two events.

2.1.2 Non-compositional Resultative Compounds

While the theoretical linguistics work focuses on compositional verb compounds, in practical UMR annotation there is a need to consistently distinguish them from non-compositional verb compounds. In non-compositional verb compounds, while both component verbs can function as standalone verbs, the meaning of the verb compound is no longer predictable from their component verbs. An example is provided in (5):

(5) 该 产业 能 带动 经济
This industry can drag-move economy
发展。
development.

"This industry can spur economic development. "

```
(x4 / 带动-01 [daidong,"drag"+"move"
                  = "spur"]
      :Arg0 (x2 / 产业 [chanye, "industry"]
            :mod (x1 / 该 [gai, "this"]))
      :Arg1 (x6 / 发展-01 [fazhan,
            "development"]
            :Arg1 (x5 / 经济 [ jingji,
                        "economy"]))
      :modstr NeutAff)
```

In (5), the meaning of verb compound 带动 [daidong, "spur"] has diverged from the meaning of their component verbs, 带 [dai, "drag"] and 动 [dong, "dong"]. While the meaning of the verb compound 带动 is abstract, the meanings of their component verbs are concrete.

In yet another type of resultative verb compounds the result verb V_2 is grammaticalized and has largely been reduced to some aspectual meaning. Yet they are not fully grammaticalized as Chinese aspectual markers 着 [zhe, PRG], 了 [le, PF], and 过 [guo, EXP]. One sign of their grammaticalization is that they tend to be productive, and can co-occur with a wide range of V_1s. Since V_2 in the verb compound is grammaticalized, its meaning in the verb compound also diverges from its meaning if it is used in isolation. In this sense, it is also non-compositional. For example, in (6), 掉 [diao] originally means "to drop" as a stand-alone verb, but when it forms a verb compound with another verb as V_2, it means finishing up something by means of V_1. 吃掉 [chidiao] in (6) thus means "eat up". Since 掉 [diao] is grammaticalized and does not alter the predicate-argument structure of the verb compound in any way, we do not annotate the argument structure of this verb. Since it is partially grammaticalized, it contributes to the aspectual value of V_1, which is *Performance* in this case. Since it is not fully grammaticalized, we still use the entire verb compound as the predicate rather than just the first verb, which would be the case if it is fully grammaticalized as the aspect markers.

(6) 小孩吃-掉 了 糖果。
Kid eat-drop PF candy.

"The kid ate up the candy."

```
(x2 / 吃掉-01 [chidiao, "eat up"]
    :Arg0 (x1 / 小孩 [xiaohai, "kid"])
    :Arg1 (42 / 糖果 [tangguo, "candy"])
    :aspect Performance)
```

Another such example is 完 [wan, "finish"], which forms "phase resultative verb compounds" with V_1 (Li and Thompson, 1981; Woo, 2021). It indicates the completion of the event denoted by V_1 and is also partially grammaticalized and does not contribute to the argument structure of the verb compound. In (7), 写完 [xiewan] means "finish writing", with 完 [wan] contributes to the completion reading of the verb compound, and this is reflected in the aspectual value *Performance* for the event.

(7) 小孩写完 了 作业。
kid write-finish PF homework.

"The kid finished doing his homework."

```
(x2 / 写完 [xie, "write"]
    :Arg0 (x1 / 小孩 [xiaohai, "kid"])
    :Arg1 (s2 / 作业 [zuoye, "homework"])
    :aspect Performance)
```

Verbs like 写完 [xiewan, "finish writing"], 听惯 [tingguan, "get used to listening"] contribute to the aspectual meaning of V_1. Since they are not fully grammaticalized, we use the verb compound as a whole as the UMR concept to avoid loss of meaning. Since V_2 is partially grammaticalized and is productive, creating separate frame file entries for these verb compounds is impractical as there is potentially a long list of such verb compounds. Since such verbs do not contribute to the argument structure of the verb compound, this means the argument structure of the verb compound as a whole is the same as the argument structure of V_1. We could exploit this property and link the argument structure of the verb compounds ending with such verbs to the argument structure of V_1 as aliases, a practice that is similar to how phrasal verbs in English like "eat up" is annotated in the Propbank (Palmer et al., 2005).

2.1.3 Variants of resultative verb compounds

One test for resultative verb compounds that have been recognized very early on is that resultative verb compounds can have an infix between V_1 and V_2 to indicate "potential". The infix can either be 得 [de, "able"] or 不 [bu, "not able"], and this is illustrated in (8):

(8) a. 柜子 打-得-开
cabinet open-ABL-open

"The cabinet can be opened."

```
(x2a / 打开-01 [dakai, "open"]
    :Arg1 (x1 / 柜子 [guizi, "cabinet"])
    :aspect State
    :MODSTR NeutAff )
```

b. 柜子 打-不-开
cabinet open-NEG-open

"The cabinet cannot be opened."

```
(x2a / 打开-01 [dakai, "open"]
    :Arg1 (x1 / 柜子 [guizi, "cabinet"])
    :aspect State
    :MODSTR FullNeg)
```

In both (8a) and (8b), the resultative verb compound is 打开 [dakai, "open"]. The compound is non-compositional in that 打 has a different meaning when used as a standalone verb than it is in the compound. In (8a), the infix adds a modal meaning to the verb compound so that it means "can be opened", while in (8b), it adds the infix 不 to mean that "cannot be opened". The modal meaning in UMR is annotated as modal strength (:MODSTR) with values FullNeg (fully negative) and NeutAFF (neutral affirmative).

2.1.4 Pseudo-resultative compounds

Some V_1 V_2 constructions look like resultative compounds in form, but upon closer examination they are not. In this section, we discuss a few such examples. In UMR annotation, it is important to separate such cases from resultative verb compounds as the semantic relation between these two verbs is not one of cause and result. One example is (9), where V_1 is an argument of V_2. In this example V_1 研制 [yanzhi, "develop"] is actually an argument of the V_2 成功 [chenggong, "succeed"], as what is successful is the research and development activity denoted by V_1. The fact that this endeavor succeeded implies the completion of the event denoted by V_1, as indicated by the aspectual value of *Performance*.

(9) 新 药 研制 成功
new medicine develop succeed

"New medicine has been successfully developed. "

```
(x3 / 研制-01 [yanzhi, "develop"]
    :Arg1 (x2 / 药 [yao, "medicine"]
              :mod (x1 /新 [xin, "new"]))
    :Arg0-of (x4 / 成功-01 [chenggong,
                  "succeed"])
    :aspect Performance)
```

Some verb compounds closely resemble resultative verb compounds but they are in fact object-oriented depictives. 买-贵 [mai-gui, "buy-expensive"] in (10) is such an example. It differs from 买-亏 [mai-kui, "buy-loss"] in (4) by one character, but has a very different interpretation. The semantic relation between V_1 and V_2 is one of temporal co-occurence (as indicated by the *:temporal* role), meaning the clothes were bought at a time when they were expensive, not that the buying event made the clothes more expensive, as would be case if there is a cause-result interpretation.

(10) 这 件 衣服 小王 买-贵 了
This CL clothes Xiaowang buy-costly PF.

"Xiaowang bought this piece of clothes at a high price."

```
(x2a / 买-01[mai, "buy"]
    :Arg0 (x1 / 小王 [Xiaowang, (name)])
    :Arg1 (x5 / 衣服 [yifu, "clothes"]
              :mod (x4 / 这 [zhe, "this"]))
    :temporal (x2b / 贵-01 [gui, "costly"]
                  :Arg0 x5 )
    :aspect Performance)
```

Another example is 挖-浅 [wa-qian] in (11), where V_2 indicates a deviation from the expected result from V_1 (Li, 2007) rather than the result. This is annotated with with the UMR abstract concept *but-91*, which captures the semantic relation between the events denoted by the two verbs.

(11) 这 口 井 小张 挖-浅 了
This CL well Xiaozhang dig-shallow PF.

"Xiaowang dug this well but it was too shallow."

```
(x5a / 挖-01 [wa, "dig"]
    :aspect Performance
    :Arg0 (i / individual-person
          :name ( n / name
                :op ''小张'' [Xiaozhang]))
    :Arg1 (x3 / 井 [jing, "well"]
              :mod (x1 / 这)
              :unit (x2 / 口 [kou, CL]))
    :Arg1-of (b / but-91
              :Arg2 (x5b / 浅 [qian,
                        "shallow" ]
                        :Arg0 x3)))
```

What we have presented above are just a few examples of apparent resultative verb compounds that have other semantic relations. They are unlikely to be exhaustive and further research is needed to uncover more such examples.

2.2 Subordinating Compounds

Syntactically subordinating compounds in Chinese are compounds where V_1 is a modifier to V_2. An example is provided in (12), where V_1 describes the manner of V_2, represented in UMR as a *:manner* relation. That is, the student bikes to school rather than by any other means.

(12) 这 个 学生 骑行 前往 学校。
this CL student cycle head-to school.

"The student bikes to school."

(x1 / 前往 [qianwang, "head to"]
:Arg0 (x2 / 学生 [xuesheng, "student"])
:Arg1 (x3 / 学校 [xuexiao, "school"])
:manner (x4 / 骑行 [qixing, "cycle"])
:aspect Habitual)

Not all V_1 indicates the manner of V_2, and some subordinating verb compounds are depictives. This is illustrated in , where 活捉 [huo-zhuo, "catch alive"] is an object-oriented depictive that means when V_2 happens, the tiger is in the state of V_1. That is, the tiger was captured while it was alive. This is indicated by the *:temporal* relation between $V1$ and V_2.

(13) 猎人 活-捉 了 这 只 老虎。
hunter alive-catch PF this CL tiger .

"The hunter caught this tiger alive."

(x1 / 捉 [zhuo, "catch"]
:Arg0 (x2 / 猎人 [lieren, "hunter"])
:Arg1 (x3 / 老虎 [laohu, "tigerl"]
:mod (x4 / 这 [zhe, "this"])
:unit (x5 / 只 [zhi, CL]))
:temporal (x6 / 活 [huo, "alive")
:aspect Performance)

Examples like 活捉 are compositional, but subordinating conjunctions can also be non-compositional. The literal meaning of (14), 三思 is "think three times", but the verb compound actually just means "think carefully". 三思 should thus not decomposed in UMR annotation and treated as a single concept.

(14) 购买前 要 三思 。
buy before should three-think

"(You) need to think carefully before (you) buy (it)"

(x4 / 三思 [sansi, "think carefully"]
:temporal (x2 / 前 [qian, "before"]
:op (x1 / 购买[goumai, buy])))
:aspect Process)

2.3 Coordinating compounds

Coordinating verb compounds are compounds in which V_1 and V_2 are viewed as equals in their importance, and they also be tend to have similar argument structures. In UMR, the two verbs in the verb compound are typically annotated as arguments to an abstract concept *and* that indicates a discourse relation, and they typically share arguments. This is illustrated in (15). In this sentence, 开发 [kaifa, "develop"] and 建设 [jianshe, "build"] share the same argument 港口 [gangkou, "port"].

(15) 开发 建设 港口.
Develop build port.

"To develop and build the port"

(s1a / and
:op1(x1 / 开发-01 [kaifa, "develop"]
:Arg1 (x3 / 港口 [gangkou, "port"]))
:op2 (x2 / 建设-01 [jianshe, "build"]
:Arg1 x3))

Compositional coordinating verb compounds like 开发-建设 should be distinguished from non-compositional verb compounds like 褒贬 [baobian, "pass judgment on"], where the meaning of the verb compound as a whole cannot be systematically predicted from the individual verbs, although it is clear they are still related. In this case, the verb compound should be treated as a single concept, as in (16):

(16) 他 喜欢褒贬 人.
he like praise-criticize others.

"He likes to pass judgment on others"

(x1 / 喜欢-01 [xihuan, "like"]
:Arg0 (x3 / individual-person
:ref-person 3rd
:ref-number Singular)
:Arg1 (x2 / 褒贬-01 [baobian, "pass judgment on"])
:Arg0 x3
:Arg1 (x4/人 [ren, "people"])))

2.4 Verb compounds that have a copula

Chinese copula include 是 [shi, "be"], 为 [wei, "be"] and 成 [cheng, "become"], and they can form a verb compound as V_2 with another verb.

Since when used in a verb compound the sole purpose of 是 and 为 is to introduce another argument to V_1, in UMR annotation, they will not be represented as a separate concept. This is illustrated as (17), where 是 simply introduces *:Arg2* of V_1:

(17) 小王 被 看作-是好 人
xiaowang PAS see-is good person

"Xiaowang is viewed as a good person."

```
(x3 / 看作-01 [kanzuo, "viewed as"]
    :Arg1 (i / individual-person
            :name (n / name
                    :op "小王" [Xiaowang]))
    :Arg2 (x5 / 人 [ren, "person"]
            :mod (x4 / 好 [hao, "good"]))
    :aspect Performance)
```

As a V_2 in a verb compound, the copula 成 [cheng, "become"] also introduces an argument to V_1, but it indicates change and has a meaning of its own. For this reason, we treat it as a separate predicate taking its own arguments, but it is also an argument itself to V_1. This is illustrated in (18):

(18) 气旋 增强-成 风暴
Cyclone intensify-become storm.

The cyclone intensifies into a storm.

```
(x2a / 增强-01 [zengqiang, "intensify"]
    :Arg1 (x1 气旋 [qixuan, "storm"])
    :Arg2 (x2b / 成 [cheng, "become"]
        :Arg0 s1x3
        :Arg1 (s1x4 / 风暴 [fengbao,
                            "storm"]))
```

In the example above, 增强 [zengqiang, "intensify"] as a verb has two arguments: Arg0 is the agent/cause and Arg1 is the thing strengthened. This verb implies a transition. Thus, we propose a new core argument Arg2 to indicate the end state of intensification. Thus, if we want to keep the copula, 成 [cheng, "become"], it would become part of Arg2.

2.5 Directional verb compounds

Modern Chinese has a closed list of direction verbs (Lu, 1977; Packard, 2000) that can serve V_2 in a verb compound, forming that has been described in literature as a directional verb compound. Here we focus on two main types of such verb compounds, compositional and partially grammaticalized verb compounds.

2.5.1 Compositional Directional Verb Compounds

In compositional directional verb compounds, both V_1 and V_2 have their own argument structures, with V_2 serving as a direction or goal of V_1. This is illustrated in (19):

(19) 老师 走-进 学校。
teacher walk-enter school.

"The teacher walked into the school."

```
(x2a / 走 [ zou, "walk"]
    :Arg0 (x1 / 老师 [laoshi, "teacher"])
    :goal (x2b / 进 [jin, "enter"]
            :Arg0 x4
            :Arg1 (x3/ 学校 [xuexiao,
                            "school"]))
    :aspect Performance)
```

2.5.2 Non-compositional Directional Verb Compounds

The direction verb in directional verbs are frequently partially grammaticalized in the sense that they no longer have their own argument structure, and only indicate a direction for V_1, sometimes literally and other times metaphorically. The examples in (20) show that while the meaning of V_1 递 in the directional verb compound 递-过来 does not change when it is in a compound (20a,b), V_2 过来 cannot be used in isolation (20c).

(20) a. 他递-过来 一 杯 水
he hand-come one cup water.

"He handed over a glass of water."

b. 他递 一 杯 水
he hand one cup water.

"He handed over a glass of water."

c. *一杯 水 过来
one cup water come.

"A glass of water came."

Partially grammaticalized verbs tend to be productive in the sense that the direction verb can cooccur with a wide range of other verbs to form verb compounds. We approach such verb compounds similarly as we do with grammaticalized resultative verb compounds by treating the verb compounds as a single UMR concept, but link the argument structure of the verb compound to that of V_1 so that we do not have create separate frame file entries for such compounds.

(21) 他递-过来 了一 杯 水
he hand-come PF one cup water

"He handed over a glass of water."

```
(x2a / 递-过来-01 [di, "hand over"]
      :Arg0 (i / individual-person
                  :ref-person 3rd
                  :ref-number Singular)
      :Arg1 (x6 / 水 [shui, "water"]
                  : quant 1
                  : unit 杯 [bei, "cup"])
      :aspect Performance)
```

2.6 Ambiguity between direction and resultative verb compounds

Some verbs in Chinese are ambiguous between a resultative reading and a directional reading, and it is not always possible to say the verb compound is resultative or directional without a specific context.

For example, the verb 开 as V_2 in (22a) means "away", while in (22b) V_2 means "open". This means that 踢开 [tikai, "kick open / kick away"] in (22) is a directional verb compound while in (22b) it is a resultative verb compound. When it is a resultative verb compound as in (22b), the verb is actually compositional, and are decomposed into two separate concepts in UMR annotation. When it is a directional verb compound, it is non-compositional as there is not an "away" sense when 开 [kai, "open"] is used as a standalone verb. It is also partially grammaticalized in the sense that it can form a verb directional verb compound with a wide range of other verbs. As such we will treat the verb compound as a whole as a UMR concept, but linking its argument structure to that of its V_1, adopting a similar approach to other directional verb compounds. What this example suggests that compositionality is tied to specific senses of a word in a particular context rather than the word as a whole.

(22) a. 小孩踢开 了 皮球
Kid kick-away PF ball

"The Kid kicked the ball away."

```
(x2 / 踢开-01 [ti, "kick away"]
    :Arg0 (x1 小孩 [xiaohai, "kid"])
    :Arg1 (x4 / 皮球 [piqiu, "ball"])
    :aspect Performance)
```

b. 小孩踢-开 了 门
Kid kick-open PF ball

"The Kid kicked the door open."

```
(x2a / 踢-01 [ti, "kick"]
      :Arg0 (x1 小孩 [xiaohai, "kid"])
      :Arg1 (x4 / 门 [men, "door"])
            :Arg0-of (x2b / 开[kai,
                              "open"])
      :aspect Performance)
```

3 Related verb constructions

Light verb constructions are also worth discussion here. When determining the type of semantic relations that hold between V_1 and V_2 in a verb compound in UMR annotation, it is important to first determine whether it is a verb compound in the first place. One construction that is similar to verb compounds in appearance is the light verb construction, which also has a verb followed by a deverbal noun that is identical in form to verbs as Chinese verbs can function as a noun without having to have a derivational suffix. This is illustrated in (23), where 进行 [jinxing "hold"] 讨论 [taolun, "discussion"] is a light verb construction in which

(23) 小王 用 图表 进行-讨论
xiaowang use graph operate-discuss

"Xiaowang use graph to discuss. "

```
(x4a / 讨论-01[taolun, "discuss"]
      :instrument (x2 / 图表[tubiao,
                           "graph"])
      :Arg0 ( i / individual-person
            :name (n / name
                  :op ''小王" [Xiaowang]))
      :aspect Performance
      :MODSTR FullAff)
```

进行 [jinxing, "process"] is a light verb in this sentence, thus it is not annotated in the graph. 讨论 [taolun, "discuss"] is treated as the predicate.

4 Related work

Theoretical discussion on V-V compounds . Chinese V-V compounds, particularly resultative verb compounds have received a lot of discussion in theoretical linguistics literature. Most of the discussion centers on the issue of whether such compounds are formed in lexicon or in syntax. (Li,

1990; Gu, 1992; Thompson, 1973; Li, 2007) generally hold that V-V compounds are produced in lexicon and it is theta identification that restricts the possible V-V constructions. However, (Lu, 1977; James Huang, 1992) hold the view that V-V compounds are generated via syntactic operations. Some other works (Cheng, 1997) charted a course in the middle, arguing that verb compounds are generated in both lexicon and syntax. There are also discussions (Paul, 2022; Lu, 1973) specifically on directional verb compounds. Most of the discussions have implicitly assumed these compounds are compositional without providing a set of criteria for how to distinguish compositional from non-compositional verb compounds. For UMR annotation, however, out of necessity we first to determine whether they are compositional or not as we have to decide what concepts to propose. The question of whether they are generated in syntax or the lexicon is of secondary importance. Here we provide a classification of different types of verb compounds in Chinese and show how compositional verb compounds can be distinguished from non-compositional verb compounds and how each type of verb compounds can be annotated in UMR.

Semantic role annotation in the Chinese Propbank, Chinese AMR, and UMR The practice of defining predicate-specific semantic roles started with the Proposition Bank (Palmer et al., 2005) and this practice has been adopted in the construction of the Chinese Propbank (Xue and Palmer, 2009). Before the argument structure of a predicate can be annotated, a frame file that defines the semantic roles for each sense of that predicate has to be created. For a language like English in which verb compounds are uncommon, the list of verbal and nominal predicates is relatively small[3]. However, for a language like Chinese where verb compounding is a common process, as we have discussed, the number of frame files can be quite large[4] if we consider each verb compound as a new predicate that needs a frame file. This issue is inherited by the Chinese AMR Project (Li et al., 2019, 2016) and the UMR project (Gysel et al., 2021) as they adopt the same approach to predicate-argument structure annotation. We propose a solution in which the argument structure of the component verbs are annotated together with the relation between them if the verb compound is compositional. This way we do not to create a new frame files every time we see a new verb compound as long as the frame files for the individual verbs are already available.

[3]See a list of frame files here: `https://verbs.colorado.edu/verb-index/`

[4]See a list of Chinese frame files here: `https://chinese-propbank.herokuapp.com`

5 Conclusion

In this paper we describe the challenge to annotate Chinese verb compounds in the Uniform Meaning Representation framework as compounding is a productive process in Chinese. We propose a solution that is based on treating different types of verb compounds differently based on compositionality, levels of grammaticalization, and productivity of these verb compounds. For compounds that are non-compositional, we annotate the argument structure of the verb compound as a whole, but for compositional verb compounds, we annotate the argument structure of their component verbs, obviating the need to create an additional frame file entry for the compound verb as a whole. For verb compounds that have highly grammaticalized verb components, we also annotate the argument structure of the verb compound as a whole, but link its argument structure to that of the primary verb in the verb compound so that there is no need to create a completely new frame file.

Acknowledgement

This work is supported in part by a grant from the CNS Division of National Science Foundation (Award No: 2213804) entitled "Building a Broad Infrastructure for Uniform Meaning Representations". All views expressed in this paper are those of the authors and do not necessarily represent the view of the National Science Foundation. We would like to thank William Croft, James Pustejovsky, Martha Palmer, James Andrew Cowell, and other collaborators of the UMR project for useful discussions. We would also like to thank annotators of the Chinese UMR team, particularly Ching-wen Chen and Alicia Tu for raising issues related to the UMR annotation of Chinese verb compounds. All shortcomings of the paper are those of the authors.

References

Laura Banarescu, Claire Bonial, Shu Cai, Madalina

Georgescu, Kira Griffitt, Ulf Hermjakob, Kevin Knight, Philipp Koehn, Martha Palmer, and Nathan Schneider. 2013. Abstract meaning representation for sembanking. In *Proceedings of the 7th linguistic annotation workshop and interoperability with discourse*, pages 178–186.

LL Cheng. 1997. Resultative compounds and lexical relational structures. *Chinese Languages and Linguistics III: Morphology and Lexicon*, pages 167–197.

Yang Gu. 1992. *The syntax of resultative and causative compounds in Chinese*. Cornell University.

Jens Van Gysel, Meagan Vigus, Jayeol Chun, Kenneth Lai, Sarah Moeller, Jiarui Yao, Timothy J. O'Gorman, Andrew Cowell, W. Bruce Croft, Chu-Ren Huang, Jan Hajic, James H. Martin, Stephan Oepen, Martha Palmer, James Pustejovsky, Rosa Vallejos, and Nianwen Xue. 2021. Designing a uniform meaning representation for natural language processing. *Künstliche Intell.*, 35:343–360.

C-T James Huang. 1992. Complex predicates in control. *Control and grammar*, pages 109–147.

Bin Li, Yuan Wen, Weiguang Qu, Lijun Bu, and Nianwen Xue. 2016. Annotating the little prince with chinese amrs. In *Proceedings of the 10th Linguistic Annotation Workshop held in Conjunction with ACL 2016 (LAW-X 2016)*, pages 7–15.

Bin Li, Yuan Wen, Li Song, Weiguang Qu, and Nianwen Xue. 2019. Building a chinese amr bank with concept and relation alignments. *Linguistic Issues in Language Technology*, 18.

Chao Li. 2007. *Mandarin resultative verb compounds: Where syntax, semantics, and pragmatics meet*. Yale University.

Charles N Li and Sandra A Thompson. 1981. *Mandarin Chinese: A functional reference grammar*. Univ of California Press.

Yafei Li. 1990. On vv compounds in chinese. *Natural language & linguistic theory*, 8(2):177–207.

John HT Lu. 1973. The verb—verb construction with a directional complement in mandarin. *Journal of Chinese Linguistics*, pages 239–255.

John HT Lu. 1977. Resultative verb compounds vs. directional verb compounds in mandarin. *Journal of Chinese linguistics*, pages 276–313.

Jerome L Packard. 2000. *The morphology of Chinese: A linguistic and cognitive approach*. Cambridge University Press.

Martha Palmer, Daniel Gildea, and Paul Kingsbury. 2005. The proposition bank: An annotated corpus of semantic roles. *Computational linguistics*, 31(1):71–106.

Waltraud Paul. 2022. Svcs in disguise. *New Explorations in Chinese Theoretical Syntax: Studies in honor of Yen-Hui Audrey Li*, 272:133.

Sandra Annear Thompson. 1973. Resultative verb compounds in mandarin chinese: A case for lexical rules. *Language*, pages 361–379.

Meagan Vigus, Jens EL Van Gysel, and William Croft. 2019. A dependency structure annotation for modality. In *Proceedings of the First International Workshop on Designing Meaning Representations*, pages 182–198.

I-hao Woo. 2021. Pedagogical and theoretical issues around the resultative verb compound construction in mandarin chinese. *International Journal of Chinese Language Teaching*, 2(1):17–35.

Naiwen Xue, Fei Xia, Fu-Dong Chiou, and Marta Palmer. 2005. The penn chinese treebank: Phrase structure annotation of a large corpus. *Natural language engineering*, 11(2):207–238.

Nianwen Xue and Martha Palmer. 2009. Adding semantic roles to the chinese treebank. *Natural Language Engineering*, 15(1):143–172.

Jiarui Yao, Haoling Qiu, Bonan Min, and Nianwen Xue. 2020. Annotating temporal dependency graphs via crowdsourcing. In *Proceedings of the 2020 Conference on Empirical Methods in Natural Language Processing (EMNLP)*.

Yuchen Zhang and Nianwen Xue. 2018. Structured interpretation of temporal relations. In *Proceedings of the Eleventh International Conference on Language Resources and Evaluation (LREC 2018)*, Miyazaki, Japan. European Language Resources Association (ELRA).

Construction Grammar Provides Unique Insight into Neural Language Models

Leonie Weissweiler[*◇], **Taiqi He**[†], **Naoki Otani**[†], **David R. Mortensen**[†], **Lori Levin**[†], **Hinrich Schütze**[*◇]

[*]Center for Information and Language Processing, LMU Munich

[◇]Munich Center of Machine Learning

[†]Language Technologies Institute, Carnegie Mellon University

weissweiler@cis.lmu.de

{taiqih,notani,dmortens,lsl}@cs.cmu.edu

Abstract

Construction Grammar (CxG) has recently been used as the basis for probing studies that have investigated the performance of large pre-trained language models (PLMs) with respect to the structure and meaning of constructions. In this position paper, we make suggestions for the continuation and augmentation of this line of research. We look at probing methodology that was not designed with CxG in mind, as well as probing methodology that was designed for specific constructions. We analyse selected previous work in detail, and provide our view of the most important challenges and research questions that this promising new field faces.

1 Introduction

In this paper, we will analyse existing literature investigating how well constructions and constructional information are represented in pretrained language models (PLMs). We provide context to support the argument that this is one of the most important challenges facing Language Models (LMs) today, and provide a summary of the current open research questions and how they might be tackled.

Our paper is organised as follows: In Section 2, we explain why LMs must understand constructions to be good models of language and perform effectively on downstream tasks. In Section 3, we analyse the existing literature on non-CxG-focused probing to determine its limitations in analysing constructional knowledge. In Section 4, we summarise the existing probing work that is specific to CxG and analyse its data, methodology, and findings. In Section 5, we argue that the development of an appropriate probing methodology for constructions remains an open and important research question (§5.1), and highlight the need for data collection and annotation for facilitating this area of research (§5.2). Finally, in Section 5.4, we suggest next steps that LMs might take if CxG probing reveals fundamental problems.

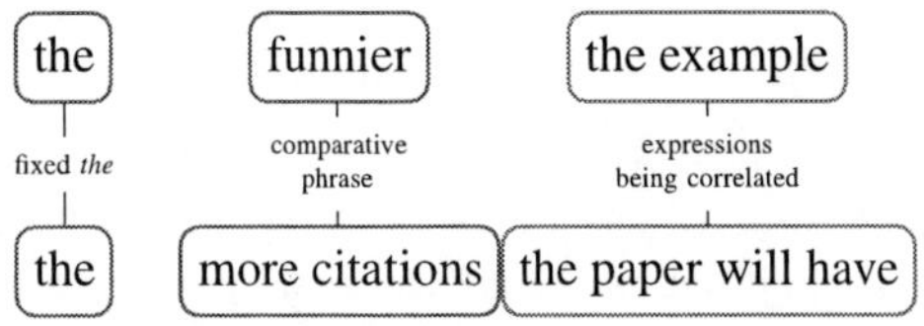

Figure 1: An example illustrating the complexity of a construction. It is an instance of the English Comparative Correlative (CC), with its syntactic features highlighted above the text and paraphrases illustrating its meaning below.

1.1 Construction Grammar

Although there are many varieties of CxG, they share the assumption that the basic building block of language structure is a pair of form and meaning. The form can be anything from a simple morpheme to the types of feature structures seen in Sign-Based Construction Grammar (SBCG) (Boas and Sag, 2012), which can be constellations of inflectional features, morphemes, categories like parts of speech, and syntactic mechanisms. Constructions with many detailed parts in SBCG include comparative constructions in sentences such as *The desk is ten inches taller than the shelf* (Hasegawa et al., 2010) and the causal excess construction as in *It was so big that it fell over* (Kay and Sag, 2012). Most importantly, the form or syntax of a sentence is not reduced to an idealized binary-branching tree or a set of hierarchically arranged pairs of head and dependants. For the purposes of this paper, we take the meaning of a construction to be a combination of Frame Semantics (Petruck and de Melo, 2014) and comparative concepts in semantics and information packaging from language typology (Croft, 2022). Because CxG does not have a clear line separating the lexicon and the grammar, the same kinds of meanings that can be associated with words can be associated with more complex structures. Table 1.1, adapted from Goldberg (2013) illustrates constructions at different

Proceedings of the First International Workshop on Construction Grammars and NLP (CxGs+NLP, GURT/SyntaxFest 2023), pages 85 - 95
March 9-12, 2023 ©2023 Association for Computational Linguistics

Construction Name	Construction Template	Examples
Word		Banana
Word (partially filled)	pre-N, V-ing	Pretransition, Working
Idiom (filled)		Give the devil his due
Idiom (partially filled)	Jog <someone's> memory	She jogged his memory
Idiom (minimally filled)	The X-er the Y-er	The more I think about it, the less I know
Ditransitive construction (unfilled)	Subj V Obj1 Obj2	He baked her a muffin
Passive (unfilled)	Subj aux VPpp (PP by)	The armadillo was hit by a car

Table 1: Standard examples of constructions at various levels, adapted from Goldberg (2013)

levels of complexity that contain different numbers of fixed lexemes and open slots.

In this paper, we ask whether PLMs model constructions as gestalts in both form and meaning. For example, we want to know whether a PLM represents a construction like the Comparative Correlative (*The more papers we write, the more fun we have*) as more than the sum of its individual phrases and dependencies. We also want to know whether the PLM encodes knowledge of the open slots in the construction and what can fill them. In terms of meaning, we want to find out whether the sentence's position in embedding space indicates that it has something to do with the correlation between the increase in writing more papers and having more fun. We would like to know whether PLMs represent the meaning of a correlative sentence as close to the meaning of other constructions in English and other languages that have different forms but similar meanings (e.g., *When we write more papers, we have more fun*).

1.2 Language Modelling

This paper is partially concerned with the fundamental questions of language modelling: what is its objective, and what is required of a full language model? We see the objective of language modelling very pragmatically: we aim to build a system that can predict the words in a sentence as well as possible, and therefore our aim in this paper is to point out where this requires knowledge of constructions. We do not take the objective of language modelling to mean that LMs should necessarily achieve their goal the same way that humans do. Therefore, we do not argue that language models need to "think" in terms of constructions because humans do. Rather, we consider constructions an inherent property of human language, which makes it necessary for language models to understand them.

2 Motivation

There has recently been growing interest in developing probing approaches for PLMs based on CxG. We see these approaches as coming from two different motivational standpoints, summarised below.

2.1 Constructions are Essential for Language Modelling

According to CxG, meaning is encoded in abstract constellations of linguistic units of different sizes. This means that LMs, which the field of NLP is trying to develop to achieve human language competency, must also be able to assign meaning to these units to be full LMs. Their ability to assign meaning to words, or more specifically to subword units which are sometimes closer to morphemes than to words, has been shown at length (Wiedemann et al., 2019; Reif et al., 2019; Schwartz et al., 2022). The question therefore remains: are PLMs able to retrieve and use meanings associated with patterns involving multiple tokens? We do not take this to only mean contiguous, fixed expressions, but much more importantly, non-contiguous patterns with slots that have varying constraints placed on them. To imitate and match human language behaviour, models of human language need to learn how to recognise these patterns, retrieve their meaning, apply this meaning to the context, and use them when producing language. Simply put, there is no way around learning constructions if LMs are to advance. In addition, we believe that it is an independently interesting question whether existing PLMs pick up on these abstract patterns using the current architectures and training setups, and if not, which change in architecture would be necessary to facilitate this.

2.2 Importance in Downstream Tasks

Regardless of more fundamental questions about the long-term goals of LMs, we also firmly believe that probing for CxG is relevant for analysing

Lang	Reference Translation	DeepL Translation
German	Sie nieste den Schaum von ihrem Cappuccino runter.	Sie nieste den Schaum von ihrem Cappuccino.
Italian	Lei ha starnutito via la schiuma dal suo cappuccino.	Starnutì la schiuma del suo cappuccino.
Turkish	Cappuccino'sunun köpüğünü hapşırdı.	Hapşırarak cappuccino'sunun köpüğünü uçurdu.

Table 2: Translations of 'She sneezed the foam off her cappuccino.' given by DeepL[1]. Translated back to English by humans, they all mean "She sneezed her cappuccino's foam.", which does not correctly convey the resultative meaning component, i.e., that the foam is removed from the cappuccino by the sneeze (as opposed to put there).

the challenges that face applied NLP, as evaluated on downstream tasks, at this point in time. Discussion is increasingly focusing on diagnosing the specific scenarios that are challenging for current models. Srivastava et al. (2022) propose test suites that are designed to challenge LMs, and many of them are designed by looking for 'patterns' with a non-obvious, non-literal meaning that is more than the sum of the involved words. One example of such a failure can be found in Table 2, where we provide the DeepL[1] translations for the famous instance of the caused-motion construction (Goldberg, 1995, CMC;): 'She sneezed the foam off her cappuccino', where the unusual factor is that *sneeze* does not usually take a patient argument or cause a motion. For translation, this means that it either has to use the corresponding CMC in the target language, which might be quite different in form from the English CMC, or paraphrase in a way that conveys all meaning facets. For the languages we tested, DeepL did not achieve this: the resulting sentence sounds more like the foam was sneezed onto the cappuccino, or is ambiguous between this and the correct translation. Interestingly, for Russian, the motion is conveyed in the translation, but not the fact that it is caused by a sneeze.

Targeted adversarial test suites like this translation example can be a useful resource to evaluate how well LMs perform on constructions, but more crucially, CxG theory and probing methods will inform the design of better and more systematic test suites, which in turn will be used to improve LMs (§5.4).

2.3 Diversity in Linguistics for NLP

Discussions about PLMs as models of human language processing have recently gained popularity. One forum for such discussions is the Neural Nets for Cognition Discussion Group at CogSci2022[2]. The work is still very tentative, and most people agree that LMs are not ready to be used as models of human language processing. However, the discussion about whether LMs are ready to be used as cognitive models is dominated by results of probing studies based on Generative Grammar (GG), or more specifically Transformational Grammar. This means that GG is being used as the gold standard against which the cognitive plausibility of LMs is evaluated. Studies using GG assume a direct relationship between the models' performance on probing tasks and their linguistic competency. Increased performance on GG probing tasks is seen as a sign it is becoming more reasonable to use LMs as cognitive models. Another linguistic reason for theoretical diversity is that if we could show that LMs conform better to CxG rather than GG, this might open up interesting discussions if they ever start being used as cognitive models.

3 Established Probing Methods Are Only Applicable to Some Aspects of CxG

Established probing methods have focused on different aspects of the syntactic and semantic knowledge of PLMs. In this section, we summarise the major approaches that were not designed specifically with constructions in mind. We show that although each of these methodologies deals with some aspect of CxG, and might even fully investigate some simpler constructions, none of them fully covers constructional knowledge as defined in Section 1.1.

3.1 Probing Using Contextual Embeddings

Various probing studies (Garcia et al., 2021; Chronis and Erk, 2020; Karidi et al., 2021; Yaghoobzadeh et al., 2019; *inter alia*) have focused on analysing contextual embeddings at different layers of PLMs, either of one word or multiple words, or both. The common thread in their methodology is that they compare the embeddings of the same word in different contexts, or of different words in the same context. From a constructional point of view, this requires finding two

[1]`https://www.deepl.com/translator`

[2]`http://neural-nets-for-cognition.net`

constructions with similar surface forms. By comparing the embeddings over many sentences, they are able to investigate if a certain word "knows" in which construction it is, which provides evidence for the constructional knowledge of a model.

While this is a useful starting point for probing, it is also limited. Sentences with similar constructions have to be identified, which is not always possible. More importantly, this methodology currently does not tell us anything about if the model has identified the extent of the construction correctly, or if the model has correctly learned how each slot can be filled.

3.2 Probing for Relationships Between Words

Some probing studies investigate whether a PLM recognises a word pair associated with a meaningful relationship of some kind (Rogers et al. (2020)). Most prominently, probing based on Universal Dependencies (UD; de Marneffe et al. (2021)) by Hewitt and Manning (2019) attempts to find out whether there is a high attention weight between words that are in a dependency relation where one word is the head and the other word is the dependent. They found different attention heads at different layers that seem to represent specific dependency relations such as a direct object attending to its verb, a preposition attending to its object, determiners attending to nouns, possessive pronouns attending to head nouns, and passive auxiliary verbs attending to head verbs.

The methodology as it was used by Hewitt and Manning (2019) looked at the one token that each token attended to the most. This made sense for the Hewitt and Manning (2019) study because they were probing for UD structures, which consist of binary relationships of heads and dependents in a hierarchical structure.

However, the methodology would have to be extended if we want to find out whether a whole construction with many construction elements is represented in the model in something other than a hierarchical set of binary relations. Most varieties of CxG recognise constructions with more than two daughters and constructions such as *thirty miles an hour* (Fillmore et al., 2012) in which no element is the head (headless constructions). As a research question, it is still unclear what patterns of attention we would consider as evidence that a model encodes a construction that may have headless and non-binary branches. An appropriate probing methodology has not yet been developed.

3.3 Probing with Minimal Pairs

Some works in probing based on Generative Grammar have relied on finding minimal pairs of sentences that are identical except for one specific feature that, if changed, will make the sentence ungrammatical (Wei et al., 2021). For example, in *The teacher who met the students is/*are smart*, a language model that encodes hierarchical structure would predict *is* rather than *are* after *students*, whereas a language model that was fooled by adjacency might predict *are* because it is next to *students*. The sentences can be safely compared, because only one feature, in this case, the verb being assigned the same number as the subject, is changed, and no other information can intervene or distort the probe. Other studies use a more complicated paradigm of minimal pairs involving filler-gap constructions, contrasting *I know what the lion attacked (gap) in the desert* and *I know that the lion attacked the gazelle (no gap) in the desert.*

These probing methodologies have led to productive lines of research and have been applied to complex constructions such as the Comparative Correlative Construction (Weissweiler et al., 2022). However, they depend on finding two minimally different constructions, which differ only in one way (e.g., singular/plural or gap/no gap), but close minimal pairs are simply not available for every construction.

4 CxG-specific Probing

We have argued that the most commonly used and straightforward probing methods are not sufficient for fully investigating constructional knowledge in PLMs. However, there have been several papers which have created new probing methodologies specifically for constructions. In this section, we will analyse them in terms of

- Which constructions were investigated? Does the paper investigate specific constructions or does it use a pre-compiled list of constructions or restrain itself to a subset?
- For the specific instances of their construction or constructions, what data are they using? Is it synthetic or collected from a corpus? If from a corpus, how was it collected?
- What are the key probing ideas?

Paper	Language	Source	Construction	Example
Tayyar Madabushi et al. (2020)	English	From automatically constructed list by Dunn (2017)	Personal Pronoun + didn't + V + how	We didn't know how or why.
Li et al. (2022)	English	Argument Structure Constructions according to Bencini and Goldberg (2000)	caused-motion	Bob cut the bread into the pan.
Tseng et al. (2022)	Chinese	From constructions list by (Zhan, 2017)	a + 到 + 爆, etc.	好吃到爆了！ *It's so delicious!*
Weissweiler et al. (2022)	English	McCawley (1988)	Comparative Correlative	The bigger, the better.

Table 3: Overview of constructions investigated in CxG-specific probing literature, with examples.

- Does the paper only investigate probing of (unchanged) pretrained models or is finetuning also considered?

For ease of reference, we provide an overview of the constructions investigated by each of the papers in Table 3.

4.1 CxGBERT

Tayyar Madabushi et al. (2020) investigate how well BERT (Devlin et al., 2019) can classify whether two sentences contain instances of the same construction. Their list of constructions is extracted with a modified version of Dunn (2017)'s algorithm: they induce a CxG in an unsupervised fashion over a corpus, using statistical association measures. Their list of constructions is taken directly from Dunn (2017), and they find their instances by searching for those constructions' occurrences in WikiText data. This makes the constructions possibly problematic, since they have not been verified by a linguist, which could make the conclusions drawn later from the results about BERT's handling of constructions hard to generalise from.

The key probing question of this paper is: Do two sentences contain the same construction? This does not necessarily need to be the most salient or overarching construction of the sentence, so many sentences will contain more than one instance of a construction. Crucially, the paper does not follow a direct probing approach, but rather finetunes or even trains BERT on targeted construction data, to then measure the impact on CoLA. They find that on average, models trained on sentences that were sorted into documents based on their constructions do not reliably perform better than those trained on original, unsorted data. However, they additionally test BERT Base with no additional pre-training on the task of predicting whether two sentences contain instances of the same construction, measuring accuracies of about 85% after 500 training examples for the probe. These results vary wildly depending on the frequency of the construction, which might relate back to the questionable quality of the automatically identified list of constructions.

4.2 Neural Reality of Argument Structure Constructions

Li et al. (2022) probe for LMs' handling of four argument structure constructions: ditransitive, resultative, caused-motion, and removal. Specifically, they attempt to adapt the findings of Bencini and Goldberg (2000), who used a sentence sorting task to determine whether human participants perceive the argument structure or the verb as the main factor in the overall sentence meaning. The paper aims to recreate this experiment for MiniBERTa (Warstadt et al., 2020) and RoBERTa (Liu et al., 2019), by generating sentences artificially and using agglomerative clustering on the sentence embeddings. They find that, similarly to the human data, which is sorted by the English proficiency of the participants, PLMs increasingly prefer sorting by construction as their training data size increases. Crucially, the sentences constructed for testing had no lexical overlap, such that this sorting preference must be due to an underlying recognition of a shared pattern between sentences with the same argument structure. They then conduct a second experiment, in which they insert random verbs, which are incompatible with one of the constructions, and then measure the Euclidean distance between this verb's contextual embedding and that of a verb that is prototypical for the corresponding construction. The probing idea here is that if construction information is picked up by the model, the contextual embedding of the verb should acquire some constructional meaning, which would bring it closer to the corresponding prototypical verb meaning than to the others. They indeed find that this effect is significant, for both high and low frequency verbs.

4.3 CxLM

Tseng et al. (2022) study LM predictions for the slots of various degrees of openness for a corpus of Chinese constructions. Their original data comes from a knowledge database of Mandarin Chinese constructions (Zhan, 2017), which they filter so that only constructions with a fixed repetitive element remain, which are easier to find automatically in a corpus. They filter this list down further to constructions which are rated as commonly occurring by annotators, and retrieve instances from a POS-tagged Taiwanese bulletin board corpus. They binarise the openness of a given slot in a construction and mark each word in a construction as either constant or variable. The key probing idea is then to examine the conditional probabilities that a model outputs for each type of slot, with the expectation that the prediction of variable slot words will be more difficult than that of constant ones, providing that the model has acquired some constructional knowledge. They find that this effect is significant for two different Chinese BERT-based models, as negative log-likelihoods are indeed significantly higher when predicting variable slots compared to constant ones. Interestingly, the negative log-likelihood resulting from masking the entire construction lies in the middle of the two extremes. They further evaluate a BERT-based model which is finetuned on just predicting the variable slots of the dataset they compiled and find, unsurprisingly, that this improves accuracy greatly.

4.4 Probing for the English Comparative Correlative

Weissweiler et al. (2022) investigate large PLM performance on the English Comparative Correlative (CC). There are two key probing ideas, corresponding to the investigation of the syntactic vs. the semantic component of CC. They probe for PLM understanding of CC's syntax by attempting to create minimal pairs, which consist of sentences with instances of the CC and very similar sentences which do not contain an instance of the CC. They collect minimal pairs from data by searching for sentences that fit the general pattern and manually annotate them as positive and negative instances, and additionally construct artificial minimal pairs that turn a CC sentence into a non-CC sentence by reordering words. They find that a probing classifier can distinguish between the two classes easily, using mean-pooled contextual PLM embeddings. They also probe the models' understanding of the meaning of CC, for which they choose a usage-based approach, constructing NLU-style test sentences in which an instance of the construction is given and has then to be applied in a context. They find no above-chance performance for any of the models investigated in this task.

4.5 Summary

In this section, we summarise the findings of previous work on CxG-based LM probing and analyse them in terms of the constructions that are investigated, the data that is used and the probing approaches that are applied.

4.5.1 Constructions Used

So far, Tseng et al.'s (2022) study is only the work that chose a set of constructions from a list precompiled by linguists. They constrain their selection to contain only constructions that are easy to search for in a corpus, and the resource they use only contains constructions with irregular syntax, but it is nevertheless to be considered a positive point that they are able to reach a diversity of constructions investigated. In contrast, both Li et al. (2022) and Weissweiler et al. (2022) pick one or a few constructions manually, both of which are instances of 'typical' constructions frequently discussed in the linguistic literature. This makes the work more interesting to linguists and the validity of the constructions is beyond doubt. But the downside is selection bias: the constructions that are frequently discussed are likely to have strong associated meanings and do not constitute a representative sample of constructions, from a constructions-all-the-way-down standpoint (Goldberg, 2006). Lastly, Tayyar Madabushi et al. (2020) rely on artificial data collected by Dunn (2017). We consider this method to be unreliable, but it has the resulting dataset has the advantage of variety and large scale.

4.5.2 Data Used

The two main approaches to collecting data are: (i) *patterns*: finding instances of the constructions using patterns of words / part-of-speech (POS) tags and (ii) *generation* of synthetic data. Tseng et al. (2022), Weissweiler et al. (2022) and Tayyar Madabushi et al. (2020) use patterns while Li et al. (2022) and a part of Weissweiler et al. (2022) generate data based on formal grammars. Patterns have the advantage of natural data and are less prone to accidental unwanted correlations. But there is a risk of errors in the data collection process, even after the set of constructions has to be constrained to even allow for automatic classification, and the data may have been post-corrected by manual annotation, which is time-intensive. On the other hand, generation bears challenges for making the sentences as natural as possible, which can eliminate confounding factors like lexical overlap.

4.5.3 Probing Approaches Used

Regarding the probing approaches, all previous work has had its own idea. Weissweiler et al. (2022) and Li et al. (2022) both operate on the level of sentence embeddings, classifying and clustering them respectively. Tayyar Madabushi et al. (2020) could maybe be classified with them, as it employs the Next Sentence Prediction objective (Devlin et al., 2019), which operates at the sentence level. On the other hand, another part of Weissweiler et al. (2022), as well as Tseng et al. (2022), works at the level of individual predictions for masked tokens.

The greatest difference between these works is in their concept of evidence for constructional information learned by a model, and what this information even consists of. Tayyar Madabushi et al. (2020) frame this information as 'do these two sentences contain the same construction', Li et al. (2022) as 'is clustering by the construction preferred over clustering by the verb', Weissweiler et al. (2022) as 'can a small classifier distinguish this construction from similar-looking sentences' and 'can information given in form of a construction be applied in context', and Tseng et al. (2022) as 'are open slots more difficult to predict than closed ones'. There is little overlap to be found between these approaches, so it is difficult to draw any conclusion from more than one paper at a time.

4.5.4 Overall Findings

We nonetheless make an attempt at summarising the findings so far about large PLMs' handling of constructional information. Regarding the structure, all findings seem to be consistent with the idea that models have picked up on the syntactic structure of constructions and recognised similarities between different instances of the same construction. This appears to hold true even when tested in different rigorous setups that exclude bias from overlapping vocabulary or accidentally similar sentence structure. This has mostly been found for English, as Tseng et al. (2022) are the only ones investigating it for a non-English language, and it remains to be seen if it holds true for lower-resources languages. Considering the acquisition of the meaning of constructions, only Weissweiler et al. (2022) have investigated this, and found no evidence that models have formed any understanding of it, but were not able to provide conclusive evidence to the contrary.

5 Research Questions

In this section, we lay out our view of the problems that are facing the emerging field of CxG-based probing and the reasons behind these challenges, and propose avenues for potential future work and improvement.

5.1 How Can We Develop Probing Methods that are a Better Fit for CxG?

Going forward, we see two directions. One is what has already been happening: keep finding new ways to get around the inherent difficulty of probing for constructions, which leads us to mostly non-conclusive and not entirely reliable evidence. The better, and more difficult way forward, is to adopt a fundamentally different methodology that would establish a standard of evidence/generalisability comparable to GG-based probing.

5.2 Data

Another reason why so little work has been done in this important field is likely the lack of data. We view the lack of data as divided into three parts: the lack of lists of constructions, the lack of meaning descriptions or even a unified meaning formalism for them, and the lack of annotated instances in corpora. We explain different opportunities for the community to obtain this data going forward below.

5.2.1 Exploiting Non-constructicon Data

Many resources are available, as already stated above, that have collected or created data with specific constructions, with the aim of making certain tasks more challenging to the models in a specific way. We can analyse those datasets and the results on them from a CxG point of view, and this can add to our pool of knowledge about what models struggle with regarding constructions. They will probably not contain any meaning descriptions, but some, like in Srivastava et al. (2022), are grouped naturally by construction, and contain instances in data, which may however be artificial.

5.2.2 Making Constructicons Available

Recently, there has been substantial work by linguists to develop constructicons for different languages (Lyngfelt et al., 2018; Ziem et al., forthcoming). Some of these constructicons are readily available online, e.g., the Brazilian Portuguese one, but many are either not available or have an interface that makes them difficult to access, e.g., because it is in the constructicon's language. Although to our knowledge, none of these constructicons contain annotated instances in text, and their meaning representations will be very difficult to unify, they are an important resource at least for lists of constructions that can be investigated by probing methods. They are especially valuable because of their linguistic diversity (English, German, Japanese, Swedish, Russian, Brazilian Portuguese), the lack of which is a major flaw in the current literature, as we stated above in §4.5.4.

5.2.3 Universal Constructicon

As a more ambitious project than simply making these constructicons available online, we firmly believe that the field would benefit greatly from an attempt to unify their representations and make them available as a shared resource. Parallels can be drawn here to UD (de Marneffe et al., 2021), a project which developed a simplified version of dependency syntax that could be universally applied and agreed upon, and then provided funding for the creation of initial resources for a range of languages, which was later greatly added to by community work in the different communities. This was a major factor in the popularisation of dependency syntax within the NLP community, to the point where it is now almost synonymous with syntax itself, due in no small part to its convenience for computational research.

As a second step after the creation of a shared online resource to access the existing constructicons, the community could consider developing a shared representation to formalise the surface form of the constructions. A dataset without meaning representation that includes multiple languages would already be a very useful resource. As a next step after that, we could think about aligning constructions across languages that encode a similar meaning. The last and most ambitious step would be unifying and linking the meaning representations, which would ideally be formalised similarly to AMR (Banarescu et al., 2013). This would enable us to develop automatic test suites that can really account for the constructions' meanings and not just their structure.

5.2.4 Annotated Instances in Text

In any stage of the development of 'construction lists' detailed above, it would be necessary to find instances of the constructions in text. Some of the probing literature described above have generated this data artificially, which is time-consuming and also removes two important advantages of precompiled construction lists: objectivity and scale. Therefore, the ideal solution would be to find resources to have data annotated for constructions. This in itself faces many challenges from a constructions-all-the-way-down perspective: annotating even one sentence completely would be very time-consuming and require many discussions about annotation schemata in advance. A more basic way of acquiring data would be to focus on a limited set of constructions, which is selected manually, and to use pre-filtering methods similar to those employed by Tseng et al. (2022) and Weissweiler et al. (2022), to acquire simply an Inside-Outside-Beginning marking in sentences that might be instances of a construction. On the downside, this is far less linguistically rigorous and also less timeless than Universal Dependencies, which guarantees that any annotated sentence has been fully annotated and will probably not need to be revised. Nevertheless, a compromise will need to be found if annotated data is to be created at all.

5.3 CxG and Transformer Architecture

As more work is done on CxG-based probing, the field will hopefully soon be able to approach the questions that we see as crucial. Current probing techniques have not yet shown that PLMs are able to adequately handle the meaning of constructions. Assuming that more comprehensive probing techniques will show conclusively that this is not the case, is it due to a lack of data? Or is there a fundamental incompatibility of current architectures and the concept of associating a pattern with a meaning? In 5.3.1 and 5.3.2, we elaborate on why the latter might be the case.

5.3.1 Non-compositional Meaning

It is possible that constructions are intrinsically difficult for LMs because they include non-compositional meaning that is not attached to a token. It is tempting to compare them to simpler multiword expressions, which also have meaning that spans several words and that is only instantiated when they appear together. They also pose a challenge to LMs because of this, as their concept of sentence meaning is often too compositional (Liu and Neubig, 2022). The key difference is in our view, that for very complex constructions, it is not clear where in the model we can search or probe for the additional meaning.

The meaning is not attached to the words instantiating the construction, but rather to the abstract pattern itself (Croft, 2001), which we can recognise, connect mentally to previous instances and store meaning for. Once we have retrieved this meaning, it is potentially applied to the whole sentence, and can therefore have consequences for the contextual meaning of words which were never even involved in it. In a transformer-based LM, this additional meaning component cannot be stored in the static embeddings and contextualised through the attention layers, because unlike for MWEs, many constructions have very open slots, so that it is impossible to say that their meaning should somehow be stored with the meaning of the words that may instantiate them. The only place to store constructional information, therefore, remains the model weights, which are much harder to investigate or alter than the model's input, and further probing might reveal that they are unable to store it at all.

5.3.2 The Language Modelling Objective

Another possibility for fundamental difficulties arises from the nature of the training objective. PLMs are typically trained either on a masked or causal language modelling objective (Devlin et al., 2019; Radford et al., 2019). It makes sense that this incentivises them to learn word meaning in context, which they will need to predict certain words, and also relationships between words, such as simple morphological dependencies. However, information about the meaning of a construction might not often be learned in a language modelling setting, simply because it will not be needed to make the correct prediction. The meaning of a construction might not be necessary information to predict one of its component words correctly when it is masked, although its structure certainly will. In contrast, finetuning on a downstream task that requires assessment of sentence meaning, such as sentence classification, might enable us to better access the constructional meaning contained in PLMs, because the finetuning objective has required explicit use of this meaning. On the other hand, this might also be thought of as a distortion of the lens, as grammatical knowledge is not typically evaluated on finetuned models, because the findings might not generalise well.

5.4 Adapting Pretraining for CxG

If we do decide that there is a fundamental problem with the current architecture and/or training regime, the next logical step would be to think about how to alter these so that acquisition of constructional meaning becomes possible. Something similar has already been considered by Tseng et al. (2022), where models are finetuned on data that has been altered to mask entire construction instances at once, and by Tayyar Madabushi et al. (2020), which collects sentences that contain instances of the same construction into 'documents' and pretrains on them. This line of thinking, which can be summarised as data modification with constructional biases, can be further expanded, to give models some help with associating sentences with similar constructions with each other.

A far more radical idea would be to think about injecting something into the architecture that could represent this additional meaning, in the style of a position embedding, or a control token (Martin et al., 2020).

6 Conclusion

We have motivated why probing large PLMs for CxG is a very important topic both for computational linguists interested in the ideal LM and for applied NLP scientists seeking to analyse and improve the current challenges that models are facing. We then summarised and analysed the existing literature on this topic. Finally, we have given our reasons for why CxG probing remains a challenge, and detailed suggestions for further development in this field, within the realms of data, methodology, and fundamental research questions.

References

Laura Banarescu, Claire Bonial, Shu Cai, Madalina Georgescu, Kira Griffitt, Ulf Hermjakob, Kevin Knight, Philipp Koehn, Martha Palmer, and Nathan

Schneider. 2013. Abstract Meaning Representation for sembanking. In *Proceedings of the 7th Linguistic Annotation Workshop and Interoperability with Discourse*, pages 178–186, Sofia, Bulgaria. Association for Computational Linguistics.

Giulia ML Bencini and Adele E Goldberg. 2000. The contribution of argument structure constructions to sentence meaning. *Journal of Memory and Language*, 43(4):640–651.

H. C. Boas and I. A. Sag. 2012. *Sign-Based Construction Grammar*. Center for the Study of Language and Information.

Gabriella Chronis and Katrin Erk. 2020. When is a bishop not like a rook? when it's like a rabbi! multi-prototype BERT embeddings for estimating semantic relationships. In *Proceedings of the 24th Conference on Computational Natural Language Learning*, pages 227–244, Online. Association for Computational Linguistics.

William Croft. 2001. *Radical construction grammar: Syntactic theory in typological perspective*. Oxford University Press on Demand.

William Croft. 2022. *Morphosyntax: Constructions of the World's Languages*. Cambridge University Press.

Marie-Catherine de Marneffe, Christopher D. Manning, Joakim Nivre, and Daniel Zeman. 2021. Universal Dependencies. *Computational Linguistics*, 47(2):255–308.

Jacob Devlin, Ming-Wei Chang, Kenton Lee, and Kristina Toutanova. 2019. BERT: Pre-training of deep bidirectional transformers for language understanding. In *Proceedings of the 2019 Conference of the North American Chapter of the Association for Computational Linguistics: Human Language Technologies, Volume 1 (Long and Short Papers)*, pages 4171–4186, Minneapolis, Minnesota. Association for Computational Linguistics.

Jonathan Dunn. 2017. Computational learning of construction grammars. *Language and cognition*, 9(2):254–292.

C. J. Fillmore, R. Lee-Goldman, and R. Rhodes. 2012. The framenet constructicon. In H. C. Boas and I. A. Sag, editors, *Sign-Based Construction Grammar*. Center for the Study of Language and Information.

Marcos Garcia, Tiago Kramer Vieira, Carolina Scarton, Marco Idiart, and Aline Villavicencio. 2021. Probing for idiomaticity in vector space models. In *Proceedings of the 16th Conference of the European Chapter of the Association for Computational Linguistics: Main Volume*, pages 3551–3564, Online. Association for Computational Linguistics.

Adele Goldberg. 2006. *Constructions at work: The nature of generalization in language*. Oxford University Press, Oxford, UK.

Adele E.. Goldberg. 1995. *Constructions: A construction grammar approach to argument structure*. University of Chicago Press.

Adele E. Goldberg. 2013. 1415 Constructionist Approaches. In *The Oxford Handbook of Construction Grammar*. Oxford University Press.

Yoko Hasegawa, Russell Lee-Goldman, Kyoko Hirose Ohara, Seiko Fujii, and Charles J Fillmore. 2010. On expressing measurement and comparison in english and japanese. *Contrastive studies in construction grammar*, 10.

John Hewitt and Christopher D. Manning. 2019. A structural probe for finding syntax in word representations. In *Proceedings of the 2019 Conference of the North American Chapter of the Association for Computational Linguistics: Human Language Technologies, Volume 1 (Long and Short Papers)*, pages 4129–4138, Minneapolis, Minnesota. Association for Computational Linguistics.

Taelin Karidi, Yichu Zhou, Nathan Schneider, Omri Abend, and Vivek Srikumar. 2021. Putting words in BERT's mouth: Navigating contextualized vector spaces with pseudowords. In *Proceedings of the 2021 Conference on Empirical Methods in Natural Language Processing*, pages 10300–10313, Online and Punta Cana, Dominican Republic. Association for Computational Linguistics.

Paul Kay and Ivan A. Sag. 2012. Cleaning up the big mess: Discontinuous dependencies and complex determiners. In H. C. Boas and I. A. Sag, editors, *Sign-Based Construction Grammar*. Center for the Study of Language and Information.

Bai Li, Zining Zhu, Guillaume Thomas, Frank Rudzicz, and Yang Xu. 2022. Neural reality of argument structure constructions. In *Proceedings of the 60th Annual Meeting of the Association for Computational Linguistics (Volume 1: Long Papers)*, pages 7410–7423, Dublin, Ireland. Association for Computational Linguistics.

Emmy Liu and Graham Neubig. 2022. Are representations built from the ground up? an empirical examination of local composition in language models. *arXiv preprint arXiv:2210.03575*.

Yinhan Liu, Myle Ott, Naman Goyal, Jingfei Du, Mandar Joshi, Danqi Chen, Omer Levy, Mike Lewis, Luke Zettlemoyer, and Veselin Stoyanov. 2019. Roberta: A robustly optimized bert pretraining approach. *arXiv preprint arXiv:1907.11692*.

Benjamin Lyngfelt, Lars Borin, Kyoko Ohara, and Tiago Timponi Torrent. 2018. *Constructicography: Constructicon development across languages*, volume 22. John Benjamins Publishing Company.

Louis Martin, Éric de la Clergerie, Benoît Sagot, and Antoine Bordes. 2020. Controllable sentence simplification. In *Proceedings of the Twelfth Language*

Resources and Evaluation Conference, pages 4689–4698, Marseille, France. European Language Resources Association.

James D McCawley. 1988. The comparative conditional construction in english, german, and chinese. In *Annual Meeting of the Berkeley Linguistics Society*, volume 14, pages 176–187.

Miriam R. L. Petruck and Gerard de Melo, editors. 2014. *Proceedings of Frame Semantics in NLP: A Workshop in Honor of Chuck Fillmore (1929-2014)*. Association for Computational Linguistics, Baltimore, MD, USA.

Alec Radford, Jeffrey Wu, Rewon Child, David Luan, Dario Amodei, Ilya Sutskever, et al. 2019. Language models are unsupervised multitask learners. *OpenAI blog*, 1(8):9.

Emily Reif, Ann Yuan, Martin Wattenberg, Fernanda B Viegas, Andy Coenen, Adam Pearce, and Been Kim. 2019. Visualizing and measuring the geometry of bert. In *Advances in Neural Information Processing Systems*, volume 32. Curran Associates, Inc.

Anna Rogers, Olga Kovaleva, and Anna Rumshisky. 2020. A primer in BERTology: What we know about how BERT works. *Transactions of the Association for Computational Linguistics*, 8:842–866.

Lane Schwartz, Coleman Haley, and Francis Tyers. 2022. How to encode arbitrarily complex morphology in word embeddings, no corpus needed. In *Proceedings of the first workshop on NLP applications to field linguistics*, pages 64–76, Gyeongju, Republic of Korea. International Conference on Computational Linguistics.

Aarohi Srivastava, Abhinav Rastogi, Abhishek Rao, Abu Awal Md Shoeb, Abubakar Abid, Adam Fisch, Adam R Brown, Adam Santoro, Aditya Gupta, Adrià Garriga-Alonso, et al. 2022. Beyond the imitation game: Quantifying and extrapolating the capabilities of language models. *arXiv preprint arXiv:2206.04615*.

Harish Tayyar Madabushi, Laurence Romain, Dagmar Divjak, and Petar Milin. 2020. CxGBERT: BERT meets construction grammar. In *Proceedings of the 28th International Conference on Computational Linguistics*, pages 4020–4032, Barcelona, Spain (Online). International Committee on Computational Linguistics.

Yu-Hsiang Tseng, Cing-Fang Shih, Pin-Er Chen, Hsin-Yu Chou, Mao-Chang Ku, and Shu-Kai Hsieh. 2022. CxLM: A construction and context-aware language model. In *Proceedings of the Thirteenth Language Resources and Evaluation Conference*, pages 6361–6369, Marseille, France. European Language Resources Association.

Alex Warstadt, Yian Zhang, Xiaocheng Li, Haokun Liu, and Samuel R. Bowman. 2020. Learning which features matter: RoBERTa acquires a preference for linguistic generalizations (eventually). In *Proceedings of the 2020 Conference on Empirical Methods in Natural Language Processing (EMNLP)*, pages 217–235, Online. Association for Computational Linguistics.

Jason Wei, Dan Garrette, Tal Linzen, and Ellie Pavlick. 2021. Frequency effects on syntactic rule learning in transformers. In *Proceedings of the 2021 Conference on Empirical Methods in Natural Language Processing*, pages 932–948, Online and Punta Cana, Dominican Republic. Association for Computational Linguistics.

Leonie Weissweiler, Valentin Hofmann, Abdullatif Köksal, and Hinrich Schütze. 2022. The better your syntax, the better your semantics? probing pretrained language models for the English comparative correlative. In *Proceedings of the 2022 Conference on Empirical Methods in Natural Language Processing*, pages 10859–10882, Abu Dhabi, United Arab Emirates. Association for Computational Linguistics.

Gregor Wiedemann, Steffen Remus, Avi Chawla, and Chris Biemann. 2019. Does bert make any sense? interpretable word sense disambiguation with contextualized embeddings. *arXiv preprint arXiv:1909.10430*.

Yadollah Yaghoobzadeh, Katharina Kann, T. J. Hazen, Eneko Agirre, and Hinrich Schütze. 2019. Probing for semantic classes: Diagnosing the meaning content of word embeddings. In *Proceedings of the 57th Annual Meeting of the Association for Computational Linguistics*, pages 5740–5753, Florence, Italy. Association for Computational Linguistics.

Weidong Zhan. 2017. On theoretical issues in building a knowledge database of chinese constructions. *Journal of Chinese Information Processing*, 31(1):230–238.

Alexander Ziem, Alexander Willich, and Sascha Michel. forthcoming. *Constructing constructicons*. John Benjamins Publishing Company.

Modeling Construction Grammar's Way into NLP: Insights from negative results in automatically identifying schematic clausal constructions in Brazilian Portuguese

Arthur Lorenzi[1], Vânia Gomes de Almeida[1], Ely Edison Matos[1], Tiago Timponi Torrent[1,2]

[1] FrameNet Brasil Lab, Graduate Program in Linguistics, Federal University of Juiz de Fora

[2] Brazilian National Council for Scientific and Technological Development – CNPq

{arthur.lorenzi,vania.almeida}@estudante.ufjf.br

{tiago.torrent,ely.matos}@ufjf.br

Abstract

This paper reports on negative results in a task of automatic identification of schematic clausal constructions and their elements in Brazilian Portuguese. The experiment was set up so as to test whether form and meaning properties of constructions, modeled in terms of Universal Dependencies and FrameNet Frames in a Constructicon, would improve the performance of transformer models in the task. Qualitative analysis of the results indicate that alternatives to the linearization of those properties, dataset size and a post-processing module should be explored in the future as a means to make use of information in Constructicons for NLP tasks.

1 Introduction

Constructional approaches to language description can be traced back to early work by Fillmore (1968), which later gave rise to a myriad of approaches sharing the common assumptions that (a) constructions are learned pairings of form and function related to one another in a network, and (b) grammar does not rely on transformations and derivation, instead it is directly associated with function (Goldberg, 2013).

From the 2000's on, computational implementations of Construction Grammar started being built both in terms of language resources comprising of collections of constructions called *Constructicons* (Fillmore, 2008; Lyngfelt et al., 2012; Ohara, 2014; Torrent et al., 2014; Ziem and Boas, 2017), and proofs of concept, namely constructional parsers (Bryant, 2008; Matos et al., 2017).

As a natural consequence of the focus of constructionist analysis on families of constructions, Constructicons typically start by modeling the same kind of phenomena, leaving more schematic and foundational language structures, clausal and phrasal constructions, respectively, for later. These kinds of constructions represent a challenge for both Constructicography, that is, the process of describing and modeling constructions in a resource (Lyngfelt et al., 2018), and for constructional parsing, since schematic clausal constructions, as opposed to idioms, are typically difficult or impossible to describe in terms of the presence of distinctive lexical fillers. Moreover, it is common for those constructions to share constituency properties. As an example, consider (1) and (2), both sentences share the same syntactic structure in Brazilian Portuguese, but express opposite types of semantic events (controlled × uncontrolled activity), thus representing instances of distinct constructions, namely `Intransitive` and `Unaccusative`. Because this difference is not derived from specific lexical fillers, if the verbs in the examples were to be changed to *dance* and *slip* respectively, the same constructions would be used to describe the sentences.

(1) *Ele correu hoje pela manhã.*
He run.PST.3SG today for morning
'He ran this morning.'

(2) *Ele morreu hoje pela manhã.*
He die.PST.3SG today for morning
'He died this morning.'

In this paper, we discuss insights from negative results obtained in an experiment for identifying schematic clausal constructions and their construction elements in Brazilian Portuguese (pt-br) by using a combination of Multilingual BERT (Devlin et al., 2019) with the computational representations of such constructions in the FrameNet Brasil Constructicon (FN-Br Ccn) (Torrent et al., 2018; da Costa et al., 2018; Almeida and Torrent, 2021). Qualitative analysis of the results indicate that alternatives to the linearization of the constructional properties modeled in resources, number of annotated sentences and a post-processing module

Proceedings of the First International Workshop on Construction Grammars and NLP (CxGs+NLP, GURT/SyntaxFest 2023), pages 96 - 109
March 9-12, 2023 ©2023 Association for Computational Linguistics

should be explored in the future as a means to make use of information in Constructicons for NLP tasks.

In the remainder of this paper, we present, in section 2, how constructions are represented in the FN-Br Ccn. Next, in section 3, we go through the steps needed to convert the FN-Br Ccn representations into a dataset that could be used for proposing the construction identification model in section 4. Sections 5 and 6 describe the experimental setup used to evaluate the model and the results. Discussion of the results is carried out in section 7, with quantitative and qualitative analyses. Section 8 presents final considerations.

2 Construction Representation in the FN-Br Constructicon

The FN-Br Constructicon (Torrent et al., 2014, 2018) is built as part of the FrameNet Brasil language resource, meaning that, similarly to lexical units, constructions in this database can have their meaning import represented in terms of frames. Therefore, the semantics of the *`Intransitive`* construction licensing (1) can be represented as the `Intentionally_act` frame in Figure (1).

The database structure of FN-Br allows for construction elements (CEs) to be mapped to frame elements (FEs), when relevant. Hence, the SUBJECT and the PREDICATE CEs in the *`Intransitive`* construction can be respectively mapped to the AGENT and ACT FEs in the `Intentionally_act` frame.

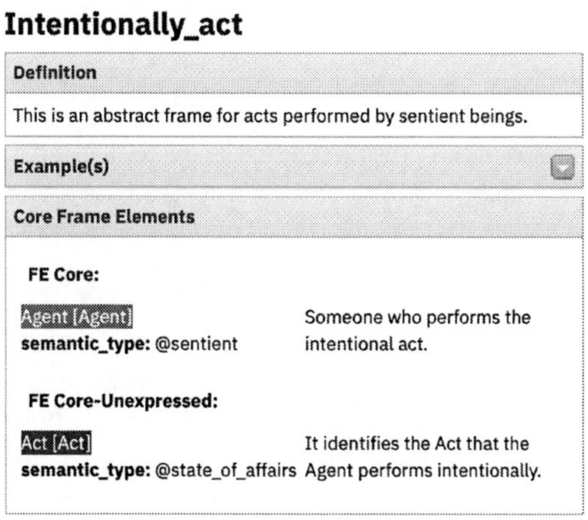

Figure 1: The `Intentionally_act` frame.

Moreover, the FN-Br Ccn allows for other types of information to be represented. First, CEs can be defined in terms of phrasal constructions licensing them. For the *`Intransitive`*, the SUBJECT CE is a `Determined_noun_phrase`, while the PREDICATE is a *`Non_complement_taking_verb_phrase`*. Furthermore, the information that the verb CE of this last construction has to be filled by a frame that inherits `Intentionally_act` can also be recorded. If instead, this slot was constrained by a child frame of `Undergoing`, then this would be an *`Unaccusative`* construction. Formal properties of the construction can also be represented, such as the fact that the SUBJECT CE usually comes before the PREDICATE, and that the first corresponds to the *nsubj* relation in the Universal Dependencies tag set (de Marneffe et al., 2021), while the latter would correspond to the *root*. All the information associated to the *`Intransitive`* construction in the FN-Br Ccn, together with the fact that it inherits a general *`Subject_predicate`* construction are shown in Figure 2.

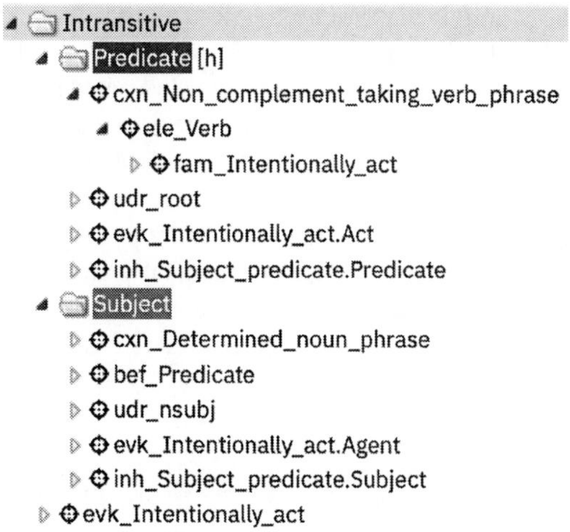

Figure 2: The *`Intransitive`* construction.

In addition to the two clausal constructions mentioned so far, work by Almeida (2022) has modeled 22 other clausal constructions and 22 phrasal and POS constructions licensing the CEs in them in the FN-Br Ccn. Many of those CEs share the same name (*e.g.* PREDICATE), but are fully separate entities in the database, each belonging to a single construction. For that reason, when applying these structures to an experiment for automatically identifying construction in corpora, the CEs can be treated as the actual labels. A model working with CEs is, arguably, more informative and easier to interpret, despite being more complex. Moreover, the frame information, used to represent the semantic part of a construction, is not lost because the CEs are directly related to the FEs of frames. The full dataset that includes pieces of the FN-Br Ccn and setup used in this work are described next.

3 Dataset

The dataset used in the experiments had to be built step by step because one of our research goals was to assess the impact of Universal Dependencies (UD) and Frame information embedding into a neural model for CE labeling, which is not a traditional NLP task. The corpus consists of 673 sentences annotated for UD, clausal constructions (and their CEs) and frames. Subsections 3.1, 3.2 and 3.3 describe how each type of data was integrated into the same dataset.

3.1 Universal Dependencies Treebank

To evaluate the impacts of UD information when labeling CEs in sentences, the model must be trained on a corpus that has both types of data. Instead of using the annotated sentences from the FN-Br Ccn and including UD annotations, we opted to use an existing, manually-annotated UD treebank and include constructional information. Using a corpus that has been reviewed by specialists reduces the chances of results being affected by poor quality UD annotations. Moreover, a manually-annotated treebank has the advantage of guaranteeing that the model results are be influenced by another system's errors. For those reasons, the UD (Brazilian) Portuguese GSD treebank was chosen [1]. It comprises 12019 sentences and 297045 tokens and was originally annotated using Stanford-style dependencies for multiple languages and later converted into UD (McDonald et al., 2013).

3.2 Constructions

To annotate the constructions for the UD pt-br GSD sentences, the FN-Br WebTool was used, as it already contains the required set of features to work with constructions and visualizing them (Torrent et al., forthcoming). We worked exclusively on the test subset of the UD pt-br GSD treebank, containing 1200 sentences. Before the annotation process was carried out, 24 construction elements from 11 argument structure constructions were selected for annotation. This set was chosen among all of the constructions modeled by Almeida (2022) because they were more likely to occur in the GSD treebank. Moreover, our aim was to identify highly schematic constructions, in opposition to constructions with many fixed slots that could be identified by hybrid or rule-based systems. In total, 673 sentences were annotated. Table 1 shows not only the counts for each construction, but also their schemata (for instance examples, see Appendix A).

It is worth noting that the `Instransitive` and `Ergative` pair discussed in section 1 is not the only in which constructions share a schema. The same happens to the `Indirect_transitive` and the `Oblique_transitive`, but the former is used by dative indirect objects, while the latter is more general. The difference between the `Elapsed_time` construction and the `Presentational_existential`, as their names suggest, is semantic. The former confirms that something happened a certain time ago, while the latter simply introduces a new entity or event to a discourse. Finally, the `Stative_nominal_predicative` and `Attributive_nominal_predicative` constructions assign states or attributes to their SUBJECTS, something closely related to the type of verbal copula present in the sentence. Other constructions are constrained by the presence existential verbs, indicating that the task of labeling CEs deals with lexical, semantic and syntactic constraints simultaneously.

In regards to their elements, the majority of the constructions considered for the experiments have only their SUBJECT and PREDICATE CEs (which are treated as distinct types of subject and predicates), with the execption of `Elapsed_time` and `Presentational_existential`, which have EXISTENTIAL VERBS, NOMINALS and SECONDARY PREDICATES. Because the variety of pt-br in the UD GSD tends to be monitored for verb inflection and SUBJECTS could be nully instantiated, in some sentences, only PREDICATE CEs were annotated. The annotation schema was designed to handle those cases. It is also worth noting that multiple constructions can occur in one single sentence. However, those instances were discarded in next steps, so that the model could be trained to label a single CE (see section 5).

[1] `https://github.com/UniversalDependencies/UD_Portuguese-GSD`

Construction	Schema	# Sent
`Active_bitransitive`	[NP [V NP [PP]]]	21
`Active_direct_transitive`	[NP [V [NP]]]	337
`Indirect_transitive`	[NP [V [PP]]]	7
`Oblique_transitive`	[NP [V [PP]]]	75
`Intransitive`	[NP [V]]	33
`Ergative`	[NP [V]]	30
`Elapsed_time`	[V_{exi} [NP [VP]]]	2
`Presentational_existential`	[V_{exi} [NP [VP]]]	8
`Locative_predicative`	[NP [V_{cop} [AdvP | PP]]]	17
`Attributive_nominal_predicative`	[NP [V_{cop} [AP | NP]]]	106
`Stative_nominal_predicative`	[NP [V_{cop} [AP | NP]]]	37
Total	-	**673**

Table 1: Constructions present in the dataset with their respective schemata and number of annotated examples. The subscripts specify that the slots must be filled by existential verbs or verbal copulas. With the exception of `Elapsed_time` and `Presentational_existential`, all constructions have SUBJECT and PREDICATE construction elements. The CEs on these two are the EXISTENTIAL VERBS, NOMINALS and SECONDARY PREDICATES.

3.3 Frames

The FN-Br Ccn represents constructions in an interconnected graph to express inheritance between them, but also to connect them to other types of entities, including frames, which can be used to explicitly define the semantics of constructions (see Appendix B). Although it would not make sense to feed this frame information to our model because it is part of the prediction objective, these frames serve as anchor nodes to identify relevant clusters in the network. Such clusters can be used to improve the quality of CE classification. The idea of using frame clusters as explicit semantic information was implemented using two algorithms that compute potentially relevant frames for each token in the sentences.

The first algorithm, responsible for frame disambiguation, has been used in previous works (Matos and Salomão, 2014; Costa et al., 2022). It consists of a variation of the spreading activation algorithm executed over the whole network. First, the system identifies and activates the nodes for the words in the sentence, then it iterates over their neighbor nodes spreading "energy". For each word that contains a potential lexical unit, the frame with the highest energy is selected as the evoked frame. The algorithm is highly dependent on FN-Br's coverage, especially of lexical items, because they act as the initial activation points.

The goal of the second algorithm is to identify a set of frames related to a token that could be relevant for label prediction. The procedure depends on a fixed set of frames, containing those related to one of the 11 relevant argument structure constructions in the database. FN-Br is also modified when running this algorithm: it is transformed in a digraph where arcs represent the inheritance, subframe and perspective relations in the original database. For each token, the system finds the minimum paths from its frame to the frames related to constructions in the digraph. In many instances, this path doesn't exist and the token is associated only to its own frame. For the others, the frame is associated to the whole cluster of potentially relevant frames.

4 Model

Figure 4 shows the general architecture of the proposed model. The system was designed and implemented in a way such that some components could be switched or just removed to facilitate testing of the various scenarios.The most important elements in the model are described next.

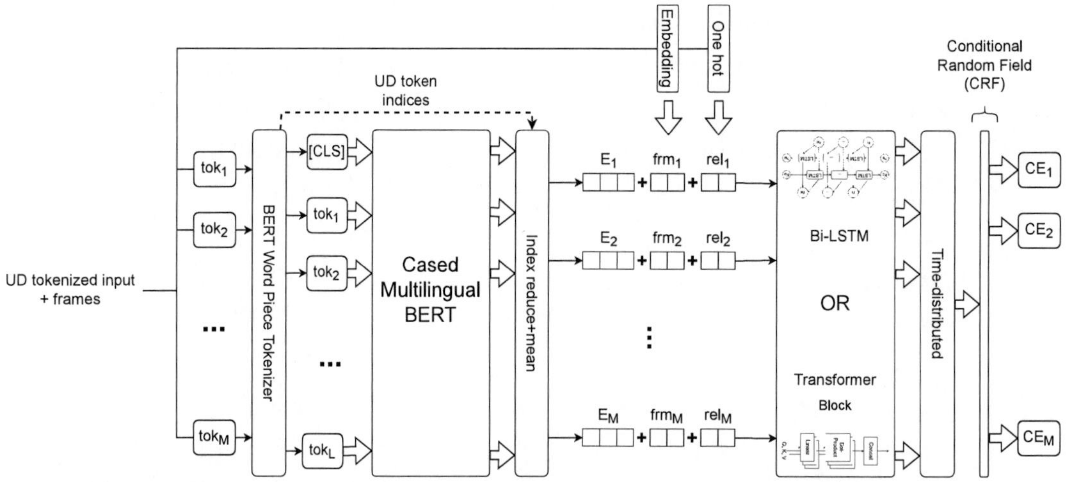

Figure 3: The complete architecture of the proposed system. Because BERT manipulates word piece tokens, the sequence size of the UD annotated sentence (M) is not the same as L. The output from BERT is transformed into a M size sequence later in the pipeline using a mapping of word piece indices to UD tokens. Each vector i in this sequence – referred as E_i in the image – is concatenated with its position frame embedding and UD relation, which is then used by other components to label the construction element in that position.

4.1 Preprocessing

As described in section 3, the dataset built for the experiment already includes tokenized sentences. In this schema, tokens correspond to words, with the exception of some special cases, such as contractions. BERT, however, is trained on sequences created by a word piece tokenizer, *i.e.*, tokens can be full words, but also subwords. During preprocessing, each sentence in the corpus went through BERT's word piece tokenizer and the resulting sequences of subwords were stored. Using those sequences and the treebank tokenized sentences, a mapping between indices was computed for each record, so that, given any subword, its complete token can be retrieved. Both the BERT tokenized sequences and the mappings serve as inputs to the model.

4.2 Encoding UD relations & Frames

Neural networks can process syntactic trees using two main approaches: having a specialized architecture to handle these complex data structures or apply some form of transformation to linearize the trees (Tai et al., 2015; Liu et al., 2017). The former has the advantage of being designed to perform this type of task, albeit being more computationally expensive and more complex to implement. In this work, the trees were linearized using a strategy very similar to the one described by Liu et al. (2017). It works by first associating each token with its one-hot encoded relation to its head. By itself, this is not enough to represent the relation because there is no information about the head. To compensate for this, the tokens are reorganized into a Breadth-first search (BFS) sequence order, which guarantees that the head of a relation will always come before its dependent tokens. The only setback is the lack of limits in the distance between two related tokens. It is important to note that this reordering of the sequence never happens before the sentence is processed by BERT, as that is not compatible with how the language model was trained.

Similarly to the UD relations, the frame clusters associated to each token in the dataset were linearized into sparse binary vectors where each position indicates the presence of a frame. Those sparse vectors of size 1136 (total number of frames) are reduced to 50-dimension vectors by a dense layer before they are used by a LSTM or Transformer Block. This linearization process does not embed any type of information about the relation between frames, but has the advantage of being easily integrated into the model without the need of a special architecture.

4.3 Pre-trained BERT

In all of our experiments, a pre-trained multilingual BERT model (Devlin et al., 2019) was used as the first component, with the goal of obtaining a sequence of vectors from a sequence of sub-words in our corpus. Although word embedding models could have been used for this step, there are advantages in using a language model. First, because of how those models are trained, vector representations of tokens are contextual, *i.e.*, there is no single word vector, but a representation of that word in a specific sentence. The added information is especially useful, considering that our final task is the identification of CEs that may be represented by multiple words in a sentence. In fact, there is evidence that constructional information can be identified and extracted from BERT vectors (Tayyar Madabushi et al., 2020). Second, the fact that a single model was trained in 104 languages makes it easier to evaluate our experiments for other Constructicons, modeled after other languages. Finally, the applicability of this type of model to many different tasks in NLP makes it a good candidate for fine-tuning in our CE labeling experiments.

For all settings presented in section 5, the BERT model was fine-tuned to each downstream task using the multilingual cased parameters as the checkpoint[2]. In this procedure, each BERT sequence output is transformed into one of smaller dimensions before feeding it to the subsequent layers. This transformation was necessary because BERT operates at the subword level, while our CE labels are assigned at the word level. For this step, we simply averaged all of the subword vectors of a single word to obtain a sequence of a smaller size.

4.4 Bi-LSTM

Long short-term memory (LSTM) artificial neural networks are designed to process sequences of data without the caveats of normal recurrent networks, especially the problem of vanishing gradients (Hochreiter and Schmidhuber, 1997). A LSTM unit processes data in sequential timesteps, taking as input the cell and hidden state from a previous timestep, as well as the actual data input and outputting new cell and a new hidden output. In theory, each output is related to a different type of information: the hidden state, when dealing with text data, is the current token output and the cell state is a more general, sentence-level memory that can always be influenced.

In our experimental setup, we used unmodified LSTM cells, containing only the forget and input gates to change the cell state, and the output gate. We also made sure to use a Bidirectional LSTM, since relevant information of a CE can be present before or after the actual CE in the sentence. During development, we have decided to use hidden (and cell) states of 20 dimensions for each direction, because greater values didn't increase performance. The forward and backward hidden states were concatenated, resulting in vectors of size 40 for each position in the sequence. In the final model, the Bi-LSTM layer input are the averaged BERT vectors concatenated with their UD and frame information and in BFS order, according to their dependency tree. This layers transforms the inputs to vectors of lower dimension to be classified by a final layer.

4.5 Transformer Block

The Transformer architecture (Vaswani et al., 2017) was proposed as a "simpler" alternative to popular sequence neural networks, relying only on attention mechanisms, instead of the recurrence observed in an LSTM network, for example. The most important mechanism in a Transformer Block is the Multi-Head Self-Attention, a series of computations that generate multiple weight matrices—generally referred to as attention filters—used to transform parts of the input based on the whole input itself. Each attention filter captures a different aspect of the information and their results are then concatenated. In NLP, this mechanism is usually exemplified as the importance that each word in a sentence has for every single word, where importance can be framed in various ways.

In BERT's architecture, the Transformer is the main unit. Hence, the use of an additional layer in our proposed model can be seen as an extension to make the language model fit the goals of our experiment. The difference between BERT's original layers and the one included in this work is on the hidden dimension size and the type of input sequence. The block still has 12 attention heads, but they manipulate hidden vectors of size 300, instead of the 768 in Multilingual BERT. This reduction was mostly motivated by hardware limitations, but also because the layer is closer to the actual output of the system, which is way smaller in dimension. In regards to the input sequence, this Transformer takes as input a sequence with the same size as the UD token sequence, not the one used by BERT. Each position in this sequence consists of the averaged BERT subword vectors concatenated with the UD relation and frame information, similarly

[2] `https://github.com/google-research/bert`

to the LSTM.

4.6 Conditional Random Fields

Conditional Random Fields (CRF) are a class of discriminative models that can classify a sample considering its contextual information. In NLP, this type of model has been used extensively for labelling tasks, such as POS tagging and NER (Chiche and Yitagesu, 2022; Li et al., 2020). Similarly to the latter, in our experiments, we decided to use a CRF layer after the final Bi-LSTM (or Transformer) layer because a CE generally spans more than a single token of the input sentence. While a simple dense layer applied to all tokens can independently predict CE labels, the CRF is parameterized to capture the internal logic of labels, which can correlate to construction constraints. For example, in the vast majority of cases in Brazilian Portuguese, a PREDICATE CE cannot be followed by a SUBJECT CE. Moreover, it can attenuate mistakes made by the model in previous layers by using both linguistic information and the labeling probabilities. In the experiments where the CRF was used, the log-likelihood was used as the loss function.

5 Experiments

In order to understand the impacts of UD and frame data in CE labeling, 9 different experimental setups were proposed, 5 variations using LSTM and 4 using Transformers. For each of those options, the effectiveness of the CRF was evaluated, with and without UD and frame data. The LSTM was the only model where the BFS sorting of tokens was tested, hence it has one more variation. This type of ordering was considered only for this architecture because, in theory, the way information vanishes in the cell states is influenced by the order of the elements in the input sequence. The Transformer can handle this problem by simply adjusting attention weights.

One of the challenges of working with the dataset described in section 3 was the number of samples annotated for each construction. For `Elapsed_time`, for example, only two examples were found in the 673 sentences. This variation in construction frequency is expected and leads to the fact that a much larger dataset would be needed to find a reasonable amount of examples for that construction. We have decided to consider only the two most frequent constructions in the UD Portuguese GSD treebank, namely `Direct_transitive` and `Attributive_nominal_predicative`, as the models could not perform consistently for the ones with less samples. This resulted in a dataset with 443 sentences and 4 CE labels that was split into train and test sets in a 8:2 ratio. Considering the relative effectiveness of BERT's fine-tuning and that constructional information can be extracted from it, this dataset can still be used to predict CE labels (Devlin et al., 2019; Sun et al., 2019; Tayyar Madabushi et al., 2020).

In all variations, the networks were implemented to predict a single CE label (or none) for each position corresponding to a token in the sequence, despite the fact that it is possible for more than one label to be true. This was done because, in our first implementation tests, we verified that only one instance of the dataset had a token with two labels. Moreover, convergence was slow during training, even after adjusting parameters, without any performance gains. For that reason, we used a softmax activation function and cross-entropy as the loss function. When the final layer was a CRF, loss is computed using the log-likelihood.

For training, we used an Adam optimizer with learning rate set to $3e-5$. Due to GPU memory limitations, batch size was set to 16 samples and the maximum number of epochs to 20, which was not a problem because of the reduced size of the training dataset. To prevent over-fitting, the loss over the validation set was monitored and after 3 epochs without any improvements, training would be stopped, resulting in less than 20 epochs per training run. Every model variation was trained 10 times so that their performance and generalization could be better analyzed. The BERT model's weights were adjusted, *i.e.* fine-tuned, in each of those runs and, in order to prevent tests from influencing one another, memory was cleaned up between executions.

Table 2 summarizes the number of parameters in each model as the difference to each of the two base model types and their average number of training epochs.

6 Results

After the execution of all of the training algorithms, model results were computed and compiled into Table 3. The main metric used for evaluation was a macro-F1 calculated by treating each label as a

Model	Δ|θ|	epochs
LSTM		
Base	0 (~180M)	10.5
CRF	+35	11.7
Frm, UDrel	+70,450	10.0
Frm, UDrel+order	+70,450	10.3
Frm, UDrel, CRF	+70,485	11.5
Transformer		
Base	0 (~206M)	10.4
CRF	+35	12.0
Frm, UDrel	+6,725,525	10.0
Frm, UDrel, CRF	+6,725,560	11.6

Table 2: Model size in number of parameters and number of epochs used on average for training.

Model	F1	
	μ	best
LSTM		
Base	.694 (.050)	**.767**
CRF	**.700 (.015)**	.720
Frm, UDrel	.647 (.081)	.709
Frm, UDrel+order	.603 (.111)	.763
Frm, UDrel, CRF	.675 (.072)	.748
Transformer		
Base	.643 (.044)	.703
CRF	.643 (.044)	.720
Frm, UDrel	.618 (.033)	.653
Frm, UDrel, CRF	.638 (.054)	**.767**

Table 3: Average and best macro-F1 scores for each model, based on the results of 10 separate training executions. Standard deviations are shown in parentheses. The best overall results for all experiments are highlighted.

binary class, computing their F1s and then averaging. The label used to indicate the absence of a CE is ignored in this calculation. The main advantage of using a macro-F1 over the micro-F1 or accuracy lies on the fact that the absence of a CE can be treated asymmetrically. This is relevant for our analysis because it can focus on the predictions where the model assigned a label in order to obtain insights.

To better understand the variations between different training iterations, the average (with standard deviation) and the best F1 scores for each configuration were observed. In terms of averages, the LSTM model with a CRF, but without frames or UDs had the best performance. This configuration also had the smallest standard deviation, indicating that training is somewhat consistent. In terms of best results, the base LSTM model without CRF and the complete Transformer model have the highest F1, with a score of .767. Of the two, the LSTM is a considerable smaller model, as shown in Table 2. Taking into consideration that the averages of the models are not that different, for a LSTM-based model, the inclusion of only a CRF seems to yield the best results. For a Transformer-based network, the extra semantic and syntactic information, along with the CRF, contributes to better results.

The worst configuration, on average, was the LSTM model where tokens were reordered using the dependency tree BFS results. In constrast, every model achieved better average F1 scores when a CRF layer was added.

7 Discussion

As previously stated, the LSTM models performed better, especially when no additional frame or UD data was embedded into the inputs. However, when using Transformers, the same type of data can increase performance. One possible explanation is that the latter has a considerably larger number of parameters, making it easier to integrate the additional information, but, at the same time, being more complex to train and, thus, having worse performance than LSTMs. Also, the difference in the results is likely affected by the small size of the training dataset, it is possible that the quality of the predictions could improve if more samples were processed by the networks.

The LSTM where the order of the tokens was changed also provides good insight on how this model used the information to make predictions and why it has the lowest average F1 score. When analyzing the average F1 scores for each construction element, it was noted that final F1 was mostly influenced by the SUBJECT CE of the `Attributive_nominal_predicative`. In the model using a CRF, the F1 for the subject was .628, for the one with the BFS ordering, it was .388. This is a strong evidence that when optimizing with few samples, for a CE that has a relatively strict position in a sentence, positional information is relevant. It also shows that the model was not able to compensate for the absence of this kind of information using only UDs and a different ordering. This type of problem can be potentially avoided by using a network architecture designed to handle graphs or trees.

We have also decided to carry out a qualitative analysis of the predictions made by the best Transformer model. All of the predictions made over the test set were transformed back to CE spans, which where then aligned to the original sentences and paired with the original human annotations. Making this side-by-side comparison, notes were taken for each record. During this process, we observed that some types of errors were way more frequent than others. For instance, 26% of the sentences had only the head words of the constructions elements labeled, while 13% had a problem of discontinuity in the CE span. These numbers agree with the F1 results displayed on Table 3 that show an improve in performance when a CRF layer is added. Because this type of layer models the relation between the classification labels, it is able to correct some of the mistakes in continuity and length of the CE spans made by the previous layers.

More importantly, these errors seem to originate from an overgeneralization made by the model over the POS of words. Despite the fact that POS tags are not part of the input to the model, this information is arguably embedded into BERT. More evidence of that is found on examples where the model labeled some word with the incorrect CE. Although rare, when it happens, the CE predicted for that word is of the same POS of a head of that CE. For example, many verbs are labeled as the predicate of a `Direct_transitive` construction, even when they are part of other type of construction. The same happens for adjectives and the `Attributive_nominal_predicative`. This happened in 8.7% of the analyzed sentences.

The problem of overgeneralization also occurs with the *conj* relation in this model. Interestingly, this seems to be the only UD relation that clearly influenced the predictions of the test set. In 8,7% of the sentences, the model labeled the tokens of a conjunct despite the fact that they are not related to a subject or predicate. In a deterministic approach, this type of error can be easily verified using the dependency trees, as the CE span nodes would not be connected.

8 Final considerations

The experiment reported on in this paper aimed at testing whether UD and frame information extracted from a Constructicon could positively influence the performance of Transformer-based models for schematic construction identification in sentences. However, the most effective models in our tests are still the smaller LSTMs, without any extra information. Furthermore, we have identified that the trained models were overgeneralizing certain aspects of the data, causing performance to degrade.

One of the limitations of our experiments is in the architecture of the network itself when these various types of information are used. For both LSTM and Transformers, there are gaps that could be filled if they were implemented to fully handle tree and graph structures instead of their linearized, thus, simplified, versions. Other changes in the network structure and training procedure are needed to prevent the overgeneralization discussed in section 7.

Another course of action to better understand how neural networks can be used to classify constructions effectively is to expand the dataset, both in number of samples, but also in representation of different clausal structures. For example, if the models were to be trained to also label the CEs of the `Unaccusative` construction, they would have to learn the semantic boundaries that differentiate an unaccusative from a transitive verb.

Finally, in spite of their limitations, it is clear that performance could be improved by using post-processing algorithms that could either find anomalous outputs (*e.g. the incorrect conjucts* and even expand the spans of the CEs based on the dependency relations. This type of procedure is adequate because the models are already able to identify most CE heads.

References

Vânia Almeida and Tiago Torrent. 2021. Construções de estrutura argumental com argumento preposicionado: uma modelagem linguístico-computacional na FrameNet Brasil. In *Anais do XIII Simpósio Brasileiro de Tecnologia da Informação e da Linguagem Humana*, pages 353–362, Porto Alegre, RS, Brasil. SBC.

Vânia Gomes de Almeida. 2022. *Modelagem e Identificação Automática de Construções de Estrutura Argumental: uma proposta para o Constructicon da FrameNet Brasil*. Ph.D. thesis, Graduate Program in Linguistics, Federal University of Juiz de Fora, Brazil.

John Edward Bryant. 2008. *Best-Fit Constructional Analysis*. Ph.D. thesis, EECS Department, University of California, Berkeley.

Alebachew Chiche and Betselot Yitagesu. 2022. Part of speech tagging: a systematic review of deep learning and machine learning approaches. *Journal of Big Data*, 9(1):1–25.

Alexandre Diniz da Costa, Mateus Coutinho Marim, Ely Matos, and Tiago Timponi Torrent. 2022. Domain adaptation in neural machine translation using a qualia-enriched FrameNet. In *Proceedings of the Thirteenth Language Resources and Evaluation Conference*, pages 1–12, Marseille, France. European Language Resources Association.

Alexandre Diniz da Costa, Vânia Almeida, Ludmila Lage, Gustavo Barbosa, Natália Marção, Vanessa Paiva, Ely da Silva Matos, and Tiago Torrent. 2018. Representação computacional das construções de sujeito-predicado do português do brasil. *Revista LinguíStica*, 14(1):149–178.

Marie-Catherine de Marneffe, Christopher D. Manning, Joakim Nivre, and Daniel Zeman. 2021. Universal Dependencies. *Computational Linguistics*, 47(2):255–308.

Jacob Devlin, Ming-Wei Chang, Kenton Lee, and Kristina Toutanova. 2019. BERT: Pre-training of deep bidirectional transformers for language understanding. In *Proceedings of the 2019 Conference of the North American Chapter of the Association for Computational Linguistics: Human Language Technologies, Volume 1 (Long and Short Papers)*, pages 4171–4186, Minneapolis, Minnesota. Association for Computational Linguistics.

Charles J. Fillmore. 1968. The case for case. In Emmon Bach and Robert T. Harms, editors, *Universals in Linguistic Theory*, pages 0–88. Holt, Rinehart and Winston, New York.

Charles J. Fillmore. 2008. Border conflicts: FrameNet meets Construction Grammar. In *Proceedings of the XIII EURALEX International Congress*, pages 49–68, Barcelona. Universitat Pompeu Fabra, Universitat Pompeu Fabra.

Adele E. Goldberg. 2013. Constructionist approaches. In Thomas Hoffman and Graeme Trousadale, editors, *The Oxford Handbook of Construction Grammar*. Oxford University Press.

Sepp Hochreiter and Jürgen Schmidhuber. 1997. Long short-term memory. *Neural Computation*, 9(8):1735–1780.

Jing Li, Aixin Sun, Jianglei Han, and Chenliang Li. 2020. A survey on deep learning for named entity recognition. *IEEE Transactions on Knowledge and Data Engineering*, 34(1):50–70.

Rui Liu, Junjie Hu, Wei Wei, Zi Yang, and Eric Nyberg. 2017. Structural embedding of syntactic trees for machine comprehension. In *Proceedings of the 2017 Conference on Empirical Methods in Natural Language Processing*, pages 815–824, Copenhagen, Denmark. Association for Computational Linguistics.

Benjamin Lyngfelt, Lars Borin, Markus Forsberg, Julia Prentice, Rudolf Rydstedt, Emma Sköldberg, and Sofia Tingsell. 2012. Adding a constructicon to the Swedish resource network of Språkbanken. In *Proceedings of KONVENS 2012*, pages 452–461. ÖGAI. LexSem 2012 workshop.

Benjamin Lyngfelt, Lars Borin, Kyoko Ohara, and Tiago Timponi Torrent. 2018. *Constructicography: Constructicon development across languages*. John Benjamins, Amsterdam.

Ely Matos, Tiago Torrent, Vânia Almeida, Adrieli Laviola, Ludmila Lage, Natália Marção, and Tatiane Tavares. 2017. Constructional Analysis Using Constrained Spreading Activation in a FrameNet-Based Structured Connectionist Model. In *The AAAI 2017 Spring Symposium on Computational Construction Grammar and Natural Language Understanding Technical Report SS-17-02*, pages 222–229, Palo Alto, CA. AAAI Press.

Ely Edison da Silva Matos and Maria Margarida Martins Salomão. 2014. Ludi: um framework para desambiguação lexical com base no enriquecimento da semântica de frames. *Revista Linguística*, 12(1).

Ryan McDonald, Joakim Nivre, Yvonne Quirmbach-Brundage, Yoav Goldberg, Dipanjan Das, Kuzman Ganchev, Keith Hall, Slav Petrov, Hao Zhang, Oscar Täckström, et al. 2013. Universal dependency annotation for multilingual parsing. In *Proceedings of the 51st Annual Meeting of the Association for Computational Linguistics (Volume 2: Short Papers)*, pages 92–97.

Kyoko Hirose Ohara. 2014. Relating frames and constructions in Japanese FrameNet. In *Proceedings of the 9th International Conference on Language Resources and Evaluation, LREC 2014*, Proceedings of the 9th International Conference on Language Resources and Evaluation, LREC 2014, pages 2474–2477. European Language Resources Association (ELRA). Copyright: Copyright 2017 Elsevier B.V., All rights reserved.; 9th International Conference on Language Resources and Evaluation, LREC 2014 ; Conference date: 26-05-2014 Through 31-05-2014.

Chi Sun, Xipeng Qiu, Yige Xu, and Xuanjing Huang. 2019. How to fine-tune bert for text classification? In *China national conference on Chinese computational linguistics*, pages 194–206. Springer.

Kai Sheng Tai, Richard Socher, and Christopher D. Manning. 2015. Improved semantic representations from tree-structured long short-term memory networks. In *Proceedings of the 53rd Annual Meeting of the Association for Computational Linguistics and the 7th International Joint Conference on Natural Language Processing (Volume 1: Long Papers)*, pages 1556–1566, Beijing, China. Association for Computational Linguistics.

Harish Tayyar Madabushi, Laurence Romain, Dagmar Divjak, and Petar Milin. 2020. CxGBERT: BERT meets construction grammar. In *Proceedings of the 28th International Conference on Computational Linguistics*, pages 4020–4032, Barcelona, Spain (Online). International Committee on Computational Linguistics.

Tiago Timponi Torrent, Ludmila Meireles Lage, Thais Fernandes Sampaio, Tatiane da Silva Tavares, and Ely Edison da Silva Matos. 2014. Revisiting border conflicts between FrameNet and Construction Grammar: Annotation policies for the Brazilian Portuguese Constructicon. *Constructions and Frames*, 6(1):34–51.

Tiago Timponi Torrent, Ely Edison Matos, Alexandre Diniz Costa, Maucha Andrade Gamonal, Simone Peron-Corrêa, and Vanessa Maria Ramos Lopes Paiva. forthcoming. A Flexible Tool for a Qualia-Enriched FrameNet: the FrameNet Brasil WebTool. *Language Resources and Evaluation*.

Tiago Timponi Torrent, Ely Edison Matos, Ludmila Meireles Lage, Adrieli Laviola, Tatiane da Silva Tavares, Vânia Gomes de Almeida, and Natália Sathler Sigiliano. 2018. Towards continuity between the lexicon and the constructicon in FrameNet Brasil. In Benjamin Lyngfelt, Lars Borin, Kyoko Ohara, and Tiago Timponi Torrent, editors, *Constructicography: Constructicon development across languages*, pages 107–140. John Benjamins, Amsterdam.

Ashish Vaswani, Noam Shazeer, Niki Parmar, Jakob Uszkoreit, Llion Jones, Aidan N Gomez, Łukasz Kaiser, and Illia Polosukhin. 2017. Attention is all you need. *Advances in neural information processing systems*, 30.

Alexander Ziem and Hans Boas. 2017. Towards a Constructicon for German. In *The AAAI 2017 Spring Symposium on Computational Construction Grammar and Natural Language Understanding Technical Report SS-17-02*, pages 274–277, Palo Alto, CA. AAAI Press.

A Argument structure constructions in the FN-Br Ccn

A.1 Active_bitransitive

This construction expresses predicates with three central participants, *i.e.* a trivalent event.

(3) *O jornal atribui o*
The news attribute.PRS.3SG the
abandono ao custo da
abandonment to_the cost of_the
ferrovia.
railroad

'The news attributes the abandonment to the cost of the railroad.'

(4) *O ministro transferiu a*
The minister transfer.PST.3SG the
sede da colônia para o
head_office of_the colony to the
Rio de Janeiro.
Rio de Janeiro

'The minister transferred the seat of the colony to Rio de Janeiro.'

A.2 Active_direct_transitive

This construction is licensed by predicates that require at least two participants, one agent and the other is patient-like.

(5) *A agência federal determinou*
The agency federal determine.PST.3SG
o início imediato dos trabalhos.
the start immediate of_the works

'The federal agency determined the immediate start of the works.'

(6) *Eu misturo o tempero e está*
I mix.PRS.1SG the seasoning and it's
pronto!
ready

'I mix the seasoning and it's ready!'

A.3 Indirect_transitive

This construction is very similar to the `Oblique_transitive` because both have the predicated object introduced by a preposition. The main difference is that the indirect object in this construction must be a dative object, *i.e.* it needs to play a beneficiary or recipient role.

(7) *O diretor respondeu aos*
The director reply.PST.3SG to_the
jornalistas.
journalists

'The director answered the journalists.'

(8) *Assim_que a carta chegou,*
As_soon_as the letter arrive.PST.3SG,
contaram para ele.
tell.PST.3PL to he

'As soon as the letter arrived, they told him.'

A.4 Oblique_transitive

The `Oblique_transitive` construction is the one used by certain verbs in Portuguese, in which the oblique/indirect object is introduced by a prepositional phrase. These complements are not optional and, semantically speaking, the event has two central participants.

(9) *A cidade precisa de uma*
The city need.PRS.3SG of a
reflexão mais profunda.
reflection more deep

'The city needs a deeper reflection [on the matter].'

(10) *A família procurou por cirurgias*
The family look.PST.3SG for surgeries
corretivas
corrective

'The family sought corrective surgeries.'

A.5 Intransitive

Construction with an agent-like subject and an unergative verb.

(11) *João Paulo concordou com a*
João Paulo agree.PST.3SG with the
fala.
statement

'João Paulo agreed with the statement.'

(12) *Eu ensinei com entusiasmo.*
I teach.PST.3SG with enthusiasm

'I taught with enthusiasm.'

A.6 Ergative

Construction with a non agent-like subject and an unaccusative verb.

(13) *O jogo começou em ritmo*
The game start.PST.3SG on pace
alucinante.
crazy

'The game started at a breakneck pace.'

(14) *A produção industrial aumentou*
The production industrial rise.PST.3SG
1,7% ante abril.
1.7% from april

'Industrial production rose 1.7% from April onwards.'

A.7 Elapsed_time

In this construction, the idea that an event occurred some time ago is expressed. In the following examples, the verb 'haver' was translated as 'have', but has the meaning of an exlcusively existential verb.

(15) *Eles moram naquela cidade*
They live.PRS.3PL in_that city
há vinte anos.
have.PRS.3SG twenty years

'They have lived in that city for twenty years.'

(16) *O crime aconteceu há*
The crime happen.PST.3SG have.PRS.3SG
três dias.
three days

'The crime happened three days ago.'

A.8 Presentational_existential

This type of construction is used to add new, entity-central, information to a discourse, *i.e.*, there's no subject being referred to, only existential predication of a nominal. Optionally, this nominal can be followed by a secondary predicate.

(17) *Existem 30 negócios na*
exist.PRS.3PL 30 businesses in_the
categoria.
category

'There are 30 businesses in the category'

(18) *Tem umas pessoas*
have.PRS.3SG some people
esperando você lá fora.
wait.PRS.PROG.3SG you there outside

'There are people waiting for you outside'

A.9 Locative_predicative

This type of construction is used to express where the SUBJECT is located.

(19) *E eles estão na cadeia, naquele inferno.*
And they be.PRS.3PL in jail, in_that hell

'And they're in jail, in that hell'

(20) *Seu pai estava em serviço na Coréia.*
his father be.PST.3SG in service in_the Korea

'His father was on duty in Korea.'

A.10 Attributive_nominal_predicative

This type of construction consists of a predicational clause where a stable object or property is being predicated and is quite similar to the `Stative_nominal_predicative`, with the only difference being the stable *vs* temporary construal.

(21) *O apoio dos fãs também será essencial.*
The support of_the fans also be.FUT.3SG essential

'The support of the fans will also be essential.'

(22) *Reichenbach é um município na Alemanha.*
Reichenbach be.PRS.3SG a municipality in_the Germany

'Reichenbach is a municipality in Germany.'

A.11 Stative_nominal_predicative

The type of construction in which a temporary state concept is predicated. In pt-br, the copula 'estar' is not exclusively but usually used for a stative construal of the SUBJECT. Being sad or hungry are very prototypical temporary states, but it is possible to have attribute-like states construed as temporary.

(23) *Os gravetos estavam todos molhados.*
The sticks be.PST.3PL all wet

'The sticks were all wet.'

(24) *Ele fica desconfiado.*
He stay.PRS.3SG suspicious

'He gets suspicious.'

B The 11 argument structure as a subgraph of the FN-Br Ccn

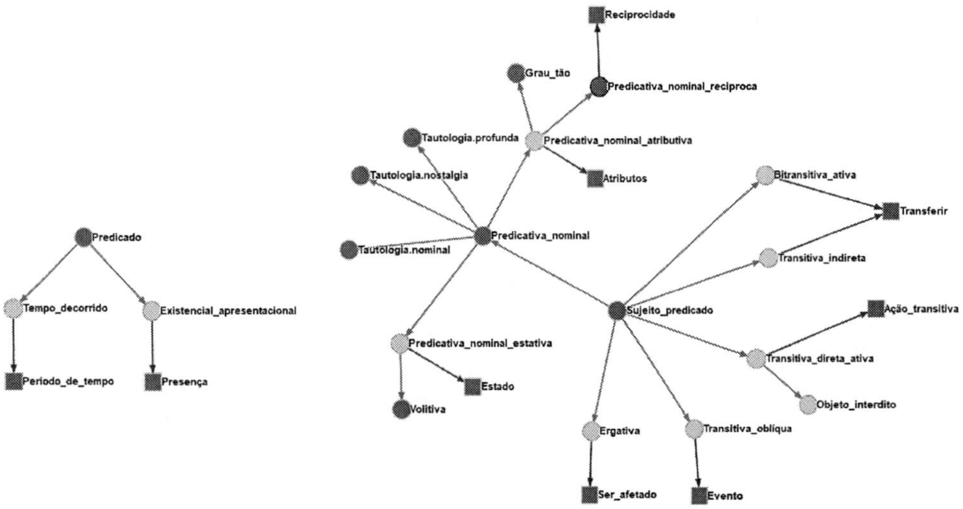

Figure 4: A subgraph of the FN-Br Constructicon containing all of the 11 argument structure selected for this paper. Their nodes are indicated in yellow, while other related constructions are green. Squares represent connections to frames, as discussed in the manuscript. Arrows in red are used for construction inheritance relations and the blue ones for frame evokation.

Author Index

Association for Computational Linguistics
209 N. Eighth Street
Stroudsburg, Pennsylvania 18360

ISBN 978-1-7138-9049-2

CURRAN ASSOCIATES INC.
proceedings.com